HISTORY MAKERS

100 MOST INFLUENTIAL PEOPLE OF THE TWENTIETH CENTURY

Books of Merit

HISTORY MAKERS

100 MOST INFLUENTIAL PEOPLE OF THE TWENTIETH CENTURY

**IAN WHITELAW &
JULIE WHITAKER**

THOMAS ALLEN PUBLISHERS

TORONTO

Library and Archives Canada Cataloguing in Publication available
upon request from http://www.collectionscanada.gc.ca/

Published by Thomas Allen Publishers,
a division of Thomas Allen & Son Limited,
390 Steelcase Road East
Markham, Ontario, L3R 1G2 CANADA

www.thomasallen.ca

Conceived, designed, and produced by:
Quid Publishing
Level 4 Sheridan House
114 Western Road
Hove BN3 1DD
England
www.quidpublishing.com

ONTARIO ARTS COUNCIL
CONSEIL DES ARTS DE L'ONTARIO

Canada Council
for the Arts

The publisher gratefully acknowledges the support
of The Ontario Arts Council for its publishing program.

We acknowledge the support of the Canada Council for the Arts, which
last year invested $20.1 million in writing and publishing throughout Canada.

We acknowledge the Government of Ontario through the
Ontario Media Development Corporation's Ontario Book Initiative.

We acknowledge the financial support of the Government of Canada through
the Canada Book Fund (CBF) for our publishing activities.

10 9 8 7 6 5 4 3 2 1

Printed and bound in Singapore

This book is dedicated to my father, George Whitaker—the greatest influence in my life.

Julie Whitaker

CONTENTS

Featured on page 112

Featured on page 120

Featured on page 118

Featured on page 152

Featured on page 180

Featured on page 198

INTRODUCTION

What precisely is it that you are holding in your hands? Well, this is as close to a definitive list of the twentieth century's most influential people as you might reasonably expect. In truth, there are countless ways of evaluating influence, and the process inevitably involves a degree of subjectivity. The authors have therefore used their own judgment to decide who should be included in the book, and for every one of the history makers that has been featured there are probably a dozen candidates that have had to be left out. What this *is* is a brief account of the lives and achievements of 100 people of the twentieth century whose thoughts, actions, ambitions, and imaginations have had a marked effect upon the world we live in, some for good and some for ill, and in many cases even that may depend upon your point of view.

Categories of Achievement

Our influential people fall into five broad fields of human activity—Politics & Leadership; Popular Culture & the Arts; Science & Technology; Business & Commerce; Writers & Thinkers—and the nature of influence in each category is completely different. It would be meaningless to make comparisons between the impact of a warmongering political leader and that of a successful entrepreneur. Decisions made by holders of political and military power can have a direct, dramatic, and lasting effect upon the lives of millions, and for this reason Politics & Leadership is the most populous category in the book, making up more than one third of the entries (34/100). Next come Popular Culture & the Arts (23), Science & Technology (18), and Writers & Thinkers (16), with Business & Commerce constituting nine percent of the entries.

Putting Influence in Order

The profiled people are ranked from 1 to 100, and here a degree of objectivity has been possible, at least in so far as we have applied the same criteria to all by assessing their importance with a simple equation. This equation can even be called democratic in that it measures interest in the history makers by regular people, using the World Wide Web to represent the populace at large. For each candidate we have "Googled" the person's name and recorded the number of hits. (Even the name has involved a degree of choice—for example, is that Franklin Roosevelt, Franklin D. Roosevelt, or FDR? For each individual we have Googled the version of the name that brings up the person's Wikipedia entry highest in the hit list.) We have then counted the number of words in the candidate's Wikipedia article and multiplied the two numbers (number of hits and number of words) together.

In order to overcome the fact that more recent personalities are likely to have a greater Internet presence, we have then divided the total by the decade in which they had their most prominent moment (1 for the 1900s, 10 for the 1990s), and we have then ranked the final scores.

It has to be admitted that it's not a perfect system. These scores inevitably change over time, sometimes quite rapidly, and events in the real world can introduce anomalies. For example, had we calculated Michael Jackson's score in the week after his death, he would have been at the top of the list with a score twice that of Albert Einstein, a result that some might have applauded but many would have challenged. Either way, it's fair to say that this system has helped identify some of the most captivating personalities of the last century—those who have truly captured our imagination and left behind remarkable legacies.

World Famous

So where do these 100 influential people come from? The answer is: from all around the globe, with 29 countries represented, from Argentina to Vietnam, and in the majority of cases each country has only one history maker on the list. Only ten nations have more than one son or daughter in this selection of 100, and some of these are surprising. Poland, for example, with less than 40 million souls (a little over half a percent of the world's population), has three of the 100 history makers—Pope John Paul II, Lech Walesa, and Marie Curie—and they are all from different categories.

Austria, with less than 9 million people (0.12 percent of the world's population) has an amazing four entries, but here there's a twist. Three of them—Sigmund Freud, Karl Popper, and Ludwig Wittgenstein—had to leave their native country (and coincidentally all ended up living in England) because of the exploits of the fourth. He, of course, was Adolf Hitler. The categories from which the famous come also throw a light on national history. France, for example, with less than one percent of the world's population, has a disproportionate seven entries, and three of these—Jean-Paul Sartre, Michel Foucault, and Simone de Beauvoir—are writers and philosophers. On the other hand, three of the five Soviet Union candidates—Joseph Stalin, Vladimir Lenin, and Mikhail Gorbachev—are political leaders.

Albert Einstein, the most influential of them all.

INFLUENTIAL CANADIANS

In keeping with the country's image around the world, Canada's most internationally famous sons and daughters are best known for doing good in the fields of medicine and politics or for bringing pleasure in the field of entertainment. These are areas in which there is perhaps the toughest competition and although Canadians do not figure in the top 100, there are many very worthy contenders who narrowly missed receiving the accolade.

Born in Scotland, Alexander Graham Bell (1847–1922) moved to Canada with his family at the age of 23 and settled in Ontario, where he continued the work that led to his invention of the telephone, transforming communications worldwide. Dr. (later Sir) Frederick Banting (1891–1941) and the success of his scientific research continue to have a daily impact upon the lives of tens of millions of diabetes sufferers. In 1927, he and his assistant Dr. Charles Best were the first to succeed in extracting and purifying the hormone insulin, the substance now used to treat this disease. Knighted in 1934 by King George V, he shared the 1940 Nobel Prize in Medicine with another insulin pioneer, John James Rickard Macleod, and he shared the award money with Charles Best.

Canada's peacekeeping role around the globe is famous, but it is less well known that it was a Canadian, Prime Minister Lester B. Pearson (1897–1972), who originally came up with the concept. His efforts to defuse the Suez Canal of 1956 through the creation and successful deployment of a United Nations Emergency Force, the first peacekeeping force, earned him the 1957 Nobel Peace Prize, and he remains the only Canadian to receive this honour.

There is no doubt that the musical landscape of the late twentieth century would have been very different—and a great deal poorer—without the Canadian contribution. As a classical pianist, composer, conductor, writer, and broadcaster, Glenn Gould (1932–1982) was influential in both North America and Europe. Renowned for his highly personal interpretations of the works of such composers as J.S. Bach, Mozart, and Schoenberg, he was also quick to embrace studio technology as a means of honing his art.

The influence of the poetry and music of Montreal-born Leonard Cohen (b. 1934) spans almost half a century. In the mid-60s his impressionistic lyrics and singular musical style made him a cult figure, especially in Canada and Europe, and the fact that there have been more than 2,000 cover versions of his songs attests to his iconic status.

In the field of sport, few have achieved the legendary status of Wayne Gretzky, widely acclaimed as the greatest hockey player there has ever been. Born in Ontario in 1961, his record-breaking career was founded less on physical prowess than on a remarkable and intelligent reading of the game that put him consistently in the right place at the right time.

HOW TO READ THIS BOOK

It isn't necessary to read this book from #100 to #1. By working through chronologically (in terms of peak year of achievement) or by category, subtle and unexpected connections between the entries become apparent and might encourage you to explore the themes further.

CHRONOLOGICALLY

#16 Marie Curie	**#4** Walt Disney
#9 The Wright Brothers	**#44** Pablo Picasso
#1 Albert Einstein	**#40** Howard Hughes
#10 Sigmund Freud	**#81** Enrico Fermi
#84 Emmeline Pankhurst	**#42** Francisco Franco
#96 Ernest Rutherford	**#27** Joseph Stalin
#50 Igor Stravinsky	**#18** Winston Churchill
#30 Charlie Chaplin	**#86** Wernher von Braun
#22 Vladimir Ilyich Lenin	**#62** Dwight Eisenhower
#2 Henry Ford	**#31** George Orwell
#25 Woodrow Wilson	**#37** Ho Chi Minh
#51 John Maynard Keynes	**#61** Robert Oppenheimer
#59 Ludwig Wittgenstein	**#89** Alan Turing
#99 Thomas Midgley Jr.	**#92** Alexander Fleming
#19 James Joyce	**#43** Harry S. Truman
#39 Coco Chanel	**#46** Eva Perón
#36 T. S. Eliot	**#83** David Ben-Gurion
#71 F. Scott Fitzgerald	**#55** Mao Zedong
#97 Edwin Hubble	**#65** Kim Il-sung
#74 Robert Goddard	**#82** Karl Popper
#58 Charles Lindbergh	**#85** Simone de Beauvoir
#52 Le Corbusier	**#57** Billy Graham
#28 Mohandas Gandhi	**#13** Marilyn Monroe
#12 Salvador Dalí	**#38** Alfred Hitchcock
#6 Adolf Hitler	**#45** Marlon Brando
#54 Franklin D. Roosevelt	**#15** James Dean
#60 Fred Astaire	**#11** Miles Davis
#91 Jesse Owens	**#5** Elvis Presley
#56 Benito Mussolini	**#80** Thomas Watson Jr.
#68 Haile Selassie	**#32** Charles de Gaulle

#21	Fidel Castro	#73	Milton Friedman
#26	Che Guevara	#63	Mother Teresa
#47	Frank Lloyd Wright	#90	Lech Walesa
#69	Jean-Paul Sartre	#29	Bill Gates
#7	John F. Kennedy	#14	Michael Jackson
#100	Ray Kroc	#53	Margaret Thatcher
#34	Andy Warhol	#72	Gabriel García Márquez
#77	Crick and Watson	#33	Oprah Winfrey
#95	Sam Walton	#23	Ronald Reagan
#8	Martin Luther King	#66	Benazir Bhutto
#20	John Lennon	#35	Dalai Lama
#87	Mikhail Kalashnikov	#3	Pope John Paul II
#17	Bob Dylan	#64	Mikhail Gorbachev
#94	Gianni Agnelli	#75	Rupert Murdoch
#88	Estée Lauder	#93	Helmut Kohl
#78	Jean Piaget	#98	Tim Berners-Lee
#76	Michel Foucault	#24	Saddam Hussein
#41	Muhammad Ali	#48	Steven Spielberg
#67	Indira Gandhi	#70	Yasser Arafat
#79	Pol Pot	#49	Nelson Mandela

BY CATEGORY

POLITICS & LEADERSHIP

#84	Emmeline Pankhurst	#55	Mao Zedong
#22	Vladimir Ilyich Lenin	#65	Kim Il-sung
#25	Woodrow Wilson	#32	Charles de Gaulle
#28	Mohandas Gandhi	#21	Fidel Castro
#6	Adolf Hitler	#26	Che Guevara
#54	Franklin D. Roosevelt	#7	John F. Kennedy
#56	Benito Mussolini	#8	Martin Luther King
#68	Haile Selassie	#67	Indira Gandhi
#42	Francisco Franco	#79	Pol Pot
#27	Joseph Stalin	#90	Lech Walesa
#18	Winston Churchill	#53	Margaret Thatcher
#62	Dwight Eisenhower	#23	Ronald Reagan
#37	Ho Chi Minh	#66	Benazir Bhutto
#43	Harry S. Truman	#64	Mikhail Gorbachev
#46	Eva Perón	#93	Helmut Kohl
#83	David Ben-Gurion	#24	Saddam Hussein
		#70	Yasser Arafat
		#49	Nelson Mandela

POPULAR CULTURE & THE ARTS

#50 Igor Stravinsky
#30 Charlie Chaplin
#39 Coco Chanel
#52 Le Corbusier
#12 Salvador Dalí
#60 Fred Astaire
#91 Jesse Owens
#4 Walt Disney
#44 Pablo Picasso
#13 Marilyn Monroe
#38 Alfred Hitchcock
#45 Marlon Brando
#15 James Dean
#11 Miles Davis
#5 Elvis Presley
#47 Frank Lloyd Wright
#34 Andy Warhol
#20 John Lennon
#17 Bob Dylan
#41 Muhammad Ali
#14 Michael Jackson
#33 Oprah Winfrey
#48 Steven Spielberg

SCIENCE & TECHNOLOGY

#16 Marie Curie
#9 The Wright Brothers
#1 Albert Einstein
#10 Sigmund Freud
#96 Ernest Rutherford
#99 Thomas Midgley Jr.
#97 Edwin Hubble
#74 Robert Goddard
#58 Charles Lindbergh
#81 Enrico Fermi
#86 Wernher von Braun

#61 Robert Oppenheimer
#89 Alan Turing
#92 Alexander Fleming
#77 Crick and Watson
#87 Mikhail Kalashnikov
#78 Jean Piaget
#98 Tim Berners-Lee

WRITERS & THINKERS

#51 John Maynard Keynes
#59 Ludwig Wittgenstein
#19 James Joyce
#36 T. S. Eliot
#71 F. Scott Fitzgerald
#31 George Orwell
#82 Karl Popper
#85 Simone de Beauvoir
#57 Billy Graham
#69 Jean-Paul Sartre
#76 Michel Foucault
#73 Milton Friedman
#63 Mother Teresa
#72 Gabriel García Márquez
#35 Dalai Lama
#3 Pope John Paul II

BUSINESS & COMMERCE

#2 Henry Ford
#40 Howard Hughes
#80 Thomas Watson Jr.
#100 Ray Kroc
#95 Sam Walton
#94 Gianni Agnelli
#88 Estée Lauder
#29 Bill Gates
#75 Rupert Murdoch

THE LIST

Counting down to the most influential individual of the twentieth century…

RAY KROC (1902–1984)

American Founder and Chairman of McDonald's

Founding father of the international fast-food industry; took the seed of a commercial idea and turned it into a global multibillion-dollar business

Ray Kroc's appreciation of the potential for a fast-food restaurant chain, combined with his innovative use of a franchising system, blanket advertising, and meticulous attention to every detail of production and presentation, led to a fundamental change in the eating habits of the American people. Branding not only the product but also the service and the whole consumer experience, he made McDonald's into the world's largest food retailing chain.

An Eye for Productivity

Raymond Albert Kroc was born into a relatively poor Czech immigrant family in Chicago, Illinois, and grew up in Oak Park, Illinois. He left public school without graduating, lied to the Red Cross about his age and trained to be an ambulance driver with the intention of serving in World War I, but the war ended before he could see active duty. He then had several jobs, first as pianist for a small radio station, then as a paper cup salesman, and then marketing a commercial milk shake mixer that so impressed him that he set up a company to be the sole distributor. The machine was able to mix several drinks at the same time, so when, in 1954, a restaurant ordered eight, he was sufficiently intrigued to pay the owners a visit.

He discovered a small chain of establishments belonging to the McDonald brothers, Dick and Mac, who had pared their menu down to a handful of items—burgers, fries, soft drinks, and milk shakes—and ran the show like an assembly line. Kroc had the genius to realize that this quick production system could be the foundation of an entire fast-food industry, and that the model could be rolled out across the nation on a franchise basis. He put a proposal to the brothers and went into partnership with them, creating McDonald's Systems Inc. (later renamed McDonald's Corporation) with him as the business manager overseeing the expansion.

 REWRITING HISTORY

Kroc's concept blazed a trail along which many other food retailing companies have since followed. Now overtaken by Yumi (owners of Taco Bell and KFC) and by Subway, McDonald's was for a long time the largest restaurant chain in the world, and it remains a byword for both the benefits and the ills of globalization and the culture of mass production.

Running with an Idea

Ray Kroc was now in his fifties and had had a relatively modest career, but he felt—quite rightly as it turned out—that he was onto something big. He quickly opened up the first of his own McDonald's outlets, in Des Plaines, Illinois, but he was already looking far into the future. He set up the Franchise Realty Corporation to purchase suitable sites for restaurants and to then lease the land to McDonald's franchisees while maintaining ownership. He soon had his first sub-franchisee, and the company, boosted by a nationwide advertising campaign, expanded rapidly. Within five years there were 200 franchises in operation.

A year later, in 1961, Kroc reached a deal with the McDonald brothers to buy the business rights to their operation for $2.7 million, and the company continued to go from strength to strength.

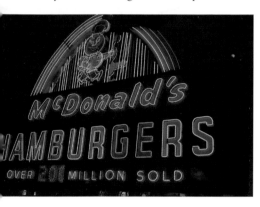

The Key to Success

At the heart of Ray Kroc's fast-food revolution was an intense focus on efficient production and uniformity of product, and Kroc has been compared to Henry Ford in this respect. Work in the restaurants was divided into specific, easily learned tasks, and unskilled teenage labor was recruited. Franchisees received intensive training at McDonald's "Hamburger University" in Elk Grove, Illinois, and every detail of the production process was defined. As well as ensuring that every burger had exactly the same weight, dimensions, and fat content, Kroc insisted that franchisees' premises conform to the company design and décor so that the McDonald's experience was always the same. He then devoted a previously unheard-of advertising budget to persuading the public that it was an experience they wanted.

The strategy brought enormous economies of scale that increased exponentially as McDonald's spread across America, throughout Europe, and beyond. At the time of Kroc's death from heart disease in 1984, there were more than 8,000 McDonald's restaurants in operation in 34 countries, and that number has now increased to over 30,000 outlets in more than 100 countries, making the golden arches a symbol of American influence around the world.

◀ Whether you're lovin' it or loathin' it, McDonald's has revolutionized the fast-food industry and become a worldwide phenomenon. The company's Golden Arches logo has become a symbol of globalization.

"I guess to be an entrepreneur you have to have a large ego, enormous pride, and an ability to inspire others to follow your lead."
Ray Kroc

- Politics & Leadership
- **Science & Technology**
- Popular Culture & the Arts
- Business & Commerce
- Writers & Thinkers

◀◀ REWRITING HISTORY

The downside of Freon was hard to predict, but Midgley was fully aware of the dangers posed by lead back in the early 1920s. In support of GM's efforts, he even demonstrated the safety of tetra-ethyl lead by breathing the fumes for one minute at a press conference and then kept quiet the fact that he had to take a year's convalescence to recover from this stunt.

THOMAS MIDGLEY JR. (1889–1944)

American Engineer, Industrial Chemist, and Inventor

Invented two key chemical compounds that appeared to offer perfect solutions to particular industrial problems; these were used worldwide and he received accolades for his work; unfortunately the compounds have caused incalculable long-term environmental damage

As the inventor of two of the world's most useful and ubiquitous chemicals, Thomas Midgley Jr. received several prestigious awards and was president and chairman of the American Chemical Society. Only with hindsight was environmental historian J. R. McNeill able to say that Midgley "had more impact on the atmosphere than any other single organism in the history of life on Earth."

A Practical Solution

Midgley was born in Beaver Falls, Pennsylvania, and grew up in Columbus, Ohio. After completing a doctorate in mechanical engineering at Cornell University, Thomas Midgley turned his considerable talents to the field of industrial chemistry. Both his father and his uncle were inventors, and Midgley soon joined the laboratory of Charles Kettering in Daytona. He worked on a research project for General Motors, looking for an additive that would prevent "knocking" (pre-ignition of gas) in car engines. This occurs when gasoline ignites as a result of compression rather than from the spark, and it was preventing the manufacturers from increasing the compression, and therefore the performance, of their engines. Working systematically through the periodic table, Midgley discovered that lead was effective, and tetra-ethyl lead ($((CH_3CH_2)_4Pb)$) was soon being used in gasoline worldwide.

Discovering the Downside

The toxic properties of lead were already well known (manufacturers were careful to call the new additive "ethyl" or TEL) and Midgley himself suffered ill-health as a result of his research. GM set up a manufacturing company with Kettering as president and Midgley as vice president, but it was soon evident that production workers were suffering the effects—hallucinations, insanity, and several deaths. However, GM successfully persuaded the authorities that tetra-ethyl lead was only toxic above a certain threshold and production continued, but over the following decades it became clear that lead released in the combustion of treated gas was entering plants, animals, and humans, and that it was having serious effects on health, including the mental development of children. The use of lead as an automotive fuel additive was eventually phased out in the 1980s, resulting in a dramatic reduction in the lead levels in children's blood.

Freon and the Ozone Layer

In the 1930s Midgley was asked to find a compound to replace the toxic sulfur dioxide and ammonia then being used in refrigeration units. He quickly came up with dichlorofluoromethane, the first of the CFCs (chlorinated fluorocarbons), which became known as Freon. Inherently non-reactive and non-poisonous substance, it did the job perfectly and was soon in use in all new fridges, inhalers, and aerosol spray cans.

It took many decades to discover that, because CFCs are inert and do not react with other chemicals, they accumulate in the upper atmosphere. There, the Sun's UV radiation breaks the molecules down and releases the chlorine, which acts as a catalyst in the breakup of ozone (O_3) molecules and destroys the ozone layer. This is the Earth's billion-year-old sunscreen, which prevents a large proportion of harmful UV radiation from reaching the Earth. The production of CFCs has now been banned, but millions of tons have been released and they will remain in the atmosphere for up to a century. The number of cases of skin cancer attributable to the reduced ozone layer has already been estimated to be in the millions.

Before the full extent of the deleterious effects of his inventions were

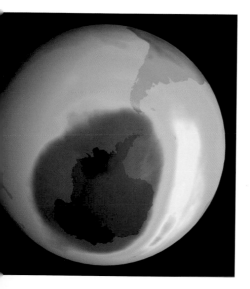

understood, Thomas Midgley died, ironically, at the hands of one of his own inventions. After contracting polio in 1940 and losing the use of his legs, Midgley designed a system of ropes and pulleys to help lift him out of bed. In the fall of 1944 he became caught up in the ropes, and the contraption strangled him.

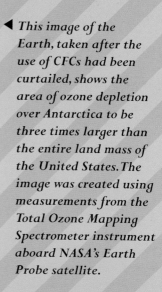

◀ *This image of the Earth, taken after the use of CFCs had been curtailed, shows the area of ozone depletion over Antarctica to be three times larger than the entire land mass of the United States. The image was created using measurements from the Total Ozone Mapping Spectrometer instrument aboard NASA's Earth Probe satellite.*

TIM BERNERS-LEE (b. 1955)

English Computer Scientist

Inventor of the World Wide Web; recipient of the Millennium Technology Prize; Knight Commander of the Order of the British Empire (KBE)

In terms of his impact upon our everyday lives, Sir Tim Berners-Lee must rank as one of the most influential people of the past 20 years. The World Wide Web, which is primarily his invention, has facilitated a previously unimaginable level of communication between individuals, businesses, and institutions around the world.

The Family Network

Sir Timothy Berners-Lee was born in London into a household steeped in computers, mathematics, and physics. Both his parents had worked on the Ferranti 1, the first commercially available electronic computer, which was based on the Mark I computer that Alan Turing helped to program at Manchester University. As a young boy he developed an early interest in the subject, and was taken by the concept of networked computers that featured in the science fiction writing of Arthur C. Clarke.

From high school he went to study physics at Queen's College, Oxford, where he built his own computer and graduated with a first-class honors degree in 1976. After a period working for British communications companies, he moved to Switzerland to be a consultant software engineer for CERN, the European nuclear research establishment, and there he took his first steps toward what was to become the World Wide Web.

Hypertext

In order to search the CERN computer database, Berners-Lee created his own data retrieval system, called ENQUIRE, based on hypertext—links between and within documents stored on CERN's computer network. At the end of his six-month contract, he went back to England, but he returned to CERN in 1984 as a Fellow. Throughout the '80s, the Internet was developing as a physical means of connecting computers around the world, and by 1989 CERN had one of the largest "nodes." Tim Berners-Lee saw the possibility of creating a hyperlink retrieval system like ENQUIRE that would be capable of searching not just the local database but also the entire Internet network,

REWRITING HISTORY

Tim Berners-Lee continues to nurture the growth of the World Wide Web, and is a strong advocate of maintaining it as a free, open, and accessible resource. He is currently working on development of the Semantic Web, in which data are stored in a form that can be understood by computers, enabling information to be searched, analyzed, and combined without human intervention.

and he put the proposal to CERN. It went ahead in 1990, and together he and the Belgian computer scientist Robert Cailliau designed and built the first Web browser and Web server. The first Web page, in which Berners-Lee and Cailliau explained what the World Wide Web is and how to use it, went on line in the summer of 1991.

The initial browser was text based and, although it was theoretically available to the public, it was initially only used by scientists and academics. A graphic interface for the Unix system was created in 1993, followed closely by versions for Windows and Macintosh, and websites and Web use began to expand exponentially. There are now in excess of 200 million websites, with more than 1.7 billion users.

Internet Issues

From the outset, Tim Berners-Lee was necessarily involved in setting standards for domain names and Web addresses (URLs), and defining the protocol by which files are retrieved and transferred (HTTP), as well as the computer language (HTML) in which Web pages are composed. He has since played a key role in the development of the Web, through his leadership since 1994 of the World Wide Web Consortium, based at the Laboratory for Computer Science and Artificial Intelligence at the Massachusetts Institute of Technology where he is a senior researcher and holder of the 3Com Founders Chair.

His achievements have been widely recognized by the international community. He has been given honorary doctorates by the Open University and the University of Southampton, and in 2004 he was awarded the first Millennium Technology Prize, with a cash prize of one million euros, and he also received a knighthood (KBE). In 2007 he was awarded the Order of Merit.

#98

Berners-Lee was using this NeXT computer at CERN when he devised the World Wide Web, and it became the first Web server. The label on the front of the CPU bears the hand-written warning, "This machine is a server. DO NOT POWER IT DOWN!!" ▼

EDWIN HUBBLE (1889–1953)

American Astronomer and Mathematician

Carried out detailed observations and measurements of distant stars and galaxies; discovered that there are galaxies beyond the Milky Way; discovered evidence that the universe is expanding; fundamentally revised our concept of the cosmos

◀◀ REWRITING HISTORY

Albert Einstein's general theory of relativity, proposed in 1917, predicted a universe that was either contracting or expanding. Unable to accept this, Einstein introduced a mathematical constant to "correct" his findings, but Hubble's discoveries showed that he had been right in the first place. Einstein regarded the introduction of the constant as his biggest blunder, and thanked Hubble for putting him right.

The astronomer Edwin Hubble made what have been described as two of the most important discoveries in the history of the human race, forcing humankind to come to terms with a universe that is infinitely larger and much older than we had believed. The orbiting Hubble Space Telescope is named in his honor.

Star Struck

Born in Missouri, the son of an insurance executive, Edwin Powell Hubble moved to Wheaton, Illinois, with his family when he was eight. At high school he made more of a mark with his athletic prowess than his academic achievements, and at the age of sixteen he broke the state high-jump record. At the University of Chicago, where he studied astronomy and mathematics, he played for the basketball team while studying for a BS, which he received in 1910. He was one of the first students to win a Rhodes scholarship to Oxford University, England, where he studied law and gained an MA degree.

Returning to the US in 1913, Hubble registered to practice law in Kentucky, but then taught for a while at a high school in New Albany, Indiana, where he also coached the basketball team. After serving with the US Army in World War I and being promoted to the rank of major, Hubble decided to return to astronomy, the subject that had fascinated him since childhood. He went to study at the University of Chicago's Yerkes Observatory at Williams Bay, Wisconsin, receiving a doctorate in astronomy in 1917, and then took a post at the Mount Wilson Observatory, high in the San Gabriel mountains near Pasadena, California.

A Crucial Discovery

At Mount Wilson, the 100-inch (254-cm) Hooker telescope (which was the world's largest telescope until 1948) had just been completed, and Hubble used it to study distant stars. At the time it was thought that the Milky Way, our home galaxy, was the full extent of the universe, but Hubble was able to show that spiral nebulae such as the Andromeda Nebula were not only tens of thousands of times further away than the stars in our own galaxy but also in fact themselves galaxies. The announcement of his findings, in 1924, altered forever the way in which we think about the universe.

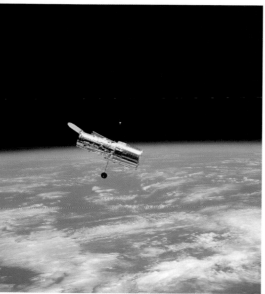

Receding Galaxies

It was already known that distant stars exhibit a red shift in the light coming from them, evidence that the stars are moving away from us (the change in the note of the siren of a passing fire truck is a similar phenomenon). Hubble's meticulous study of galaxies, in which he classified them according to various criteria, led him to the discovery that the extent of the red shift in the light from a galaxy is directly proportional to its distance away from us, and this was initially formulated in 1929 as the Redshift Distance Law. It has since become known as Hubble's Law.

A New Cosmology

The implication of Hubble's Law is both inescapable and monumental—the universe is expanding. The fact that the speed at which two galaxies are moving apart is proportional to the distance between them does not mean that the galaxies are flying outward through space at different speeds, but that space itself is expanding. This possibility, based on Einstein's work on general relativity, had been proposed by Georges Lemaître a couple of years earlier, but this was the first observational support for the idea. The "Big Bang" theory, which holds that the universe—including time and space, as well as matter and energy—came into existence at a single point, follows logically from Hubble's evidence of an expanding universe. This theory is now broadly accepted throughout the scientific community and is at the heart of modern cosmology. Hubble's discoveries had overturned humanity's vision of an eternal and immovable universe although, interestingly, Hubble always wished to keep open the possibility that no expansion was happening and that another explanation would be found for the red shift phenomenon.

◀ *Named after the pioneering astronomer, the Hubble Space Telescope has been orbiting the Earth every 96 minutes, 360 miles (575 kilometers) above the planet's surface, since 1990. From its position outside Earth's distorting atmosphere, this space-based observatory sends back uniquely clear images of our expanding universe.*

- Politics & Leadership
- **Science & Technology**
- Popular Culture & the Arts
- Business & Commerce
- Writers & Thinkers

◀◀ REWRITING HISTORY

Rutherford was quick to realize that the half-lives of elements provided a means of dating rock by measuring the relative amounts of an element and its decay products, coming up with an age for the Earth of at least 3.4 billion years. This gave a considerable boost to Charles Darwin's evolutionary theory by providing a plausible timescale over which for it to have taken place.

ERNEST RUTHERFORD (1871–1937)

New Zealand-Born British Nuclear Physicist

First to explain radioactivity; first to correctly describe the structure of the atom; discovered the existence of the proton; first to split the atom and transmute one element into another; recipient of the Nobel Prize in Chemistry; knighted and made a life peer

An enthusiastic and charismatic man, Ernest Rutherford can justifiably be called the father of atomic physics. His clear-minded approach to the scientific questions of the day, always looking for the simplest explanation and designing elegant ways of testing hypotheses, led to some of the most fundamental breakthroughs in the field.

Waves to Particles

Ernest Rutherford was born near Nelson, New Zealand, the son of a successful Scottish farmer who had emigrated from England. After attending Nelson College, Rutherford took a bachelor of science degree at Canterbury College in Christchurch, followed by a master's degree in math and physics. He then stayed on for a further year, carrying out research into the detection of electromagnetic waves, and displayed a remarkable talent for well-designed experiments. In 1895, at the age of 24, Rutherford went to England to become the first research student of the eminent physicist J. J. Thomson at Cambridge University's Cavendish Laboratory, doing particle research. Continuing his own work, Rutherford succeeded in sending and receiving electromagnetic signals—or radio waves—over a distance of 2 miles (3 km). Impressed with his abilities, Thomson asked for his assistance investigating X-ray induced conduction of electricity through a gas—work that resulted in Thomson's discovery of the electron.

Radioactive Studies

Henri Becquerel had only recently discovered radioactivity, and Rutherford, like Marie Curie, decided to conduct research into this strange phenomenon. He began by studying the radiation from uranium, and discovered not only that it would ionize a gas but also that two different kinds of radiation, with different powers of ionization and penetration, were being emitted. These he named alpha and beta radiation.

In 1898, Rutherford was given the professorship of physics at McGill University in Montreal, Canada, and there he made a very significant discovery while working on thorium oxide. He found that the compound produced a radioactive gas whose radioactivity halved every minute, and that when in contact with a metal plate the gas would produce a deposit that in turn had a "half-life" of about eleven hours. These half-lives were unaffected by any external conditions. In partnership with chemist Frederick Soddy, he was able to show that in the process of emitting an alpha or beta particle, atoms of one element were changing into atoms of another. He was also able to show mathematically that the process released considerable amounts of energy from within the atom. In 1904 Rutherford delivered a lecture to the Royal Society of London entitled "The Succession of Changes in Radioactive Bodies," in which he presented in detail his theory of radioactive decay. This "new alchemy" was a major breakthrough and it turned Rutherford into an academic celebrity overnight. He was awarded the Nobel Prize in Chemistry for this work in 1908.

The Atomic Model

In 1907, Rutherford returned to England as professor of physics at Manchester University, where he set about investigating alpha particles. Again, using simple yet ingenious experiments, he showed that alpha particles attracted free electrons to form helium atoms, and the particles were later shown to be identical to helium nuclei, consisting of two protons and two neutrons. From the results of the "gold foil experiment," carried out under his direction by Hans Geiger and Ernest Marsden and in which alpha particles were occasionally bounced back by a thin gold foil, Rutherford hypothesized that atoms consisted of a dense positively charged nucleus surrounded by orbiting electrons, contradicting Thomson's "plum pudding" model of negatively charged electrons embedded in a ball of positive charge. His new model was taken up and expanded by Niels Bohr, and it still forms the basis of our understanding of the atom today. As if this were not enough, in 1919 Rutherford succeeded in artificially transmuting nitrogen into oxygen by bombarding it with alpha particles, the first time this had been achieved.

In 1911, Ernest Rutherford (standing, fourth from right in this composite picture) found himself among an illustrious group of eminent scientists at the first Solvay Conference on Physics in Brussels. Attendees included Hendrik Lorentz, Marie Curie, Henri Poincaré, Max Planck, and Albert Einstein.
▼

SAM WALTON (1918–1992)

American Entrepreneur

Pioneer of the "pile 'em high and sell 'em cheap" school of retailing; founder of American retail store chain Wal-Mart Stores, Inc., one of the world's largest companies; the richest man in America in the late 1980s

Sam Walton, the founder of Wal-Mart, built a retailing empire by constantly finding ways to cut costs and increase scale. His innovative vision changed the face of the retail industry not only in the US, but around the globe. Today, Wal-Mart is the world's largest public corporation in terms of revenue.

Personal Work Ethic

Sam Walton was born to farming parents near Kingfisher, Oklahoma, but the farm provided a poor income. The family moved to Missouri when Sam was five and his father returned to his former occupation of loan appraiser. Walton's capacity for hard work and commitment was evident even during his high school years. He was vice president and then president of the student body, and also an honors student. At graduation he was voted the "Most Versatile Boy." After majoring in economics at the University of Missouri in 1940, Walton immediately joined the department store chain J. C. Penney as a management trainee, but left in 1942 and went to work in a munitions factory in anticipation of joining the US Army, and there he met his future wife, Helen Robson. He entered the US Army Intelligence Corps in 1943, supervising security at POW camps and aircraft factories.

Going Up

With money saved from his army service and a loan from his in-laws, Walton bought the lease on a variety store in Newport, Arkansas—a franchise of the Butler Brothers chain—and he quickly put into practice his own ideas of how to make a store profitable. Staying open for longer hours than his competitors, he sought out the lowest priced suppliers and passed the savings on to his customers. The quantities that he was able to sell enabled him to further improve his deals with suppliers, and he was soon turning in the highest profits in the Butler Brothers chain. When the landlord refused to renew the lease, he sold the business to him at a good price and opened Walton's Five and Dime in Bentonville, Arkansas, and by 1962 he and his brother owned sixteen such stores in Arkansas, Kansas, and Missouri. Managers were encouraged to invest in the stores, giving them a share of the profits and a strong incentive to implement Walton's successful—and carefully researched—retailing formula, consisting of quality, value, customer satisfaction, helpful and knowledgeable service, and a pleasant shopping environment.

The Next Level

Sam Walton was convinced that the future of retailing lay in large-scale, out-of-town, discount, big-box stores, and he had the courage to put his own money into making it happen. The first Wal-Mart store opened in Rogers, Arkansas, in 1962. Within five years there were 24 such discount outlets, and by 1980 the number had increased to 276, before the acquisition of 92 Big K stores. Ten years later, with more than 1,200 stores in 35 states, Wal-Mart was the largest retailer in the US, and the company went international the following year, opening a retail outlet in Mexico City. As with all successful entrepreneurs, Sam Walton coupled huge ambition with vision, and he was able to anticipate change ahead of his major rivals. The very nature of his business model—cutting prices at all stages of the merchandising chain, from suppliers onwards—cut hard into his margins and ensured that sales had to grow relentlessly. Achieving this demanded continual innovation, sharpening up practices in order to increase efficiencies and cut costs. Walton was an early pioneer in the use of computerized systems to manage stock control, bringing the corporation greater flexibility despite its increasing size, and setting a precedent which every major retail corporation since has followed.

This remarkable success has not been achieved without criticism. Wal-Mart has been accused of driving local independent retailers out of business—and with them a sense of local community—by offering prices that they are simply unable to match. In his defense, some would say that a figure like Sam Walton anticipated what were inevitable changes and simply sped them up. The rise of internet retail would seem to give weight to this argument. What is unarguable, however, is that consumers sided overwhelmingly with Wal-Mart. Low prices and unparalleled consumer choice is the legacy that Sam Walton leaves behind.

#95

Sam Walton gives a motivational speech to staff at a newly opened Hypermart in the US.
▼

GIANNI AGNELLI (1921–2003)

Italian Motor Industry Magnate

Italy's leading capitalist and playboy; influenced Italy's postwar economy; industrial and political mover and shaker at home and overseas; renowned as a stylish socialite

- ▪ Politics & Leadership
- ▪ Science & Technology
- ▪ Popular Culture & the Arts
- ▪ **Business & Commerce**
- ▪ Writers & Thinkers

◀◀ **REWRITING HISTORY**

The outwardly ideal life of this urbane and highly successful man was marked by a series of personal tragedies. He lost his father in a plane crash when he was just 14, his mother died in a car crash in the same year that his grandfather died, and in 1997 his young nephew and chosen heir, Giovanni Alberto Agnelli, died of cancer. His son Edoardo committed suicide three years later.

Giovanni "Gianni" Agnelli was born into a wealthy family, the grandson of the founder of Fiat. Taking control of the company in his thirties, he turned Fiat into a global force through astute business decisions, international alliances, and political maneuvering. He himself became an icon of power, wealth, and elegance to Italians.

Privileged Playboy

The son of a wealthy industrialist father and aristocratic mother, Gianni had a privileged upbringing. After studying law at the University of Turin he fought in the Italian Army in World War II, and later served as an interpreter for the occupying US forces.

Fabbrica Italiana Automobili Torino, later known as Fiat, had achieved success under the leadership of Gianni's grandfather (also called Giovanni) through acquisitions and political expedients. After the war, Giovanni the elder had to relinquish his position as head of Fiat, which had been the principal manufacturer of military vehicles for Mussolini's government, and when he died in 1945, Gianni inherited the family business. However, he wasn't yet ready for responsibility and instead joined the international jet set, indulging his passion for fast cars, expensive sports and high society, and leading the life of a playboy until he was in his thirties. He was renowned for his "conquest" of several of the world's most beautiful and high-profile women, but after a serious car accident in 1952 that left him with a permanent limp, he began to settle down, marrying Princess Marella Caracciolo di Castagneto and joining Fiat—initially in a junior role—to learn the ropes.

Taking up the Reins

In 1966, after serving as vice-chairman and managing director, Agnelli became chairman of Fiat, and he quickly demonstrated a flair for adroit political and business decisions. Under his guidance, Fiat soon took over the Italian luxury carmaker Lancia, and acquired a significant stake in Ferrari. It later acquired Alfa Romeo, making Fiat virtually the sole car producer in Italy.

As the oil crisis of the 1970s bit, harming car sales and profit margins, Agnelli solved the company's cash problems by selling a ten percent stake to Libya's Colonel Gaddafi. When threatened job cuts brought workers out on strike and halted production, Agnelli met the unions head-on, eventually breaking the strike and fundamentally altering Italian labor relations by reducing the power of the unions.

A Force to be Reckoned with

As well as consolidating Fiat's position at home, extending Fiat's model range dramatically, and decentralizing management, Agnelli also sought to put Italy back on the world economic map, pursuing new markets overseas, especially the US, and opening manufacturing plants in Poland, Russia, and Brazil. By the early '90s the Fiat group was employing 300,000 people, and its portfolio included not only car and truck manufacture but also retail stores, food and insurance, publishing, wine production, and the Juventus soccer team (a share in which was later sold to Colonel Gaddafi). At its peak the group was responsible for more than four percent of Italy's GNP, employed more than three percent of industrial workers, and was the largest car manufacturer in Europe.

Throughout his life, Agnelli was famous for his fashion sense and was regarded as a style icon, combining a taste for the very best quality in designer clothing with a dash of eccentric flair. His hallmark touches included wearing his wristwatch over his shirt cuff, or even over the cuff of his jacket, and wearing his tie loosened and pulled off center with studied carelessness. His bespoke Caraceni suits were tailored with such care and attention to detail that they still looked fashionable when his grandson wore them. Agnelli, who was the richest man in Italy, owned several opulent designer homes and a fabulous art collection, which he left to the city of Turin. An Italian senator for life, he was dubbed "Il Re"—his country's uncrowned king. Internationally, he became a key player on the world's commercial, social, and political stages, with friends in the highest places who helped him fulfill his ambitions for the company and for the Agnelli dynasty.

#94

◀ *Fiat's Lingotto production plant in Turin opened in 1923 and was the largest car factory in the world. Cars moved up through the five storeys as they passed along the assembly line, emerging at roof level, where there was a test track. Lingotto closed in 1982.*

HELMUT KOHL (b. 1930)

Chancellor of the Federal Republic of Germany

Played a key role in the creation of the European Union and the reunification of Germany; Minister President of the state of Rhineland-Palatinate (1969–76); chairman of the Christian Democratic Union (CDU) political party (1973–98)

- Politics & Leadership
- Science & Technology
- Popular Culture & the Arts
- Business & Commerce
- Writers & Thinkers

◀◀ REWRITING HISTORY

If Helmut Kohl had been born a year earlier, he would have seen active military service on the side of Nazi Germany and would not have had the untainted credentials to represent the new Germany on the political stage as he did. As it was, he was able to achieve reconciliation with many of his nation's former enemies, including France.

Hailed by President George H. W. Bush as "the greatest European leader of the second half of the twentieth century," Helmut Kohl brought about momentous changes to the political map of postwar Europe, seizing the moment to reunify East and West Germany, rebuilding relations with his nation's neighbors, and working to bring about the European Union.

A Child of War

Helmut Josef Michael Kohl was born in Ludwigshafen am Rhein, a small industrial city in the Rhine Neckar region of Germany. His father was a civil servant, and the family were conservative Roman Catholics. The last of three children, he was too young to see combat, but his brother was killed as a soldier in World War II. He joined the newly formed Christian Democratic Union party (CDU) at the age of 16, graduated from the Gymnasium in 1950 and then studied law at Frankfurt University before attending the University of Heidelberg and gaining a degree in history and political science. He received his PhD from Heidelberg in 1958 with a doctoral thesis on postwar political development in his home region.

Political Career

Increasingly active in the CDU, he was elected to the state legislature in 1963, becoming state Prime Minister in 1969 and Chairman of the CDU's federal executive in 1973. Three years later he was elected to the Bundestag, the German parliament, and in 1982, after Helmut Schmidt's resignation following a vote of no confidence in his minority government, Helmut Kohl was voted Chancellor of the Federal Republic of Germany. This was confirmed in elections the following year.

Kohl's first few years as Chancellor were unremarkable, continuing Schmidt's move away from Keynesian economic policies, cutting public spending, and adopting a less popular monetarist approach. Foreign policy continued to focus on Germany's relations with the US and the rest of Western Europe. In the general elections of 1987, his party was returned with a smaller majority, and its popularity continued to decline. The beginnings of a revolution which was stirring in the East, however, would soon arrive in Germany, bringing with it monumental change.

Reunification of Germany

Throughout 1989, democratic movements began to prosper across the Soviet Bloc. Solidarity—the trade union organization led by Lech Walesa—came to power in Poland, then Hungary returned to a non-Communist government, and in East Germany, after a visit from Mikhail Gorbachev urging reform, and widespread riots against the curtailment of freedom, the authorities bowed to the inevitable and allowed free passage across the Berlin Wall. The western European powers were paralyzed by the speed of events, but Chancellor Kohl took decisive action. Two years earlier he had received Erich Honecker, the then East German leader, indicating his wish for a rapprochement, and now he seized the chance. Without consulting either his partners in government or the Western Alliance, he put together a plan for bringing the two countries together, sought guarantees from Gorbachev that the Soviet Union would not stand in the way, and in May 1990 signed a preliminary social and economic treaty with East Germany. On October 3 1990, with the approval of the former World War II Allies for its reintegration, and for the expansion of NATO into its territory, East Germany ceased to exist and Germany was reunified.

European Unity

Two months later, in the first democratic all-Germany elections for almost 60 years, Helmut Kohl was returned to power with a landslide majority that demonstrated the German people's approval of his actions, although there proved to be many unforeseen and unwelcome social and economic consequences of reunification. Throughout his remaining years as Chancellor, Kohl strove for a stable and united Europe, formally dropping German claims to Polish and Czech territory, becoming one of the chief architects of the Maastricht Treaty that brought the European Union into existence, and providing impetus toward the adoption of a single European currency. When he stepped down in September 1998, the impact of his leadership could be seen throughout the continent.

#93

▲
A line of bricks and periodic metal plaques marks the course of the former Berlin Wall through the city. Helmut Kohl played a key role in the removal of this brutal division between East and West.

- Politics & Leadership
- **Science & Technology**
- Popular Culture & the Arts
- Business & Commerce
- Writers & Thinkers

 REWRITING HISTORY

Fleming's discovery is often depicted as being solely a surprising piece of good luck. In fact, the whole of his research for the previous ten years had been focused on finding exactly such a substance as penicillin. Few other scientists working at that time would have been primed to notice, or qualified to identify and analyze, the chance event that led to his discovery.

ALEXANDER FLEMING (1881–1955)

Scottish Bacteriologist

Discovered the antibiotic penicillin; carried out important research into the use of antiseptics; knighted in 1944; shared the Nobel Prize in Medicine in 1945

Renowned primarily for his fortuitous discovery of penicillin, Alexander Fleming displayed, throughout his career, an attention to detail and a flair for experimental research that led him to make important contributions in several other areas of bacteriology and biochemistry. Health care worldwide is still reaping the benefits of his work.

The Formative Years

Alexander Fleming grew up as part of a large family on a farm called Lochfield in East Ayrshire, Scotland. He attended local schools and then spent two years at Kilmarnock Academy before going to work in a shipping office. In 1901, when he was twenty, he inherited a sum of money from his uncle and decided to follow in the footsteps of his elder brother and study to be a medical doctor. He attended medical school at St Mary's Hospital in Paddington, London, qualified in 1906, and joined the hospital's research department as a bacteriologist working under Sir Almroth Wright, a specialist in vaccines and immunization. After gaining further degrees, he became a lecturer at the teaching hospital, and then served in the Army Medical Corps on the Western Front during World War I. In the field hospitals he found that many of the wounded soldiers were dying of septicemia, despite the copious use of antiseptics. Using his medical skills, bacteriological training, and research experience, he designed ingenious experiments that showed the use of antiseptics on deep wounds was doing more harm than good. The chemicals failed to reach the deep bacteria but destroyed leukocytes, part of the body's own defenses, and encouraged gangrene. He recommended reduced use of antiseptic and the removal of all dead tissue from wounds. His conclusions, published in *The Lancet*, were supported by Almroth Wright, and the work boosted his reputation as a fine researcher, but few physicians acted on his suggestions.

The Major Breakthrough

Fleming returned to St Mary's Hospital after the war, and continued his research, trying to find substances that would kill bacteria without damaging the leukocytes. In 1921 he discovered that nasal mucus, tears, and egg white all contained such a substance, an enzyme that he called lysozyme, because it dissolved, or "lysed," the cell walls of the bacteria. While most bacteriologists thought that the action was mechanical, Fleming was convinced that it was a chemical process, and he was later proved right. He continued his work on lysozyme until 1927.

Fleming was elected Professor of Bacteriology in 1928, and in that year he made his major breakthrough. Being somewhat untidy in his laboratory, he left several culture dishes containing *Staphylococcus* bacteria stacked up on the bench when he went on summer vacation. On his return he noticed that a mold was growing on one of the dishes, and that the *Staphylococci* had been

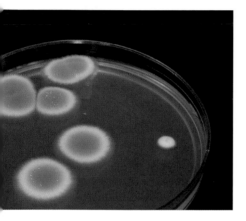

killed in a circle around it. He was able to identify the mold as *Penicillium notatum*, and he later named the antibacterial substance penicillin.

Experimenting with the substance, he realized that although it was effective, it soon lost its potency and could not be injected without being purified and concentrated. He lacked the chemical expertise

to do this, and so looked to others for a solution. He published his findings in the *British Journal of Experimental Pathology* in 1929, but his experiments with lysozyme had not proved fruitful (although much more is now known about this important group of enzymes) and the medical profession was therefore skeptical about the potential of penicillin. It wasn't until 1939 that Australian pathologist Howard Florey and German-British chemist Ernst Chain, using the newly developed technique of freeze-drying, were able to produce pure penicillin, a million times more powerful than Fleming's extract. By 1943 it was being manufactured commercially for use by the Allied military in World War II, and the drug has since revolutionized health care. It remains the world's most widely used antibiotic and is estimated to have saved 200 million lives. In 1944 Alexander Fleming and Howard Florey both received knighthoods, and Fleming shared the Nobel Prize in Medicine with Florey and Chain in 1945. He was awarded $100,000 by the US pharmaceutical companies for his contribution to medicine, which he donated to St Mary's research department. On his death he was cremated, and his ashes were buried in St Paul's Cathedral in London.

#92

◀ *Fleming had been working with culture dishes containing the common bacterium* **Staphylococcus aureus** *when one of them became infected with* **Penicillium** *mold. The spores had probably drifted up from the office of mycologist C. J. La Touche, which was situated below Fleming's.*

"No man, except Einstein in another field, and before him Pasteur, has had a more profound influence on the contemporary history of the human race."
André Maurois

JESSE OWENS (1913–1980)

American Track and Field Athlete

Held world records in 100-yard dash, broad jump, 220-yard dash, and 220-yard low hurdles; won four Olympic gold medals at the 1936 Summer Olympics in Berlin; awarded the Presidential Medal of Freedom and the Congressional Gold Medal

- Politics & Leadership
- Science & Technology
- **Popular Culture & the Arts**
- Business & Commerce
- Writers & Thinkers

 **REWRITING HISTORY**

According to Olympic myth, Hitler stormed out of the stadium after Owens' gold-medal victory so that he wouldn't have to congratulate the black athlete. Owens told his biographer a different story: "Hitler didn't snub me—it was FDR who snubbed me. The president didn't even send me a telegram." Hitler, in fact, had chosen not to honor any athlete personally after the Games' first day.

Jesse Owens was a four-time Olympic gold medalist and world record holder in track and field events. He came from a life of poverty in America's Deep South to achieve lasting fame as the first black sporting hero. Despite his success, he continued to face racial discrimination at home and was not invited to the White House until 40 years after his Olympic triumph.

Running from Racism

Owens was born into a large family in Alabama in 1913, the son of a sharecropper and grandson of a slave. Like most black children at the time, Owens encountered racism from an early age. James Cleveland Owens took the name "Jesse" after his school teacher misheard him say his initials "J. C.". In 1922, the family moved to Cleveland, Ohio. Owens attended Fairmont Junior High, where he came to the attention of track coach Charles Riley after running the 100-yard dash in ten seconds flat. Realizing the boy's potential, Riley began training Owens before school so that Owens could keep his after school job in a shoe repair store. Owens set Junior High records in the high jump and the broad jump (now called the long jump) before moving to East Technical High School. At East Tech, Owens continued his meteoric rise in athletics, gaining the accolade of the nation when he equaled the world record of 9.4 seconds in the 100-yard dash and long-jumped 24 feet 9 ½ inches (7.56 m) at the 1933 National Interscholastic meet in Chicago.

Setting Records

Although Owens was actively recruited by a number of colleges, he was not offered a track scholarship. He eventually attended Ohio State University (OSU) after the university found his father a steady job. Owens, too, held a number of part-time jobs to support himself and his young wife, Ruth. While at OSU, Owens continued to experience racism—he had to live off campus and was denied the same treatment as his white team mates while at track events. Such incidents only served to motivate him further. On May 25, 1935, at the Big Ten meet in Ann Arbor, Michigan, he set three world records (a Long Jump of 26 feet 8¼ inches (8.13 m); 220-yard sprint in 20.7 seconds; and the 220-yard low hurdles in 22.6 seconds) and equaled a fourth (the 100-yard sprint in 9.4 seconds), all within the space of 45 minutes. His long jump record remained unbroken for 25 years.

Olympic Glory

In 1936, Owens was part of the US Olympic team that went to Germany. He qualified to run the 100 and 200 meters as well as the long jump and the men's 4x100m relay team. The Games were held at the Berlin Stadium, with Adolf Hitler in attendance. From the outset, Owens showed that he was an athlete of unparalleled skill, equaling the Olympic 100-meter record

in the first round. Owens went on to win an unprecedented four gold medals, a feat that remained unmatched until Carl Lewis's performance at the 1984 Los Angeles Games. Owens' victories came in the 100 meters, 200 meters, long jump, and 4x100 meters relay. In the latter race, the US team set a world record that remained for 20 years. Owens single-handedly shattered Hitler's claim that the German Aryan race was mentally and physically superior, and the Berlin audience gave Owens one of the greatest ovations of his career, much to the consternation of the Nazi party hierarchy. Owens returned home to a ticker-tape parade in New York, though he still had to take the freight elevator to attend his hero's reception at the Waldorf Astoria.

◀ Jesse Owens at the start of the men's 200 meters in the 1936 Olympic Games held in Berlin. Owen's time of 20.7 seconds broke the Olympic record and the black athlete was acclaimed a hero by the German crowd.

Against the Odds

Owens was America's first black sporting superstar, though he never received the riches that he so deserved, and indeed had difficulty carving out a living after his triumphant return from Berlin. Owens paved the way for other black athletes to achieve their dream, proving that race has no place in the world of sport. Not only was Owens the first Olympic athlete to win four medals, he did so during a period of deep racial segregation in America. Owens had to wait many years before his achievements were truly recognized in his own country, receiving the Presidential Medal of Freedom in 1976 from President Gerald Ford and posthumously the Congressional Gold Medal in 1990.

LECH WALESA (b. 1943)

Trade Unionist and President of Poland

Cofounded the trade union Solidarity, which contributed to the end of communism in Europe in the late 1980s; awarded the Nobel Prize for Peace; served as President of Poland.

- Politics & Leadership
- Science & Technology
- Popular Culture & the Arts
- Business & Commerce
- Writers & Thinkers

◀◀ REWRITING HISTORY

The fragile trade union movement that emerged in Poland in the 1970s might never have begun had it not been for the negotiating ability and charismatic personality of electrician-turned-activist Lech Walesa. Without Solidarity, Eastern Europe may well have remained under communist rule and millions of Europeans would still be dreaming of freedom.

With his trademark mustache and ability to rouse a crowd, Lech Walesa was a charismatic figure in Poland's Gdansk shipyard. As the leader of the trade union movement Solidarity (Solidarnosc), Walesa did much to precipitate the downfall of communism within the Eastern bloc in the late 1980s. Although his success as President of Poland was limited, his legacy of a free Europe is undeniable.

From Electrician to Trade Union Activist

Lech Walesa was born in 1943, in Popowo, Poland, the son of a carpenter. After completing military service from 1963 to 1965, Walesa moved to Gdansk, where he worked as an electrician at the Lenin shipyard. He became involved in workers' rights, seeking to address workers' grievances peacefully with the authorities. In 1970, the rising cost of food and other daily essentials resulted in the outbreak of riots and strikes in Poland, which were brutally repressed by government forces with loss of life. Elected chair of the Strike Committee, Walesa was involved in subsequent negotiations with the communist government. After the authorities reneged on agreed concessions, Walesa became increasingly vocal in his anti-government views and he was dismissed from his job in 1976. He continued to be involved in workers' rights through his involvement with illegal underground trade union movements as well as legal government trade unions. In July 1980, rising meat prices caused strikes to break out again throughout Poland, including in the Lenin Shipyard. Walesa climbed the perimeter fence of his former workplace to join the strike. Feisty and charismatic, Walesa was soon leading the Strike Coordination Committee. His negotiations with the Deputy Prime Minister ended with the government granting workers both the right to form independent trade unions and the right to strike, the first such concessions within the Eastern Bloc.

Solidarity

Solidarity, a national organization of independent trade unions, quickly evolved out of the Strike Coordination Committee, with Walesa as chairman.

By the time of its first congress meeting in September 1981, Solidarity had nearly 10 million members. The movement became increasingly radical, demanding free elections and the end of the Soviet-backed communist government. In December 1981, martial law was declared in Poland and Walesa was placed under house arrest for an 11-month period. Solidarity was forced underground. By the end of 1982, Walesa had returned to his electrician job at the shipyard and also resumed covert leadership of the Solidarity movement. Internationally, Walesa became a heroic figure in the fight against communism and in 1983 he was awarded the Nobel Prize for Peace. Backed by fellow countryman Pope John Paul II and the US, Walesa continued to keep the Solidarity movement alive. The arrival of reformist Mikhail Gorbachev in the Kremlin signaled new hope, and in 1988 Walesa organized another strike at the shipyard, calling for the re-legalization of Solidarity. The Polish communist government was cajoled into entering new negotiations with the Solidarity leader, which led to limited free elections and the election of the first non-communist government within the Soviet bloc. It was the first of Europe's so-called Velvet Revolutions and the beginning of the end of communism.

Presidency and its Aftermath

In 1990, Walesa was elected President of Poland, a post he held until 1995. His term in office was marked by controversy and he appeared less comfortable in the role of being head of state than among the workers of Poland. Internal struggles within his political party caused Walesa to declare a "war at the top" against his former colleagues, and he was criticized for acting in an authoritarian manner. Accusations of the illegal prosecution of Polish conservatives and right-wing groups furthered his unpopularity, and in 1995 he lost a bid for re-election to former communist Aleksander Kwasniewski.

He ran again for office in 2000 but only received one percent of the vote. Although he may have lost the people's support in later years, Walesa's place in Polish, and European, history is assured. Perhaps more than any other individual, his actions started the process of liberation that spread rapidly throughout Europe.

The Polish food riots of 1970 led to the deaths of more than 40 protesters and marked the beginning of mass unrest in Poland. This monument to the fallen was erected near the Gdansk shipyard in 1980.
▼

ALAN TURING (1912–1954)

British Mathematician and Computer Scientist

Pioneer in computers and artificial intelligence; led the British World War II team that broke the German Enigma code; built the first programmable computer; designed the Turing test to recognize intelligence in a machine

- Politics & Leadership
- **Science & Technology**
- Popular Culture & the Arts
- Business & Commerce
- Writers & Thinkers

REWRITING HISTORY

Alan Turing's extraordinary talent and contribution have not received the recognition that they deserve, partly because of the shadow cast by his homosexuality, which was a crime in England at the time. He was convicted in 1952 and sentenced to hormone treatment. He died after ingesting poison in 1954. In Britain, a public campaign and petition led to an official apology from the government in September 2009.

A mathematician, logician, and cryptanalyst, Alan Turing made major contributions in all these fields and helped to break the German machine-generated codes during World War II. His concept of a stored-program calculating machine laid the groundwork for the computer as we know it, and he was among the pioneers of artificial intelligence.

Mathematical Genius

Alan Mathison Turing was born in London, England, and he and his elder brother spent much of their childhood staying with family friends, as their father was a civil service administrator in India. His intellectual ability was evident at an early age, his elementary school teacher proclaiming him a genius, and at Sherborne private boarding school, at the age of 16, he studied—and fully understood—Einstein's theory of relativity. He went on to revel in the newly discovered quantum theory of matter, which appealed to his inclination toward logic and order. Perhaps unsurprisingly, he had difficulty fitting in with his schoolmates and became somewhat reclusive.

His mathematical talent came to the fore during his years at King's College, Cambridge, graduating in 1934 with a distinguished degree, and becoming a Fellow of the college. In 1936, his paper entitled "On Computable Numbers" gained him wide acclaim for having solved a fundamental problem in pure mathematics. To deal with the problem, he imagined a theoretical "Universal machine" (now known as a Turing machine) that was, in essence, a programmable computer that used algorithms and operated on a binary number system—a thought experiment that provided the foundations for the electronic computer.

Extraordinary Codebreaker

After receiving a Proctor fellowship to visit Princeton University, he spent three years there writing his PhD dissertation before returning to England shortly before the start of World War II. He had already been working on a Government Code and Cipher School (GCCS) project to break coded communications enciphered by the German Enigma machine, and when Britain declared war on Germany, Turing reported to GCCS headquarters at Bletchley Park, north of London. He spent the war working there as part of an elite group of codebreakers, and he played a pivotal role. His first achievement was the design of an electromechanical machine, called the Bombe, to help break the Enigma code. The first of these giant machines was up and running by March 1940, and more than 200 of them were in use by the end of the war.

Turing went on to solve other, more complex, forms of German coding, and also spent six months in the US advising the Navy on the construction of a Bombe to break Naval Enigma encoding. It is thought that his contribution to code-breaking techniques and equipment, enabling the British to decode hundreds of crucial German communications, may have shortened the war by as many as two years, although this was not revealed until after his death.

After the War

In 1945, building on his experience at Bletchley Park, Turing went to work on electronic computer design at the

National Physical Laboratory, and in 1946 he presented detailed designs for ACE, the first stored-program computer. There were administrative delays in getting the project underway, however, and by the time Pilot ACE was built and operating, Turing had left to become chief programmer for the Mark 1 computer at Manchester University. There he created programs for math, games, language translation, codebreaking, and other non-computational functions. He also published papers on artificial intelligence and designed "Turing's test" to identify intelligence in a machine. In the last two years of his life he worked on mathematical biology, studying patterns in the growth of living things, yet another of the many fields in which he made a seminal contribution.

▲
The Bombe codebreaking machine, built by Alan Turing at Bletchley Park during World War II, was used to decipher German messages that had been encrypted using Enigma encoding machines.

 REWRITING HISTORY

With her astute business sense, Estée Lauder helped structure the company's IPO in such a way that the family was able to sidestep a $95-million capital gains tax bill. The federal tax laws were amended two years later in order to close the loophole.

ESTÉE LAUDER (1906–2004)

Founder and Former Chairman and CEO of Estée Lauder Companies

Innovative and far-sighted business woman; revolutionized the cosmetics industry with novel marketing methods; turned a backstreet operation into a multibillion-dollar enterprise

From humble beginnings, Estée Lauder used her business skills, relentless drive, and a keen understanding of women and beauty to build an international cosmetics empire. The New York-born daughter of immigrant parents became one of America's wealthiest self-made women and is regarded by many as a shining fulfillment of the American dream.

Humble Beginnings

Josephine Esther Mentzer was the ninth child born to European Jewish immigrants Max and Rose Schotz Mentzer in Queens, New York, where the family lived above their hardware store. After World War I her mother's brother, John Schotz, came from Hungary to join them, and he continued his work as a chemist, developing and producing skin-care products on a small scale in a homemade laboratory in the back yard. Estée, as the family called her, soon became involved in the preparation, packaging, and selling of the concoctions, and she worked alongside her uncle until 1930, when she married textile salesman Joseph Lauter (the family later changed their name to Lauder) and moved to Manhattan. The couple's first son was born three years later, but even as a young mother Estée continued to work on perfecting her uncle's skin creams, broadening the range of cosmetics and successfully selling her products in increasing numbers through small outlets in Manhattan despite the effects of the Depression. Much of her success was due to the marketing methods that she pioneered, including make-up demonstrations and giving free samples, which quickly gained her a reputation. In 1939 she and Joseph were divorced, and Estée moved to Miami Beach, Florida, where her upmarket products soon won over a wealthy clientele.

Into the Stores

Returning to New York in 1942, she remarried Joseph and their second son was born in 1944. Joseph joined her business venture as its full-time financial manager, and the two of them founded Estée Lauder Inc. in 1946. Two years later, Lauder achieved a major breakthrough when she persuaded Saks Fifth

Avenue to grant her counter space. This was a major step forward, and from then on she made it her strategy to open sales points in every top department store throughout America and personally train quality sales assistants, whom she saw as the all important link with her customers.

International Success

Initially, the full range of products consisted only of extremely rich all-purpose cream, creme pack, cleansing oil, and skin lotion, but in 1953—in keeping with her message to women to pamper themselves—Estée Lauder created Youth Dew, a perfumed bath oil. It proved to be an immediate bestseller in its own right, but it also attracted new customers to the Estée Lauder brand and helped to boost sales of the rest of the range. In 1960 the company opened its first sales point overseas, in Harrod's department store in London, and opened an office in Hong Kong the following year. Throughout the '60s Lauder continued to introduce new and successful products, including Aramis fragrance for men and the Clinique range of skin care products that laid claim to sound medical research and laboratory testing. In the late 1960s, using inexpensive black and white photography in advertising campaigns, she launched "the Lauder look" that evoked elegance and femininity and identified the brand with wealthy society, a look that was embodied throughout the '70s by model Karen Graham. Estée remained CEO until 1983, when she handed the reins to her son Leonard.

Company sales had already topped a billion dollars, and by the late '80s Estée Lauder Inc. controlled one third of the prestige cosmetics market in the US and was becoming truly international—the company's products became available in the USSR in 1981. Estée resigned as chairman in 1995, and the company launched an initial public offering (IPO) that raised more than $450 million. When, in 1998, *Time* magazine published its list of the 20 most influential business figures of the twentieth century, the only woman on the list was Estée Lauder. Building on the foundation that she put in place, Estée Lauder Companies Inc., which is still controlled by the Lauder family, now has worldwide annual sales in excess of US$8 billion.

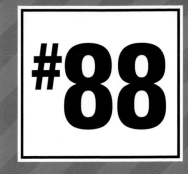

#88

Seen here applying the Lauder look to a New York customer in 1966, Estée Lauder made her mark by taking her product to the people and creating a team of well-trained marketing assistants to represent her.
▼

Russian Designer of the AK-47 Automatic Assault Rifle

Tank commander/mechanic in the Red Army; light weapons designer; twice honored as Hero of Socialist Labor; recipient of the Stalin Prize, Lenin Prize, three Orders of Lenin, Order of the Red Banner of Labor, Order of the Great Patriotic War of the First Class, Order of the Red Star

- Politics & Leadership
- **Science & Technology**
- Popular Culture & the Arts
- Business & Commerce
- Writers & Thinkers

REWRITING HISTORY

After Soviet troops had invaded Afghanistan almost without bloodshed, their fortunes changed dramatically when they found themselves faced with thousands of Chinese-made AK-47s supplied to guerilla fighters by the CIA, who chose these weapons because they were cheap and could not be traced to the US. Ironically, the rifles have since been turned against US troops by the Taliban.

During World War II, Mikhail Kalashnikov set out to design a tough and reliable submachine gun that could be produced cheaply in large quantities. He succeeded beyond his wildest dreams, and his brainchild has been the principal weapon on one or both sides in every war and skirmish worldwide since the 1960s.

Practical Talent

Born shortly after the October Revolution, in the Altai region of southern Russia, Mikhail Timofeyevich Kalashnikov was the eighth child of peasant parents. He was just ten years old when he and his family were forcibly deported to Siberia as part of Stalin's collectivization program. The young Mikhail was good with his hands, building toys, model houses, and, in his teens, a wooden grain mill. In 1938, after working briefly as a clerk on the railways, he was drafted into the Red Army and joined a tank division as a driver and mechanic, where he came up with several inventions. These included a device to count the number of shells that had been fired, using the recoil from the barrel, and a meter to record how long the tank had been running. In 1941 he was commanding a tank at the front line in Battle of Bryansk when he was injured by shrapnel. During his recuperation in a military hospital, he reflected on the slaughter that had been suffered by his comrades and resolved to design an automatic weapon with which the Russian Army could better defend themselves.

The Ultimate Rifle

Having seen at first hand the failings of the Russian armaments, Kalashnikov had a clear idea of what was required. The ideal rifle had to be light, rapid firing, cheap and easy to mass produce, simple to clean and maintain, and able to function in the mud and dust of battlefield conditions in all temperatures. He began by studying previous rifle designs and models, and by the time he left hospital for a period of convalescence he had worked out his own design. Engineers at the railway workshop in his home town made up a prototype, which he took to the Moscow Aviation Institute to test it and refine the design before presenting it at the Army's Ordnance Academy. It was not accepted, but his evident talents earned him a position in the artillery research establishment, and over the next few years he developed the weapon, finally winning a competition for rifle design in 1946. By 1949, after extensive fields trials, the AK-47 (Avtomat Kalashnikova 1947) had been adopted as the Red Army's assault weapon.

#87

A Weapon of Choice

Kalashnikov went on to design a number of small firearms for use by the Russian military, producing an entire family of weapons, but his name is now synonymous with the AK-47, the weapon that has changed the face of warfare and helped determine the outcome of conflicts for half a century.

Supplied to the North Vietnamese fighters by the Soviet Union, it proved far more effective than the US M-16 rifle, and played a major role in the progress of the Vietnam War. This light, cheap, and deadly automatic rifle has undergone a series of modifications over the years to make it even lighter

and more effective. It has since become the weapon of choice for more than 50 legitimate armies and countless freedom fighter and terrorist groups around the globe, notably in Africa and Latin America. It is frequently seen in political graffiti, and several countries and groups even feature the rifle's recognizable profile on their flags. An estimated 100 million AK-47s have now been manufactured—the majority under license—but the simple design has made it possible for the gun to be built in backstreet workshops around the world. Kalashnikov's are estimated to account for some 250,000 deaths per year, making this the most prolific and effective killing machine in history. His invention has brought Mikhail Kalashnikov the gratitude of his country, and he has twice been honored as a Hero of Socialist Labor (1958 and '76). He was awarded the Stalin Prize (1949) and the Lenin Prize (1964), and has received countless other decorations and medals. In 1994, on the occasion of his 75th birthday, he was decorated by Russian President Boris Yeltsin "For Distinguished Services for the Motherland" and promoted to the rank of Major-General.

"I shot with it a lot. I still do now. That is why I am hard of hearing."
Mikhail Kalashnikov

WERNHER VON BRAUN (1912–1977)

German-American Rocketry Pioneer

Leading rocket developer and proponent of space exploration; worked on the German V-2 rocket; came to the US in 1945; became a naturalized US citizen in 1955; instrumental in the US space program, working for the US Army and NASA

- Politics & Leadership
- **Science & Technology**
- Popular Culture & the Arts
- Business & Commerce
- Writers & Thinkers

REWRITING HISTORY

The immigration and employment of von Braun posed a moral dilemma for the US. On the one hand he had been a member of the Nazi party and an SS officer, the V-2 rocket killed more than 6,000 civilians, and he had been aware of the inhuman conditions under which they were built. On the other hand, the US was anxious not to let his expertise fall into the hands of the Russians, he had never been an "ardent" Nazi, and he played no direct part in the use of slave labor.

One of the bright lights of rocket research during the 1930s, Wernher von Braun had his sights set on space exploration, but became involved in Nazi Germany's war effort. Brought to the US after the war, he directed the design and building of the Redstone ballistic missile, the Jupiter C vehicle used to launch the first US satellite, and the giant Saturn V rocket that powered the Apollo space program.

Looking Skyward

Wernher von Braun was the second of three sons born to relatively wealthy parents in Wirsitz, Germany, (now Wyrzysk, Poland). His father was a civil servant and later Minister of Nutrition and Agriculture under the Weimar Republic, and his mother was a member of the minor aristocracy. Whilst studying, Hermann Oberth, one of the fathers of rocketry, inspired him to pursue his interest in math and physics. As a teenager he joined the German "Society for Space Travel," of which Oberth was a member, and in 1930 he enrolled at the Technical University of Berlin, where he helped Oberth with his experiments on liquid-fueled rockets. Oberth, like other rocket scientists, had been influenced by the work of Robert Goddard, and had benefited from the free flow of information coming from America.

Wernher von Braun gained his bachelor's degree in 1932 and then worked for the Ordnance Department of the German Army on the development of ballistic missiles, at the same time receiving his PhD from the University of Berlin in 1934. The Nazi Party had recently come to power in Germany, and the potential military applications of his work were obvious. Indeed, his doctoral thesis, entitled "Construction, Theoretical, and Experimental Solution to the Problem of the Liquid Propellant Rocket," was kept classified by the German army. Under the direction of Walter Dornberger, von Braun worked on the Aggregat series of rockets, incorporating design elements from Goddard's published plans, and following the success of the first two rockets in the A series, they began to work toward a much larger rocket.

Nazi War Effort

Wernher von Braun had an impressive combination of talents. Beside his academic credentials, he showed a remarkable ability to assimilate and analyze data, but he also had excellent leadership skills, and in 1937 he was made technical director of the Peenemünde Rocket Center on the Baltic coast, founded on Hitler's orders. The Treaty of Versailles explicitly forbade Germany from developing or possessing certain types of weapon, but rockets were not mentioned, so these became the focus of R&D. At Peenemünde, von Braun and his team brought together the necessary technologies—especially the guidance systems—needed to develop the V-2 rocket. The V stood for Vergeltungswaffe, meaning retaliation weapon, and it was to be Hitler's response to the sustained Allied bombing of German cities. These giant flying

bombs, which were the first missiles to achieve space flight, were built by forced labor at the Mittelwerk factory, where some 20,000 people died of malnutrition, maltreatment, and execution for acts of sabotage. Some 3,000 V-2 rockets were launched, killing more than 7,000 people, mainly in Antwerp, Belgium, and London, England. When it became clear that Germany would be defeated, von Braun took his team of more than 100 engineers and fled ahead of the advancing Russian troops in order to surrender to the Americans, the only Allied nation that he felt was likely to have a space program. He and his team, together with 100 V-2 rockets, 300 train car loads of V-2 spare parts, and copious technical data, were taken to the US, installed at Fort Bliss in Texas, and given a mandate to continue their research.

◀ A prominent spokesman for space exploration, von Braun became director of NASA's Marshall Space Flight Center (MSFC) in 1960 and played a key role in the race for space. He is seen here in his MSFC office, together with models of some of the rockets he helped to develop.

The US Space Program

For more than 20 years, Wernher von Braun made a major contribution to military ballistic missile development (first at Fort Bliss and then at the Redstone Arsenal near Huntsville, Alabama, where they built the Army's Redstone and Jupiter missiles) and to the American space program after the establishment of NASA in 1960. A strong advocate of space exploration, von Braun was made director of NASA's Marshall Space Flight Center and he directed the development of the Saturn V multistage liquid-fuel rocket that took Americans to the Moon. He died in 1977.

"I have learned to use the word 'impossible' with the greatest caution."

Wernher von Braun

- Politics & Leadership
- Science & Technology
- Popular Culture & the Arts
- Business & Commerce
- **Writers & Thinkers**

◀◀ REWRITING HISTORY

As a teenager, Simone attended a Catholic school that prepared girls for their traditional roles in society, and her education might have gone no further had her maternal grandfather, a banker, not gone bankrupt. The family's circumstances were greatly reduced, and her father encouraged her to gain an academic qualification to avoid poverty.

SIMONE DE BEAUVOIR (1908–1986)

Author of Le Deuxième Sexe (The Second Sex)

Philosopher and writer; leading member of the existentialist movement; founding mother of the women's liberation movement; winner of the prestigious Prix Goncourt for literature

Best known, ironically, for being Jean-Paul Sartre's partner, Simone de Beauvoir was a remarkable and independent woman who had the strength and courage to disregard convention and to use her personal experience as the basis for an honest literary and philosophical examination of what it is to be human and, more importantly, a woman.

A Meeting of Minds

Simone-Lucie-Ernestine-Marie Bertrand de Beauvoir was born in the artistic Montparnasse district of Paris, the first of two daughters in a relatively wealthy family. She showed a talent for many subjects at school and, after passing her baccalaureate exams in math and philosophy, she went on to study math and then literature before reading philosophy at the Sorbonne with a view to becoming a teacher. When she obtained her *agrégation* in that subject in 1929, she was the youngest person, and only the ninth woman, to do so. In the final examinations she took second place to Jean-Paul Sartre, who was to become known as France's leading existential philosopher. Their meeting was the start of a deep and lifelong, if unconventional, relationship. In keeping with the existentialist philosophy to which Sartre and de Beauvoir both subscribed and by which they tried to live, stressing freedom of choice and responsibility for the consequences of one's acts, the couple rejected marriage as an inauthentic act of conformity, and instead made their own conjugal, but not monogamous, bond.

Close to the Bone

From an early age, Simone de Beauvoir had wanted to be a writer, and while working as a teacher she wrote two novels and a collection of short stories, none of which were published at the time. In 1943, during World War II and after the year-long incarceration of Sartre in a prisoner of war camp, she wrote her first acclaimed book, *She Came to Stay*. This frank metaphysical work is a fictionalized account of the complex relationship between herself, Sartre, and two sisters, with one of whom Sartre had a sexual relationship and the other of whom later married one of de Beauvoir's ex-lovers. (Sartre actually continued to give financial support to the sisters for the rest of his life.) In it, the sisters are melded into a single character—Xavière—who joins partners Françoise and Pierre in a *ménage à trois*, which profoundly affects the couple's relationship. Using this thinly veiled construct, de Beauvoir explores themes of love, lust, and jealousy that underpin the relationships between the characters—emotions that were painfully real to the author.

This was also the year in which Sartre published *L'Être et le Néant* (*Being and Nothingness*), an existentialist treatise that became central to de Beauvoir's personal philosophy. In the course of the next few years she wrote several more books, two of which explored the moral aspects of Sartre's existentialism, but it was in 1949 that she published the work for which she is best known.

Cultural v Biological

The Second Sex looks at the way that women have been defined throughout history in male-dominated culture. Written from an existentialist perspective, it was one of the first works to talk about gender as a cultural rather than biological phenomenon. In it, de Beauvoir not only examines the externally imposed myths and perceptions that women accept and adopt (and here she criticizes the constraints that marriage and motherhood impose), but she also attempts to arrive at a positive and authentic feminine identity. *The Second Sex* is considered to be a seminal work of feminist literature and one of most influential books of the twentieth century. Throughout the rest of her life de Beauvoir remained actively involved in the feminist cause, and continued to write until the end of her life. She died in Paris, of pneumonia, in 1984.

"*The most mediocre of males feels himself a demigod as compared with women.*"
Simone de Beauvoir

◀ *A fitting tribute to a woman who sought to escape the limitations of social definitions, the Simone de Beauvoir footbridge in Paris, built in 2006, links the elegance and sophistication of the Seine's Right Bank with the creativity and bohemianism of the Left.*

- Politics & Leadership

- Science & Technology

- Popular Culture & the Arts

- Business & Commerce

- Writers & Thinkers

 REWRITING HISTORY

Sylvia Pankhurst, in **The Suffrage Movement** *(1931), argues that her mother betrayed the movement by changing her stance after the outbreak of World War I, whereas Christabel Pankhurst, in* **Unshackled: The Story of How We Won the Vote** *(1959), paints her as selflessly devoted to the cause.*

EMMELINE PANKHURST (1858–1928)

Founder of the Women's Social and Political Union

High-profile leader in the earliest days of the feminist movement; campaigned for social and political reform in Britain, North America, and Russia; won women's right to vote in the United Kingdom

Today's younger generation may associate the struggle for women's rights with the '60s and '70s, but those were second-wave feminists, heirs of a woman who, by the standards of her time, was far more radical. Emmeline Pankhurst began her campaign for women's suffrage in the nineteenth century, but she achieved her goal in the twentieth.

Women of Substance

Those who remember Audrey Hepburn in *My Fair Lady* may retain an image of late-Victorian and Edwardian ladies as impossibly elegant and demure, moving from well-appointed sitting room to well-appointed drawing room in a rustle of satins and silks, or strolling through the park under fantastic picture hats, with parasols deployed against the sun. Although the clothing bore some similarity, for women such as Emmeline Pankhurst, and her fellow suffragettes, demure did not enter into it. In 1889 she founded the Women's Franchise League, the first women's organization to campaign for universal suffrage, which in 1894 achieved partial success in securing for married women the right to vote in local elections. From 1895 she held several municipal offices in her native city of Manchester. But her goal was nothing less than achieving an equal franchise for men and women in both local and national elections. By the end of the century, there had been three bills for women's suffrage presented to Parliament, but each time the all-male House of Commons had voted them down. Pankhurst decided that it was time for a change of tactics, and in 1903, she founded the Women's Social and Political Union (WSPU).

"Rush the House of Commons!"

The Union first attracted wide attention on October 13, 1905, when two of its members, Emmeline's daughter, Christabel, and Annie Kenney were thrown out of a Liberal Party meeting for demanding a statement about votes for women and then arrested for assaulting the police. After refusing to pay their fines, they were sent to prison, the first martyrs to the cause of suffrage. From 1906, Emmeline Pankhurst directed WSPU activities from London.

Regarding Britain's Liberal government as the main obstacle to woman suffrage, she campaigned against the party's candidates at elections, and her followers interrupted meetings of Cabinet ministers. In 1908–9 Pankhurst was jailed three times, once for issuing a leaflet calling on the people to "Rush the House of Commons!" A truce that she declared in 1910 was broken when the government blocked a "conciliation" bill on women's suffrage.

Playing Cat and Mouse

From July 1912, the WSPU turned to extreme tactics, mainly in the form of arson directed by Christabel from Paris, where she had gone to avoid arrest for conspiracy. Pankhurst was imprisoned once again. It was during this time that imprisoned suffragettes staged hunger strikes, and were notoriously force-fed by prison staff. Pankhurst described prison as "a place

of horror and torment." In her autobiography, she wrote: "I shall never while I live forget the suffering I experienced during the days when those cries were ringing in my ears." Under the Prisoners (Temporary Discharge for Ill-Health) Act of 1913 (also known as the "Cat and Mouse Act"), by which hunger-striking prisoners could be freed for a time and then re-imprisoned as soon as they were well again, she was released and rearrested twelve times within a year, serving a total of thirty days.

After the outbreak of World War I in 1914, Emmeline and Christabel called a halt to the suffrage campaign, and the government released all suffragettes from prison. During the war Pankhurst lectured on women's rights in the US, Canada, and the Soviet Union. She lived in the US for several years after the war. In 1926, after returning to England, she was selected to be the Conservative candidate for a London parliamentary seat, but her campaign became mired in controversy when one of her daughters, Sylvia Pankhurst, gave birth out of wedlock. This was further complicated when Emmeline fell seriously ill, effectively ending the campaign. The Representation of the People Act of 1928, which established equal voting rights for men and women, became law a few weeks before her death. In the press coverage that followed, the *New York Herald Tribune* called her "the most remarkable political and social agitator of the early part of the twentieth century and the supreme protagonist of the campaign for the electoral enfranchisement of women."

#84

◀ *Emmeline Pankhurst addressing a crowd in New York, USA. Pankhurst visited the US on numerous occasions, including the Bryn Mawr College in Pennsylvania, which was known for its involvement with the suffrage cause.*

DAVID BEN-GURION (1886–1973)

Prime Minister of Israel

Played a pivotal role in the establishment of the independent state of Israel; elected as the first Prime Minister of Israel; led Israel during the Arab-Israeli war of 1948

◀◀ REWRITING HISTORY

Ben-Gurion was a lifelong friend of Yitzhak Ben-Zvi, the second President of Israel. In 1912, the pair went to Turkey, where they studied law together at Istanbul University. After being expelled from Palestine in 1915, Ben-Gurion and Ben-Zvi traveled to New York where they co-wrote the Yiddish book **The Land of Israel Past and Present.**

A fervent Zionist from an early age, David Ben-Gurion played an important part in the establishment of the state of Israel. He was elected the country's first Prime Minister, and helped to lead Israel to victory in the 1948 Arab-Israeli War. As Prime Minister, Ben-Gurion presided over the rapid economic and social development of the country.

Zionist Beginnings

David Ben-Gurion was born David Grün in 1886, in Plonsk, Poland, then part of the Russian Empire. He was educated at a traditional Hebrew school established by his lawyer father. Ben-Gurion grew up to be an ardent Zionist, becoming leader of a Hebrew-speaking Zionist youth group "Ezra" while in his teens. When he was 18 years old, Ben-Gurion moved to Warsaw, where he taught at a Jewish school and joined the Poelei Tziyon (Workers of Zion) Socialist Zionist movement. Outraged at the anti-Semitic pogroms in Eastern Europe, he moved to Ottoman Palestine in 1906, where he became a prominent leader of Poelei Tziyon. He also helped to establish the first agricultural workers' commune and worked as a volunteer for HaShomer, a Jewish defense organization. After the outbreak of World War I, Ben-Gurion was expelled from Palestine as an enemy alien and he traveled to New York, where he met his future wife Paula Monbesz. In 1918, Ben-Gurion joined the Jewish Legion, then part of the British Army, returning to Palestine after the end of the war. In 1920, Palestine was placed under British mandate by the League of Nations.

Fighting for a Jewish Homeland

Ben-Gurion helped to found the Jewish Federation of Labor (the Histadruth) in 1921, and also became head of the Mapai Labor Party, representing its interests at the World Zionist Organization. In 1935, he became chairman of the Jewish Agency for Palestine, the official representative of the Jewish community. During the Arab Revolt (1936–39), Ben-Gurion urged a policy of restraint, and he supported the Peel Commission recommendation in 1937 to partition Palestine into Jewish and Arab areas. However, after the

British White Paper of 1939, which severely limited Jewish immigration and placed restrictions on their right to purchase land, Ben-Gurion abandoned his policy for peace and began to prepare for war. Terrorist attacks by various paramilitary groups such as Haganah and Irgun made Britain's Palestine Mandate unworkable, and the British quit Palestine in 1948. On May 14, 1948, Ben-Gurion declared the independence of the state of Israel, and he became the new country's first Prime Minister. Shortly afterward, he led Israel to victory in the 1948–49 Arab-Israeli war, gaining additional territory for the new state.

Political Life

As Prime Minister, Ben-Gurion helped to set up the nation's employment, education, health, and trade services, as well as establish new towns and settlements. In 1953, he left office to retire to Kibbutz Sde Boker in the Negev desert region. However, he returned to politics two years later as Defense Minister, and was soon re-elected to the premiership. During his second term in office, Ben-Gurion controversially reestablished relations with West Germany and led the Israeli occupation of the Sinai Peninsula during the Suez Crisis. He resigned as Prime Minister in 1963 over the Lavon Affair (an Israeli covert operation in Egypt), though he remained in politics. Increasing tensions with his successor Levi Eshkol resulted in Ben-Gurion establishing a new party, Rafi, in 1965. In 1968, Rafi merged with Mapai but Ben-Gurion refused to reconcile with his former party and instead formed another party, Hareshima Hamamlachti (The State List), which won four seats in the 1969 election. The following year, Ben-Gurion retired from politics and returned to Sde Boker, where he remained until his death in 1973.

▲
David Ben-Gurion was the first Prime Minister of the independent Israeli state. He is pictured here with Yitzhak Katz (center) and Abba Eban (left).

A Life's Work

Ben-Gurion had a messianic vision of a Jewish homeland from an early age, and he spent his entire life creating his dream. A gifted orator, he presented an inspiring vision of a state that would provide a permanent home for Jews all over the world. During his period in office, more than a million Jews from over 80 different countries emigrated to Israel, bringing with them the skills and determination to build a modern democratic country based on parliamentary rule. Ben-Gurion also established a well-equipped army to protect his people from its enemies, and he forged strong international ties with the US and other Western countries to further Israeli interests.

KARL POPPER (1902–1994)

Austrian Philosopher, Teacher, and Writer

Instrumental in establishing the philosophy of science as a distinct and vibrant branch of philosophy; influential in both the material and social sciences

■ Politics & Leadership

■ Science & Technology

■ Popular Culture & the Arts

■ Business & Commerce

■ Writers & Thinkers

◀◀ REWRITING HISTORY

Popper directly influenced many other key thinkers in the philosophy of science, particularly Paul Feyerabend and Imre Lakatos, whom he taught at the Department of Philosophy, Logic, and Scientific Method at the London School of Economics. Thomas Kuhn, who wrote **The Structure of Scientific Revolution,** *was also inspired by Popper's ideas.*

Karl Popper was one of the most important thinkers in the philosophy of science in the twentieth century and made a major contribution to our understanding of the nature and justification of scientific knowledge. He replaced science's claims of infallibility and authority with a more humble quest to increase the scope of testable knowledge, with theories as a tentative tool in that quest.

Child Prodigy

Born to Jewish parents in Vienna, Austria—one of the cultural capitals of Europe—Karl Popper was brought up in an intellectual environment. His father, a lawyer, had an interest in classical literature, philosophy, and politics, and his mother passed on to him her love of music. Popper left for the University of Vienna at the age of just 16, although he didn't formally enroll until four years later. In 1919 he encountered two influences that were to shape his intellectual development. The first of these was Marxism, to which he was drawn through his membership of the Association of Socialist School Students, and which he studied thoroughly. The second was the psychoanalytic movement, and especially the work of Freud and of Adler, under whom Popper worked for a while with deprived children.

Science vs Non-science

Popper became disenchanted with Marxism, partly due to its perceived dogmatism and for its links to authoritarian regimes, but also because Marxist theory was constantly being amended to fit the facts and explain away anything that appeared to prove it false. Popper perceived similar problems in the psychoanalytic school. Practitioners claimed that its ability to explain all psychological processes reflected its inherent strength as a science, but Popper saw this as its failing—it could not provide specific predictions and, crucially, its theories could not be falsified. This key distinction led him to question the nature, and begin a philosophical exploration, of scientific knowledge.

The problem came into focus for Popper when he attended a lecture given by Albert Einstein. Einstein's theories led to seemingly wild and improbable implications, but those implications were testable and falsifiable and therefore, in Popper's view, "scientific." Advocates of Marxism and introspective psychology, on the other hand, found confirmation of their theories in all outcomes, so although the theories might be enlightening, they were non-falsifiable and therefore "non-scientific."

All Life is Problem Solving

This apparently simple distinction has profound implications. Popper was contesting the contemporary scientific method, which was based upon observation and the use of inductive reasoning, and consisted of the testing of hypotheses by means of a search for corroboration. In Popper's view, expounded in works such as *The Logic of Scientific Discovery* (1934), science is about problem solving, and the scientific endeavor must go beyond pedestrian observation and proceed by creative imagination, of which Einstein was a good example. According to Popper, a theory is scientific only if it prohibits certain possible occurrences—if such an occurrence is observed, the theory is false, but a scientific theory can never be proven true because the possibility of finding an exception always exists. Verifiability is unattainable. Refuting the views of the positivists, who claimed that the only reliable source of pure knowledge was sense experience, Popper said that observation was always selective and laden with theoretical perspective.

◄ *Karl Popper is seen here in conversation with Ralf Dahrendorf, who was one of his researchers at the London School of Economics in the early 1950s. Popper's lectures inspired a new generation of thinkers and had a major influence on the philosophy of science.*

In a career that took him from teaching math and physics in schools, to teaching philosophy at Canterbury University College, New Zealand, and then at the University of London, Popper developed a philosophy of science that he called critical rationalism. His thinking has fundamentally influenced not only the "hard" sciences, but also social and political sciences and the study of history in the second half of the twentieth century. He received a knighthood in 1965.

- Politics & Leadership
- **Science & Technology**
- Popular Culture & the Arts
- Business & Commerce
- Writers & Thinkers

 REWRITING HISTORY

Enrico Fermi was just 53 years old when he died of stomach cancer, almost certainly caused by his work on the building of the first nuclear pile. Two of his assistants also died prematurely of cancer. The hazards of the work, dealing with radioactive material on a daily basis and carrying out experiments with uncertain outcomes, were understood and accepted by many dedicated workers in this important field.

ENRICO FERMI (1901–1954)

Italian-American Nuclear Physicist

Theoretical and experimental nuclear physicist; Nobel Prize winner; one of the architects of the Manhattan Project; led the team that produced the first sustained nuclear chain reaction; became a US citizen in 1944; recipient of the Presidential Medal for Merit

As the preeminent nuclear physicist of the time, Enrico Fermi was a key player in ushering in the Atomic Age. Equally at home with theory and practice, he displayed an almost intuitive understanding of what was happening at the subatomic level, and had the mathematical, statistical, and experimental skills to develop some of the most important theoretical explanations in nuclear science.

Early Talent

Enrico Fermi was born in Rome, Italy, where his father worked for the Ministry of Railroads. His talent for mathematics and physics were evident in his teens, and he was awarded his PhD from the University of Pisa at the age of just 21, by which time he had already extended Albert Einstein's general theory of relativity into the field of electrodynamics. He was the first person to point out that Einstein's famous equation $E = mc^2$ implied that the nucleus of an atom was potentially the source of a vast amount of energy. In the course of studying and teaching at several European universities, he made a major breakthrough in particle physics, discovering that certain subatomic particles obey particular statistical rules. These particles are now known as fermions, and the rules, called Fermi-Dirac statistics after the two men who independently made the discovery, remain an important part of physics, helping to explain such diverse phenomena as the collapse of stars and conductivity in metals.

Nuclear Breakthroughs

Fermi was given the chair of theoretical physics at the University of Rome at the age of just 24, and in the following years he focused on using spectroscopy to investigate the behavior of subatomic particles. He was elected to the Royal Academy of Italy in 1929. In the early 1930s he turned his attention to experiments in nuclear physics, attempting to induce radiation in a range of elements by bombarding them with neutrons, and this led him to develop his theory of beta decay, in which a neutron in the nucleus is split to form a proton, an electron (or beta particle), and a neutrino, which has no mass and no charge. The existence of this hypothetical particle was not verified until 20 years later.

In 1934, Fermi and his team succeeded in inducing radioactivity in a sample of fluorium, and went on to find that slower neutrons induced greater radioactivity, a discovery that was to prove crucial in the development of nuclear fission. In December 1938, Fermi was awarded the Noble Prize in Physics, in Stockholm, and he took the opportunity to escape from fascist Italy and emigrate with his family to the US, where he was given a position at Columbia University.

The US War Effort

Reports that nuclear fission had been achieved in Germany had already reached the US, and the Columbia team, which included Fermi, began fission experiments in January 1939, soon verifying that it was possible. In the push to create an atomic bomb before Germany succeeded in doing so, the quest for controlled nuclear fission was paramount, both to further the scientists' understanding of the process and in order to create the plutonium needed for the bomb itself. In 1942, Fermi was put in charge of building the first atomic pile, at Chicago University, and after six months of planning and building, he and his team produced the world's first self-sustaining nuclear chain reaction.

0.016 SEC.
N

100 METERS

Fermi's work was crucial to the successful development of the atomic bomb. Fermi joined Robert Oppenheimer at Los Alamos in New Mexico in 1944 and was present at the explosion of the Trinity test bomb. Fermi then continued to work on perfecting nuclear reactors and producing further weapon-grade radioactive material. After the end of the war, he was appointed director of the Institute for Nuclear Studies (later named the Enrico Fermi Institute) at the University of Chicago, where his research interest moved to high-energy particle physics. As with the other pioneers in nuclear physics at the time, Fermi's legacy will forever be associated with the atomic bomb., but the impact of his work stretches far beyond its military uses.

▲
On July 16, 1945, as the shock wave from the Trinity nuclear test explosion reached him and the rest of the team, Fermi dropped small pieces of paper, and from their deflection he estimated the yield of the bomb to be equivalent to 10,000 tons of TNT. It was actually twice as powerful as that.

THOMAS WATSON JR. (1914–1993)

CEO and President of IBM

Turned a punch card tabulating machine company into the world's largest computer manufacturer; dubbed "The Most Successful Capitalist in History" by Fortune *magazine; recipient of the Presidential Medal of Freedom; wartime and civilian pilot; US Ambassador to the Soviet Union*

Despite being afflicted by depression as a youngster and plagued by self-doubt as a young man, Tom Watson Jr. had the guts to take over the leadership of IBM from his awe-inspiring father and then gamble both his reputation and a great deal of money on changing the direction of the company completely. The gamble more than paid off.

A Difficult Start

Thomas Watson Jr. was born in Summit, New Jersey, in 1914, the year in which his father joined a 400-strong company called the Computing Tabulating Recording Corporation as general manager. International Business Machines, as his father renamed the company in 1924 when he took control of it, was a major part of the lives of Tom, his two sisters, and his younger brother. Tom made visits to the factory from the age of five onward, and even accompanied his father on business trips to Europe. Attending a private school in Princeton, NJ, he had difficulty reading and suffered from depression, and subsequently struggled with his studies. Without his father's influence, it is unlikely that he would have been accepted into further education. Graduating from Brown University with a BA in Business Studies in 1937, he joined his father's company as a salesman, but showed no great enthusiasm or flair for the job.

Spreading His Wings

In 1940, Watson Jr. joined the Army Air Force and was trained as a pilot. It turned out to be something he enjoyed and was good at—a fact that provided a timely boost to his self-esteem. At the end of the war he was pilot for the AAF inspector general Major General Follett Bradley, and it was Bradley who, surprised at Watson's declared intention to become an airline pilot, told the young man he had the abilities to run IBM and gave him the confidence to return to his father's company. This time he showed considerable aptitude, and within a year he was Vice President and a board member. In 1949 he was made Executive Vice-President, becoming President in 1952. By this time, under his father's leadership, the company had become

---

◀◀ REWRITING HISTORY

Watson spent an extremely busy retirement. In 1977 his friend President Jimmy Carter asked him to chair the General Advisory Committee on Arms and Disarmament, and from 1979 to 1981 he was US Ambassador to the Soviet Union. A keen sailor, he retraced the route around the Pacific taken by Captain Cook, and in 1986 he flew the breadth of the Soviet Union with personal permission from Mikhail Gorbachev.

a major force in American business, with IBM owning or leasing more than 90 percent of all tabulating machines in the country. Tom Jr, however, believed that the future lay in electronic computing machines and, despite his father's unwillingness, he was already investing in research. In 1953, the IBM 700 series of Electronic Data Processing Machines, the first commercially available computers, was unveiled. This vacuum tube technology was followed by the transistorized 7000 series, and by the early '60s IBM was leading the market by several lengths.

A Long-Term Vision

The key elements in Watson's strategy were a decentralization of the company's organization, a high-pressure management style, and, crucially, a massive increase in research and development, recruiting literally hundreds of top scientists and spending more on R&D than most companies made in gross profits. Five billion dollars went into the development of the 360 series, the first computers to use integrated circuits. The series was a family of computers all sharing the same software, allowing growing companies to upgrade easily, but they rendered older IBM machines obsolete, so the risk was high. The far-sighted R&D policy paid off—the new computers were so far ahead of the competition that other manufacturers went to the wall, and it was a decade before any real challengers appeared.

After 1970, ill-health eventually forced Watson to step down as chairman, but he remained everpresent. Watson's focus on research, and his policy of employing only the best and the brightest, advanced computer technology immeasurably, keeping his company at the leading edge of progress in the field. The Nobel Prize in Physics has several times been awarded to IBM researchers, and an IBM Fellow received the prestigious A. M. Turing Award in 2007.

#80

◀ *One of the 700 series of Electronic Data Processing Machines, this IBM 704 was used to make computations for aeronautical research at the Langley Research Center (later part of NASA) in the late 1950s.*

POL POT (c.1928–1998)

Leader of the Khmer Rouge Movement in Cambodia

Elected Secretary-General of the Cambodian Communist Party; led the Khmer Rouge forces in the overthrow of Cambodia's military dictatorship; served as Prime Minister of Cambodia between 1975 and 1979; oversaw the genocide of millions of his own people

- ■ Politics & Leadership
- ■ Science & Technology
- ■ Popular Culture & the Arts
- ■ Business & Commerce
- ■ Writers & Thinkers

 **REWRITING HISTORY**

In later life, Pol Pot's bourgeois upbringing caused him to deny that he was Saloth Sar, the son of a prosperous small landowner. His family and upbringing was a source of embarrassment to the communist leader, clashing as it did with the fundamental principles of the Communist Party.

Pol Pot was the infamous totalitarian communist leader of Cambodia during the 1970s. More than a million Cambodians died during his regime as he attempted to put in place an agrarian society totally devoid of Western influence. After he lost power in 1979, he remained leader in exile of the Khmer Rouge army until put under house arrest by former colleagues in 1998.

From Prosperity to Rebellion

Pol Pot was born Saloth Sar in 1928 in Prek Sbauv, a small fishing village in northeastern Cambodia. His family was relatively wealthy and enjoyed social and political connections with the royal family. Pol Pot was educated at a private Catholic school in Phnom Penh and later at a technical college in Kompong, where he earned the opportunity to study radio electronics in France. From 1949 to 1953 he studied in Paris, where he became involved in left-wing political groups. On his return to Cambodia, Pol Pot joined various radical leftist groups, though he became increasingly resentful of the heavy Vietnamese influence within Cambodia's communist party, the Khmer People's Revolutionary Party (KPRP). In 1954, Cambodia gained independence from French colonial rule, with King Sihanouk as its head. Elections held the following year were generally considered fraudulent and convinced Pol Pot and his comrades that armed struggle was inevitable if they were to gain political power, though they were not yet in a strong enough position to launch a rebellion.

Gaining Political Power

In 1960, leaders of the KPRP, including Pol Pot and his political mentor Tou Samouth, held a clandestine meeting at a Phnom Penh railroad station, where they founded the Workers Party of Kampuchea (WPK). Samouth was appointed secretary-general and Pol Pot became one of the Central Committee members. Samouth disappeared in mysterious circumstances in 1962, and Pol Pot was chosen as his successor the following year. For 13 years or so, Pol Pot worked to consolidate his power, gradually lessening the influence of Vietnamese Communists within Cambodia, while courting the support of China. In 1966, the WPK changed its name to the Communist Party of Kampuchea (CPK), which was also commonly known as the Khmer Rouge. Opposition to the Sihanouk regime grew until civil war broke out in 1967. As the war intensified, Pol Pot began the transformation that was to make him into the absolute ruler of the Khmer Rouge movement and the subject of a personality cult. In 1970, a right-wing coup overthrew the Sihanouk regime, and installed Lon Nol as Cambodia's president. Most of the subsequent fighting in 1971 against the Cambodian government was led by Vietnamese forces, backed up by Pol Pot and his supporters. During this period, Pol Pot started to invest resources into the training and indoctrination of recruits and the Khmer Rouge army soon swelled in ranks, though he restricted party membership to the peasant classes alone, rejecting students and middle class recruitment. In 1972, the Vietnamese began to withdraw from the conflict, leaving the way open for the Khmer Rouge to take power. By mid-1973, the Khmer Rouge had control of two-thirds of the country and 50 percent of the population.

#79

Totalitarian Rule

On April 17, 1975, communist forces took control of the capital Phnom Penh and changed the country's name to Democratic Kampuchea. The Khmer Rouge ordered the immediate evacuation of Phnom Penh, forcing city dwellers to move to the country. Anything deemed remotely Western or foreign was destroyed, including temples and libraries, and health care fell to a minimum. After a power struggle within various factions, Pol Pot was appointed prime minister in May 1976. He immediately began to implement radical policies to achieve his dream of an agrarian utopia. The forced evacuation of cities continued, and tens of thousands were sent to work on agricultural projects, many dying *en route* from hunger and fatigue. Pol Pot also began a series of purges of perceived enemies, including white collar workers, intellectuals, and former political appointees. Victims were beaten to death or buried alive in mass graves that came to be known as Cambodia's "Killing Fields." By the time Pol Pot was deposed in 1979, nearly 20 percent of the country's population had lost their lives, with many more displaced. Ethnic minority groups had suffered disproportionately—nearly half the population of Cham Muslims died under the regime. Pol Pot has gone down in history as one of the worst mass murderers in history. After years of living underground, Pol Pot was captured in 1997 by former comrades. He died in custody the following year— possibly from suicide or deliberate poisoning—while waiting to be handed over to an international tribunal.

During the Khmer Rouge regime, tens of thousands of Cambodians were held at the notorious Security Prison 21 (S-21) in Phnom Penh. The prison is now known as the Tuol Sleng (meaning "Hill of the Poisonous Trees") Genocide Museum and commemorates the prisoners who were tortured and killed during Pol Pot's period of power.

▼

◀◀ REWRITING HISTORY

Although Piaget spent much of his life applying his ideas on the acquisition of knowledge to education and promoting the idea of active learning, many modern teaching methods fail to take this into account. Paradoxically, some of the criticized interactive technologies, such as multimedia, hypermedia, and virtual reality, are in line with Piaget's criteria.

JEAN PIAGET (1896–1980)

Swiss Psychologist

Specialist in cognitive development and the basis of knowledge; author of more than 60 books and many hundreds of articles; director of the International Bureau of Education, UNESCO; founder of the International Centre for Genetic Epistemology, Geneva

One of the most significant psychologists of the twentieth century, Piaget brought together philosophy, biology, and psychiatry in an approach that explored the interaction between thinking, knowledge, and the real world. He ascertained that the acquisition of knowledge develops along a biologically determined timeline. His theories influence many of the social sciences, but especially education.

Biology and Psychology

The first child of a university professor of medieval literature, Jean Piaget was born in Neuchâtel, Switzerland. The young boy was keen on natural history, and when he was ten he published his first scientific "paper," a single page describing his observation of an albino sparrow. By the time he was 16, he had published several well-respected papers, mainly on mollusks (he was a keen collector of shells), and he had a part-time job at the Natural History Museum, Neuchâtel. Bewildered by what he perceived as the childishness of religious discussion, he became interested in the basis of knowledge, looking first toward philosophy and then psychology, which he went on to study at the University of Neuchâtel. While there, he formulated the concept that, "In all fields of life (organic, mental, social) there exist 'totalities' qualitatively distinct from their parts and imposing on them an organization." The idea that thought and knowledge conform to structuring principles that are rooted in biology was to underpin his academic work for the rest of his life.

Investigating Learning

Piaget received his Doctorate in Science in 1918, and then spent a year working in a psychology lab and a psychiatric clinic before teaching psychology and philosophy at the Sorbonne in Paris. Here he carried out research into intelligence and, dissatisfied with the intelligence tests of the time, he began interviewing school children using the techniques he had seen used in psychiatry. His objective was to assess not whether they gave right or wrong answers but how they reasoned. The results indicated to Piaget that young children revealed similar patterns of mistakes, and that these were not found in older children. Further research at the Institut J. J. Rousseau in Geneva led to the publication of his first book on child psychology, and this was followed by three further volumes based on close observation of his own three children. Taking up the post of director of UNESCO's International Bureau of Education, where he was to stay for almost 40 years, Piaget initiated a large-scale collaborative research project to investigate cognitive development in children. The findings were to provide the basis for a theory that had profound implications in many fields, especially education.

Cognitive Development

Piaget demonstrated that our knowledge of the world grows in stages parallel to the stages of our mental growth. At each developmental stage we have a particular skill set, or schema, that enables us to acquire certain kinds of knowledge by assimilating new experiences, and by adapting our schema to incorporate new kinds of information. He identified four stages of cognitive development. The first one, lasting from birth until the age of about two years, is the "sensory-motor stage," whereby the child interacts with the world via the senses and primary motor skills. Between the ages of two and six or seven, in the "pre-operational stage," the child has mental representations, but he can only see things from his own perspective. In the "concrete operational stage," which lasts until the age of 11 or 12, the child gradually achieves the ability to use and manipulate symbols logically, and in the "formal operational stage," from adolescence onward, the child can apply logical operations to abstract events. One of the crucial consequences of Piaget's work is an understanding of the active role of the child in learning, and Piaget's cognitive stages are still a part of teacher-training.

"Intelligence organizes the world by organizing itself."
Jean Piaget

Jean Piaget's influence extends across a wide range of sciences, and has instructed research in fields as diverse as evolutionary biology and artificial intelligence. His research into cognitive development has helped shape innovation in education and remains a central influence on the field.

▲
Jean Piaget's studies of the ways in which children reason revealed that our cognitive abilities develop through a series of stages, and his findings continue to influence teachers' interactions with children in the classroom today.

- Politics & Leadership
- **Science & Technology**
- Popular Culture & the Arts
- Business & Commerce
- Writers & Thinkers

REWRITING HISTORY

Linus Pauling might have found the correct answer first had the US government not prevented him from traveling to conferences overseas and meeting with fellow scientists. This was the McCarthy era, and he was accused of un-American activity for voicing his antiwar opinions. Ironically, he received the Nobel Prize for Peace in the same year that Crick and Watson received their Nobel Prize.

CRICK (1916–2004) AND WATSON (b. 1928)

Molecular Biologists

Discovered the double-helix structure of DNA; revolutionized the biological sciences, with major implications for medicine and genetics; their work formed the basis for the Human Genome Project; they were awarded the Nobel prize for their achievements

In the spring of 1953, Francis Crick and James D. Watson published a short paper in the journal *Nature* in which they suggested a structure for DNA, the molecule that carries genetic information. "This structure," they said, "has novel features which are of considerable biological interest." That was, to say the least, an understatement.

The Key to Life

The story of DNA goes back to the mid-nineteenth century, when the Swiss doctor Johannes Friedrich Miescher discovered that the cells from many living organisms contained the same chemical, which he called "nucleic acid." In the first half of the twentieth century, it was known that there were two forms of this chemical, and scientists suspected they carried the information that conveyed inherited characteristics. By the 1950s the search to find out how these chemicals functioned was of vital importance to biologists, as they clearly held the key to many life processes. The molecular structure of the chemicals was central to the research, and scientists in several countries were working on the problem in different ways. Crick and Watson—a 35-year-old British physicist turned chemist/biologist and a 22-year-old American molecular biologist—came together at Cambridge University's Cavendish Laboratory.

Pair Bonding

It was to prove a fruitful partnership. Both men were fascinated by DNA and had a powerful drive to solve what they saw as the central question in biology, and with complementary academic skills and perspectives they were a perfect fit. Rather than carrying out laboratory research, the two men pieced together the puzzle by analyzing the findings of scientists who were approaching the problem from various angles, and they worked to develop a physical three-dimensional model that would fit the facts. This form of physical modeling had been pioneered by the eminent chemist Linus Pauling at the California Institute of Technology, one of the main contenders in the race to solve the riddle. He had already proposed that DNA was a triple helix, but there were clear flaws in his hypothesis.

A vital clue for Crick and Watson was an image of the DNA molecule made using X-ray crystallography. Taken by Rosalind Franklin, a researcher at King's College, London, who was also on the trail of DNA, the image was shown to the pair without her knowledge. It helped the Cambridge researchers not only to realize that the molecule is a double helix, but also to understand the bonding between complementary base pairs that holds the two strands of the molecule together. Remarkably, they were not just right—they were absolutely right, and although their model has been fine-tuned by further research, it has not needed any correction. This is unusual in the sciences, and has been compared with Newton's understanding of gravity.

Self-Replicating DNA

In the paper that Crick and Watson quickly published in the scientific journal *Nature*, they stated: "It has not escaped our notice that the specific pairing we have postulated immediately suggests a possible copying mechanism for the genetic material." Crick and Watson had found that the DNA molecule is structured in such a way that if the two helical strands are separated, each will attract the complementary chemicals in the right sequence to complete itself again. In other words, it does carry the genetic information and it is self-replicating.

◀ *Adorning the grounds of Clare College, Cambridge, Charles Jencks' DNA double helix sculpture pays homage to Crick and Watson's discovery, which has had an impact on virtually every branch of the biological sciences.*

The impact of this discovery on almost every branch of biology was enormous, illuminating reproduction, genetics and inheritance, and cell division and growth, among many others. In 1962 the Nobel Prize in Physiology or Medicine was awarded jointly to Crick, Watson, and Maurice Wilkins—Rosalind Franklin's coresearcher. She herself had died of cancer in 1958, and at that time the prize could not be awarded posthumously.

◀◀ REWRITING HISTORY

Foucault's homosexuality, which became clear to him while at the ENS, undoubtedly influenced his intellectual perspective, isolating him and forcing him to experience the exclusion created by society's sexual mores. He was working on the third volume of his **History of Sexuality** *when he died of AIDS, one of the first high profile cases in France.*

MICHEL FOUCAULT (1926–1984)

French Historian and Philosopher

University lecturer and writer; associated with the structuralist and post-structuralist movements; influenced philosophy but had an even greater impact on the humanities and social sciences

A student at a critical period in the development of postwar French philosophy, Foucault brought his powerful intellect to bear on the works of Hegel, Heidegger, Marx, and Sartre, among others, and developed his own incisive critique of cultural history. His influence is still felt across a wide range of academic disciplines.

Beyond Existentialism

Paul-Michel Foucault was born and raised in Poitiers, France, into a moderately wealthy bourgeois family. His father, with whom he was not close, was a surgeon with a high reputation in the area, and he pressed the boy to do well. When, in 1940, his results at the Lycée de Poitiers were inadequate, Foucault was sent to the strict Jesuit College of St Stanislas, where he took his baccalaureate examinations in 1942–3, excelling in most subjects. Ignoring his father's wishes for him to follow the same career, he then went to Paris to enroll in the elite École Normale Supérieure (ENS) but failed the entrance exams in 1945. To prepare to retake the exams he then attended the highly prestigious Lycée Henri-IV. There he was taught by, among others, the philosopher Jean Hyppolite, an expert on Hegel and a friend of Jean-Paul Sartre. Drawing together Hegel, Marx, and existentialism, and focusing on the concept of alienation and the importance of the historical perspective, Hyppolite had a strong influence on the 19-year-old Foucault, who passed the highly competitive humanities entrance exam for the ENS in July 1946, ranking fourth among only 38 students to do so.

Personal and Academic

Foucault studied at the École for the next four years and proved himself to be a brilliant student, despite suffering frequent bouts of depression. His efforts to find an effective treatment for this condition led him to become familiar with psychiatry, which in turn prompted his eventual interest in psychology. He was awarded a degree in psychology in 1949, received his *agrégation* in philosophy in 1951, and then taught psychology at the ENS, gaining a diploma in psychopathology from the Institut de Psychologie of Paris in 1952. In

1954 he published his first book, *Mental Illness and Personality*, and he then left teaching for several years, holding a position of French cultural delegate at the universities of Uppsala, Warsaw, and Hamburg, before returning to Paris in 1960 to submit his doctoral thesis. *Folie et déraison* (published in English as *The History of Madness in the Classical Age*), the text of his major thesis, attracted considerable attention when it was published in 1961 and revealed a radical new approach. Tracing the development of the modern concept of mental illness, Foucault demonstrated that contemporary medical treatments mask a means of controlling behavior seen as a challenge to society. Portrayed as scientific objectivity, psychiatry in fact has a hidden agenda.

Archeology and Genealogy

The Birth of the Clinic (1963) took a similar approach to clinical medicine, and in *The Order of Things* (1966) he demonstrated that in every period of history, the discourse taking place can only be understood in terms of the conditions surrounding it at that time. The book raised Foucault's stature as an intellectual and had repercussions for the study of cultural history.

It also gained him the label of "structuralist," which he rejected. He explained his methodology in *The Archeology of Knowledge*, but in his subsequent books, such as *Discipline and Punish* (a study of the history of the prison system), he used what he referred to as a genealogical, rather than archaeological, approach—examining and explaining the ways in which systems of thought change in response to the social and political conditions of the time.

Foucault's work, calling into question the basis of our knowledge of other times and places, and indeed our notion of truth itself, has had a deep and lasting impact on thinking throughout the social sciences.

◀ *His experience at the Lycée Henri-IV school in Paris brought Foucault into contact with the vital issues of French philosophy and set him on the path to a shining, but short, career as an academic and author.*

"The main interest in life and work is to become someone else that you were not in the beginning."
Michel Foucault

RUPERT MURDOCH (b. 1931)

Australian-American Publishing Magnate

Head of the world's largest media conglomerate; multibillionaire founder of News Corporation; major holdings include Fox Broadcasting Company in the US and BSkyB in the UK

- Politics & Leadership
- Science & Technology
- Popular Culture & the Arts
- **Business & Commerce**
- Writers & Thinkers

◀◀ REWRITING HISTORY

Grudges can take you a long way. Part of Murdoch's strategy can be seen as getting his own back—fighting to make sure control of his empire cannot be taken from him, as it was from his father; snatching deals from under the nose of Robert Maxwell, who had made derogatory comments; publishing low-brow papers in which to print sensational stories about the British upper classes who had regarded him as uncultured in his Oxford days.

In the world of communications media, Rupert Murdoch stands head and shoulders above the rest—a self-made man who, through hard graft, an acute business sense, and aggressive risk taking, has come to dominate almost all forms of print and digital news and entertainment media around the globe.

A Newspaper Background

Keith Rupert Murdoch was born into a relatively wealthy family on a farm to the south of Melbourne, Australia, the son of renowned war correspondent, journalist, and newspaper owner Sir Keith Murdoch. After a boarding school education, Rupert, as he has always been known, went to Worcester College, Oxford, where he spent more time socializing and gambling than he did studying. His politics were left-wing and he was an eloquent speaker, and in 1950 he was elected president of Oxford's Labour Club. When his father died in 1952, he returned to Australia to discover that his father had lost control of the most profitable of his chain of papers, and several others had to be sold in order to pay death duties. After a year spent at London's *Daily Express*, under the tutelage of family friend and newspaper owner Lord Beaverbrook, he took on the running of two struggling newspapers in Adelaide.

Brought up in a journalistic household, Murdoch had always envisaged a career in communications media, and he threw himself wholeheartedly into the business, learning about every aspect of newspaper production and quickly raising circulation figures by adopting a sensationalist, low-brow editorial approach. His company, News Limited, was soon able to start making acquisitions, taking over a rival paper in Adelaide, another in Perth, and then breaking into the big league in Sydney with the purchase of *The Daily Mirror*. In each case his popularizing formula turned losses into profit, and he was soon looking at alternative media.

Looking Abroad

By 1968, Murdoch had moved into TV with the purchase of what became Southern TV in Australia, had founded *The Australian*, a more serious newspaper, and had a foothold in New Zealand after outsmarting rival bidders for control of *The Dominion* newspaper. With an empire worth close to US$50 million, and backed by considerable borrowing power, he turned to Britain, purchasing the already successful *News of the World* ahead of rival media tycoon Robert Maxwell. This was followed by his acquisition of the *Sun*, which he turned into a tabloid, introducing punchy headlines, sex, scandal, and half-naked "Page 3 Girls," and quadrupling the circulation. Next came *The Times* and *The Sunday Times*, much to the consternation of the English establishment, which had been highly critical of his down-market approach. On the political front, Murdoch now sided with right-wing Prime Minister Margaret Thatcher, and when his move to automated production in 1986 led to strikes, he met the unions head-on, sacking 6,000 employees and building an entirely new plant. Throughout the 1980s Murdoch's News International (later News Corp.) invested heavily in satellite television, and BSkyB is now the UK's number one pay-TV provider.

The US and Asia

Murdoch began investing in the States in the 1970s, buying and founding newspapers there, and becoming a US citizen in 1985 in order to circumvent regulations preventing foreigners owning TV companies. News Corp., which is now based in the US, has stakes in countless US newspapers and magazines, as well as top-rated cable news network Fox News, DirecTV, Intermix Media Inc., Dow Jones, and many others. It also owns Star TV, one of Asia's largest satellite TV networks.

For almost 60 years, Rupert Murdoch has negotiated commercial, political, and regulatory hurdles with consummate skill to go from being the proprietor of a small Australian newspaper to the head of the world's largest media conglomerate and one of the wealthiest men alive, with a personal fortune of some $4 billion.

#75

◀ *The rivalry between* ***Rupert Murdoch*** *and* ***Robert Maxwell*** *(pictured here) began over the acquisition of the London newspaper* **The News of the World,** *but continued for many years, driving both men to ever greater success—and failure.*

ROBERT HUTCHINGS GODDARD (1882–1945)

American Physicist and Mathematician

Pioneer of rocket propulsion; first to explore the possibility of space travel; proved that rocket propulsion works in a vacuum; designed and built the first liquid-fueled rocket; influenced the development of missiles and guidance systems

- Politics & Leadership
- **Science & Technology**
- Popular Culture & the Arts
- Business & Commerce
- Writers & Thinkers

◄◄ REWRITING HISTORY

The German military were quick to spot the potential of rocket flight, ultimately incorporating information from Goddard's technical papers and his many patents in the design of the V2 rockets that wrought havoc on London in 1944. It is said that when Goddard was examining a captured V2, an assistant commented, "It looks like one of ours," to which Goddard replied "Yes, it seems so."

Robert H. Goddard had both the creative imagination and the scientific intelligence to have a dream and know that it was realizable. Knowledgeable in many different areas of physics, he solved countless practical problems to become the father of rocket power and, ultimately, of space flight.

Young Dreamer

Robert Hutchings Goddard was born in Worcester, Massachusetts, in 1882, and was an only child (his younger brother having died in infancy). Encouraged by his father, Robert became interested in science at an early age, especially in flight, and as a teenager he began by experimenting with kites and balloons, developing the useful habit of keeping records of all his work. It was while sitting in the branches of a cherry tree in 1899, at the age of 16, that he first imagined sending a rocket into space, and the idea had such an impact on him that ever afterward he celebrated that date—October 19—as Anniversary Day. He frequently missed school due to ill-health, and fell behind his classmates, but he kept up his studies by reading books—especially science books—from the library, and he did well at school when he returned to full-time education. He was also popular, twice being elected class president, and he was chosen to give the valedictory speech at graduation in 1904. He then attended Worcester Polytechnic Institute, where his enthusiasm for the subject led the head of the physics department to employ him as a tutor and laboratory assistant. In 1907 he wrote a paper, published in *Scientific American*, describing a method for stabilizing an aircraft in flight, an area of interest that was to prove useful later in his career.

Graduating with a bachelor of science degree in 1908, he spent a year teaching and then went to Worcester's Clark University, where he studied traditional powder-powered rockets and researched ways of increasing efficiency by using liquid fuels. He received his master's degree in 1910, and his PhD in 1911, both from Clark.

Working on the Theory

Over the next two years, while a research fellow at Princeton University, he developed the mathematical means of calculating the speed and trajectory of a rocket, taking into account its changing weight as the fuel was burnt. The next step was to build a working prototype. While recuperating from tuberculosis, Goddard worked on, and patented, the designs for a multistage rocket and for a liquid fuel rocket. These were to prove crucial in the development of rocketry.

Back at Clark University, Goddard designed an experiment that showed conclusively that a rocket could fly in a vacuum—in other words, that the space travel of which he dreamed was indeed theoretically possible—although the idea was so far from mainstream scientific thinking that Goddard continued to talk only of using rockets to investigate the upper atmosphere. In 1916 he received research funding from the Smithsonian Institution and from Clark University, and in 1919 he submitted a report to the Smithsonian entitled "A Method of Achieving High Altitudes," which the Smithsonian published. With its description of his experiments and their outcomes, and discussion of the enormous increases in efficiency that Goddard had been able to achieve by using the de Laval nozzle (developed by Swedish inventor Gustaf de Laval for use in steam turbines), this small book was read around the world by other rocket scientists and was extremely influential. This was a fairly dry exposition, but at the end of it Goddard ventured to suggest that a rocket might one day be sent to the moon. The press got hold of this and pounced, deriding the idea and even suggesting that Goddard didn't understand basic physics if he thought a rocket would work without any atmosphere to push against. The effect of this ridicule was to make Goddard much more cautious about discussing his work publicly.

Putting Theory into Practice

In the early 1920s, Goddard experimented with liquid fuels and bench-tested a prototype using liquid oxygen and gasoline, and in 1926, at his aunt's farm in Auburn, Massachusetts, he set up the first test

#74

Convinced that liquid fuel was the way of the future, Robert H. Goddard stands beside his first rocket prior to ignition on March 16, 1926, at Auburn, Massachusetts. Tubes on each side carry fuel from the tank at the bottom to the engine at the top. ▼

- Politics & Leadership
- **Science & Technology**
- Popular Culture & the Arts
- Business & Commerce
- Writers & Thinkers

▶ *Goddard's rockets and test flights became increasingly sophisticated, and here he is seen outside his control shack preparing to launch a rocket from the launch tower. He is using an electrical remote control panel to fire the rocket.*

flight of a liquid-fuel rocket. A framework of pipes, with the engine at the top and the fuel tank at the bottom, it only made a two-and-a-half second flight and landed in a frozen cabbage field, but Goddard had made a crucial breakthrough. The liquid-fuel propulsion system worked!

Over the next few years he developed and flew ever larger and more powerful rockets, but his flights were attracting public attention (and sometimes scorn) and he needed to find a more remote site. With the help of the heroic pilot Charles Lindbergh, who foresaw the role of rocket power in aviation and had become a close ally, Goddard sought further funding, but this was the period of the great stock market crash and investors were hard to come by. It was the Guggenheim family that came to the rescue, guaranteeing funding for four years, and Goddard and his wife moved to Roswell in New Mexico in 1930 to establish a new research center.

Military Rejection

For the next 12 years, with occasional pauses in the funding, Goddard and his team of technicians worked on improving rocket design. The outer casing of the rockets was by now similar to the shape of modern missiles—long, smooth, and pointed, with fins at the tail. Much of the research work focused on improving the efficiency of the propulsion system and on stabilizing, and ultimately guiding, the rocket using gyroscopes and vanes positioned in the jet of exhaust gases.

Goddard had already been involved in the development of what was to become the bazooka (which later evolved into the rocket-propelled grenade, or RPG), and it was clear to him and to others involved in the project that large rockets offered military possibilities as delivery systems. In the early '30s he, the Guggenheim Foundation, and the Smithsonian approached the Army and the Navy and offered Goddard's services, but they were rebuffed. Even the scientific community within the US was largely uninterested in the research being conducted at Roswell, but Goddard responded helpfully to a stream of requests for information and advice that came from scientists in Germany, who clearly appreciated the importance of his work.

Unfinished Business

By 1935, Goddard was working on rockets up to 15 feet (4.5 m) in length, and one of them broke the sound barrier and achieved an altitude of almost a mile. Experiments with even larger rockets in the late 1930s suffered from engine problems, and Goddard returned to smaller designs, with one of these reaching an altitude of almost 1.7 miles (2.75 km), the highest that any of his rockets flew.

Goddard continued to refine rocket propulsion throughout World War II, although none of his work was used in military applications. In 1945 Goddard was diagnosed with throat cancer, and he died a few months later without ever seeing his work come to fruition. It was not until 1959 that the Soviet spacecraft Luna 2 reached the surface of the Moon.

A True Visionary

Robert H. Goddard stands as the father of the space age, not only because he was one of the key practical pioneers of rocket propulsion but also because he was a visionary who believed that space travel was possible. As early as 1920 he wrote about the possibility of sending rocket-powered probes to photograph the moon and the planets, and using solar power on spacecrafts. He even predicted the design of the heat shields that are used to protect spacecraft reentering the atmosphere.

#74

When he first suggested that mankind would one day explore space using rocket power, Goddard was met with derision, but as the Apollo missions and the space shuttle Discovery (seen here landing at the Kennedy Space Center) have demonstrated, he was absolutely right.
▼

MILTON FRIEDMAN (1912–2006)

American Economist

Founder of monetarism; university lecturer and researcher; government adviser; writer and television personality; vocal advocate of laissez-faire capitalism; recipient of the Nobel Prize in Economics

The most influential economist of the latter part of the century, Friedman was no ivory tower theoretician. Believing that economics was a practical science that could reveal and affect the way the world works, he shared his monetarist approach to macroeconomic problems with governments and the public alike, and saw his theories implemented around the world.

Challenging Views

Friedman was born in Brooklyn, New York, to Jewish parents who had recently immigrated from northeast Hungary. When he was less than a year old, the family moved to Rahway, New Jersey, where his parents ran a dry goods store. At school he had a flair for mathematics, and his parents were determined that their fourth child and only son should go to college. He graduated before he was 16 and went to study mathematics and economics at Rutgers University in New Jersey, receiving several scholarships and working to pay for his living expenses.

There he became convinced that economics provided a means of understanding the real world, and when he graduated with a bachelor's degree in 1932, in the depths of the Great Depression, he chose to follow economics and go to the University of Chicago, where he gained his MA in a year and met his future wife. After a year studying statistics at Columbia University, he took up the first of a series of research posts that involved him increasingly with the quantitative and empirical side of economics. Franklin D. Roosevelt's New Deal economic package, intended to stimulate the economy, was in place, and the results of Friedman's research made him critical of its efficacy, believing that the money supply should have been expanded instead.

In 1937 he joined the staff of the National Bureau of Economic Research in New York, where he conducted research into income and wealth distribution.

◀◀ REWRITING HISTORY

In a book that Friedman co-wrote with Anna J. Schwartz in 1963, he claimed that the Great Depression would have been just a severe recession had the Federal Reserve not reduced the money supply. The claim was vigorously denied, but in 2002, Federal Reserve governor Ben Bernanke stated, "I would like to say to Milton and Anna: Regarding the Great Depression, you're right. We did it. We're very sorry."

Contradicting Keynes

At the Treasury Department during World War II, he helped to introduce changes to the federal tax system and then went to Columbia University, applying statistical methods to questions of weapon design and military tactics. After the war he took a staff position with both the Bureau of Economic Research (where he carried out a long-term study into the role that money played in the business cycle) and the economics department at the University of Chicago, where he was to remain until the mid 1970s. Contradicting the economic theories of John Maynard Keynes, Friedman saw money supply as a critical factor, and advocated its control as government's primary economic policy tool, claiming that other forms of intervention were actually counterproductive. His monetarist approach quickly gained ground, and by the 1960s, after publishing several highly influential books, he was advising presidential candidates, writing a regular column for *Newsweek*, and becoming involved in a much wider range of policy issues. He saw government interference as an infringement of civil rights, and he supported relatively free markets, freely floating exchange rates, the legalization of drugs, an end to conscription, and freedom of access to a much improved education system.

Going Global

In the US during the '70s, the phenomenon of "stagflation"—a stagnant economy with inflation and unemployment both rising—contradicted Keynesian theory and confirmed Friedman's ideas, which were increasingly adopted. He also took his free-market policies abroad, lecturing in Chile, South Africa, Zimbabwe, and China, in the hope of encouraging movement toward more democratic government. In 1976, he received the Nobel Prize in Economics, and the following year he was made Senior Research Fellow at Stanford University's Hoover Institution on War, Revolution, and Peace. In 1980, his theories were the subject of a television series that brought him even greater public attention, and the accompanying book was a bestseller.

He gained an international reputation in the course of the 1980s, when his ideas on privatization, deregulation, and monetary policy were put into practice not only in the US under President Reagan, but also by Margaret Thatcher in the UK, and in China. In 1988, the creator of the dominant economic theory, one that has had a transforming effect in many societies, was awarded the Presidential Medal of Freedom.

#73

Shortly before his 90th birthday, Milton Friedman, together with his wife Rose, attended a ceremony at the White House at which President Bush honored his achievements, saying , "All of us owe a tremendous debt to this man's towering intellect and his devotion to liberty."
▼

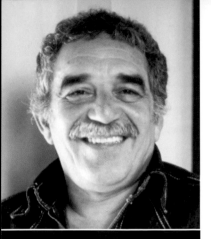

GABRIEL GARCÍA MÁRQUEZ (b. 1928)

Columbian Author, Screenwriter, and Journalist

Worked as a journalist in Colombia and Europe; published his first work Leaf Storm; *achieved international fame with the publication of* One Hundred Years of Solitude; *awarded the Nobel Prize for Literature.*

Considered the greatest living writer in Latin America, Colombian author Gabriel García Márquez is most famous for *One Hundred Years of Solitude*, a tour de force in the magical realism genre. Awarded the Nobel Prize for Literature in 1982, García Márquez is also a master short-storyteller and an accomplished journalist and screenwriter.

Literary Beginnings

Gabriel García Márquez was born in 1928, in the coastal town of Aracataca, located in a tropical region of northern Colombia, between the mountains and the Caribbean Sea. García Márquez's father was a pharmacist and shortly after Gabriel's birth, his parents moved to Barranquilla, leaving him in Aracataca to be raised by his maternal grandparents in a house that was rumored to harbor ghosts. His grandparents were great storytellers, which made a lasting impression upon García Márquez. His grandfather was a retired colonel with liberal views, and his bloody stories from the civil war shaped García Márquez's socialist politics. By contrast, García Márquez's grandmother lived in a world filled with folk beliefs and superstition, and she and her numerous sisters filled the young boy's head with tales of ghosts, premonitions, and omens. Such experiences provided the fodder for García Márquez's magical-realism style of writing. The town of Aracataca itself provided much inspiration for García Márquez's mythical town of Macondo. Márquez moved to Barranquilla in the late 1940s, studying law at the Universidad Nacional in Bogotá and also working as a journalist for a local newspaper. In 1954, he began working for the liberal newspaper *El Espectador* in Bogota, where his antiestablishment articles during the time of conservative dictatorships courted controversy. As a result, García Márquez was sent to Europe to work as a foreign correspondent. Since then he has lived mostly abroad, in Paris, New York, Barcelona, and Mexico.

The Short Stories and Novels

In 1955, García Márquez published his first novella, *Leaf Storm*, which marked the debut of the fictional town of Macondo. His reputation in the

◀◀ REWRITING HISTORY

Gabriel García Márquez's maternal grandfather was Colonel Nicolás Ricardo Márquez Mejía, a veteran of Colombia's War of a Thousand Days. In his youth, the Colonel shot and killed a man in a duel. He once told his young grandson that there was no burden greater in life than to have been responsible for the death of a man, words that García Márquez would later put into the mouths of his characters.

Spanish-speaking world grew with the publication of *Nobody Writes to the Colonel and Other Stories* (1961), *In Evil Hour* (1962), and *Big Mama's Funeral* (1962), but it was *One Hundred Years of Solitude* (1967) that propelled him to international fame. Considered one of the greatest books to have come out of Latin America, *One Hundred Years of Solitude* has been translated into 27 languages and is the best-selling Spanish language novel of all time. The novel tells the story of the rise and fall of the village of Macondo through the eyes of the Buendia family over a five-generation span. The town of Macondo is considered a microcosm for Colombia, and indeed for the whole of Latin America. He followed this masterpiece with *The Autumn of the Patriarch* (1975), *Chronicle of a Death Foretold* (1981), and a short-story collection entitled *Innocent Eréndira, and Other Stories* (1978). In 1982, García Márquez was awarded the Nobel Prize for Literature. He subsequently published the hugely popular *Love in the Time of Cholera* (1985), followed by *The General in his Labyrinth* (1989), *Strange Pilgrims* (1993), *Of Love and Other Demons* (1994), and

Memories of My Melancholy Whores (2004). García Márquez also continued to work as a journalist as well as writing screenplays. In 2002, he published the first of a proposed three-part autobiography entitled *Living to Tell the Tale*.

Magical Realism

One Hundred Years of Solitude rapidly propelled Gabriel García Márquez towards international fame. His writing, which has helped popularize a "magical realist" style, taps into a rich tradition of Latin American folklore, blurring the distinction between the real and the mythical. In his novels, Márquez elevates the smallest details of rural life to center stage, so that they became richly emblematic of a forgotten heritage. In this way, he is credited with helping to redefine questions of national identity in South America. His left-wing political views, and outspoken defense of Latin American cultural and economic autonomy, have led Márquez to become a figurehead for the region—an intellectual to rival the brightest stars in America and Europe. Over 40 years since *One Hundred Years of Solitude*, he remains one of the most globally successful and influential writers of the century.

◀ *In 1982, Gabriel García Márquez was awarded the Nobel Prize for Literature "for his novels and short stories, in which the fantastic and the realistic are combined in a richly composed world of imagination, reflecting a continent's life and conflicts." He received the prize from the Swedish monarch King Carl Gustav.*

◄◄ REWRITING HISTORY

Zelda Fitzgerald also wrote a novel. **Save Me the Waltz** *(1932) is a semi-autobiographical account of her marriage. When F. Scott Fitzgerald saw the manuscript he was outraged, as it contained much of the material that he intended to use in* **This Side of Paradise,** *and he forced Zelda to revise it considerably before publication.*

F. SCOTT FITZGERALD (1896–1940)

American Author

One of the leading proponents of the Lost Generation literary movement; published five novels and numerous short stories; Scott and Zelda Fitzgerald were defining figures of the Jazz Age

F. Scott Fitzgerald was an American writer, renowned for his depiction of the young and rich during the 1920s Jazz Age. He finished four novels, the most acclaimed of which is *The Great Gatsby*, and had another published posthumously. Fitzgerald and his wife, Zelda Sayre, became a celebrity couple, fêted for their wealth and beauty.

Early Works

Francis Scott Key Fitzgerald was born in St Paul, Minnesota, into an upper middle-class family of Irish descent. He was named for Francis Scott Key, a distant relative and the writer of the US national anthem "The Star-Spangled Banner." Fitzgerald spent part of his childhood in Buffalo, New Jersey, where his father worked as a salesman. In 1908, the family moved back to Minnesota and Fitzgerald attended St Paul Academy, where he began writing. His first published work, a detective story entitled "The Mystery of the Raymond Mortgage," appeared in the Academy's student newspaper when he was 13 years old. In 1913, Fitzgerald enrolled at Princeton University, where he wrote scripts for the Princeton Triangle Club and became friends with many future writers and critics including Edmund Wilson and John Peale Bishop. However, he was a poor student and dropped out of university to enlist in the US army in 1917. In 1918, he met Zelda Sayre, whom he married in 1920. After leaving the army, Fitzgerald moved to New York City, where he worked in advertising, simultaneously developing his first novel, *This Side of Paradise*, which was published in 1920.

Major Works

Scott and Zelda Fitzgerald led a flamboyant and glamorous lifestyle at their Connecticut home, gaining a reputation for wild and drunken parties. Their marriage was turbulent from the outset; Zelda flirted outrageously and Scott was jealous. To sustain enough income for their partying and for his more serious work as a novelist, Fitzgerald wrote short stories for magazines and sold the publishing rights of his stories to Hollywood studios. In 1920, he published a collection of short stories, *Flappers and Philosophers*, followed by

Tales of the Jazz Age in 1922. His second novel, *The Beautiful and the Damned*, also appeared in 1922. The Fitzgeralds traveled extensively in Europe during the 1920s, particularly to Paris and the French Riviera, where they befriended fellow American expatriates including writer Ernest Hemingway. In 1925, Fitzgerald wrote *The Great Gatsby*—a masterpiece of modern fiction that explores themes of isolation and loneliness in an outwardly respectable and affluent American suburb. The Fitzgerald marriage continued to be dysfunctional, worsened by Scott's alcoholism and Zelda's mental deterioration. It did, however, provide inspiration for Fitzgerald's writing, and much of his work is semi-autobiographical and even includes extracts from Zelda's private diaries. In 1930, Zelda suffered a mental breakdown and was subsequently diagnosed with schizophrenia. She spent the rest of her life in and out of mental institutions, eventually dying during a fire at one such hospital. Fitzgerald continued to write short stories but did not publish another novel until 1934 when *Tender is the Night* appeared. He spent much of the '30s working on scripts for the Metro-Goldwyn-Mayer movie company, though his continued dependency on alcohol frequently disrupted his working life. He fell in love with movie critic Sheilah Graham during this period, and it was at her Hollywood apartment that Fitzgerald had a fatal heart attack in 1940. He was just 44. His fifth novel *The Last Tycoon* was published posthumously the following year.

The Jazz Age

Fitzgerald begins one of his short stories by saying, "Let me tell you about the very rich. They are different from you and me." Both Fitzgerald's lifestyle and writings have come to characterize the hedonistic days of the Roaring Twenties. In the early postwar period, the US economy was booming and women were enjoying a new-found freedom. Fitzgerald wrote about this new generation, the flappers, and their rich and privileged lifestyle. Throughout his work, though, runs a central motif of disillusionment, placing him squarely as one of the major figures in the "Lost Generation" literary movement, which appeared in the aftermath of World War I. Fitzgerald remains one of the defining writers of the first half of the twentieth century, and *The Great Gatsby* remains one of the most popular novels in American fiction. Writers influenced by Fitzgerald include J. D. Salinger and Hunter S. Thompson.

#71

F .Scott Fitzgerald wrote his first published novel **This Side of Paradise** *while living in this brownstone row house located on Summit Avenue in St Paul, Minnesota.*
▼

- Politics & Leadership

- Science & Technology

- Popular Culture & the Arts

- Business & Commerce

- Writers & Thinkers

REWRITING HISTORY

With his army fatigues, keffiyeh headdress and pistol by his side, Arafat seemed far from a family man. He was too wrapped up in the armed struggle to marry until 1991, when he secretly wed his 28-year-old secretary Suha Tawil. However, he had previously adopted 50 Palestinian orphans. He and Suha also had a daughter Zahwa, born in Paris in 1995.

YASSER ARAFAT (1929–2004)

Chairman of the Palestine Liberation Organization and President of the Palestinian National Authority

Served in the 1948 Arab-Israeli war; cofounded the Al-Fatah underground movement; Chairman of the PLO; awarded the 1994 Nobel Prize for Peace; elected President of the Palestinian National Authority

Yasser Arafat was a Palestinian freedom fighter who spent much of his life engaged in terrorist action against Israel. In his later years, Arafat accepted the existence of Israel and entered into negotiations to end the decades-long war between Israel and the PLO. He was awarded the Nobel Peace Prize for his efforts at the Camp David Summit and Oslo Accords.

The Birth of a Freedom Fighter

Yasser Arafat was born Mohammed Abdel Rahman Abdel Raouf Arafat al-Qudwa al-Husseini in 1929, the sixth of seven children. Arafat claimed a Jerusalem birth, but records show that he was born in Cairo, Egypt. His parents were from long-established Palestinian families and his father worked as a textile merchant. His mother died when Arafat was five years old, and he was sent to live with his uncle in Jerusalem. Arafat was an active resistance fighter from an early age, helping to smuggle arms to Palestine for use against the British and the Israelis. In 1948, he abandoned his engineering studies at the University of Faud I (now Cairo University) to fight in the 1948 Arab-Israeli War. The establishment of the state of Israel left Arafat determined to commit himself to full-time revolutionary activities. After graduating, he moved to Kuwait, where he cofounded Al-Fatah, an underground movement committed to armed struggle against Israel.

The PLO

In 1964, the year Arafat moved to Jordan, the Palestine Liberation Organization (PLO) was formed, which organized the various existing groups under common leadership. According to the Palestine National Charter of 1968, its goal was the liberation of Palestine and the destruction of Israel through armed struggle. After the Arabs were defeated in the 1967 Six-Day War, Fatah emerged as the dominant group within the PLO, and in 1969 Arafat became Chairman of the PLO. Under Arafat's leadership, the PLO became a dominant political force, establishing a "state within a state" in Jordan, and establishing its own militias. As well as continuing raids on Israel, the PLO also began targeting civilians, earning worldwide condemnation and causing tension with Jordan's King Hussein. In 1970, the Popular Front for the Liberation of Palestine (PFLP), one of the factions within the PLO, hijacked five planes, blowing up three of them. The hijackings damaged Arafat's reputation and the Jordanian army moved to rid the country of the Palestinian militias, expelling them all by 1971. Terrorist attacks continued into the early 1970s, including the murder of 11 Israeli athletes at the 1972 Munich Olympic Games. Although Arafat denied any direct involvement, he was held responsible by Israel and its supporters.

Change of Policy

Arafat's image began to change in 1974 however, when he was the first representative of a nongovernmental organization to address the UN General Assembly. After the Israeli invasion of Lebanon in 1982, the Palestinian armed struggle lost most of its impetus, and Arafat was forced to change tack and move his operations to Tunis. In November 1988, the PLO announced the

establishment of the State of Palestine, to which Arafat was elected President in 1989. The following month he finally recognized Israel's right to exist and denounced terrorism. His move marked a major shift in policy and paved the way for direct negotiation with Israel. In 1993, Arafat held secret peace talks with Israeli leaders Yitzhak Rabin and Shimon Peres in Oslo, Norway. The Oslo Peace Accords gave the Palestinian Authority limited self-rule and jointly earned the three leaders the 1994 Nobel Peace Prize. The following year, Arafat set foot on Palestinian soil for the first time in 26 years and was subsequently elected president of the Palestinian National Authority. Failing health dogged Arafat and in October 2004 he was airlifted to Paris where he died of an undiagnosed illness.

◀ Yasser Arafat fought long and hard for Palestinian freedom during his lifetime and the image of him wearing his trademark black-and-white keffiyeh became an icon of Palestinian defiance. Here Arafat is portrayed in a mural on an Israeli security wall in the West Bank.

Arafat's Legacy

A charismatic figure, Arafat's presence on the world stage could not be ignored. Labeled a terrorist by Israel, Arafat was regarded as a freedom fighter by the Arab people. The truth is probably somewhere in between. As leader of the PLO, he was certainly behind some of the terrorist atrocities of the 1970s, but in the 1980s Arafat took on the role of senior statesman, using the diplomatic route to negotiate with Israel. Arafat did not live to see an independent Palestinian state within his lifetime but his efforts ensured that the dream lives on for the thousands of displaced Palestinian people.

JEAN-PAUL SARTRE (1905–1980)

French Existentialist Philosopher

A leading figure in twentieth century French philosophy; political activist; writer; playwright; awarded (but refused to accept) the Nobel Prize in Literature

◀◀ REWRITING HISTORY

There are those who have criticized Sartre's wartime resistance activities, which consisted of writing and distributing pamphlets and putting on subversive plays, as being inadequate for someone in his philosophical position. In 1964, Sartre himself renounced literature as a bourgeois substitute for real commitment in the world and rejected the Nobel Prize that he had been awarded.

Probably the most renowned philosopher of the twentieth century, not only in France but internationally, Sartre spent his life in an honest and tireless investigation of individual existence. Increasingly involved in political issues, he was at the centre of a creative group of intellectuals that helped to shape the national debate in post-World War II France.

Early Existence

Jean-Paul Charles Aymard Sartre was born in Paris, the son of a French Naval officer who died when the boy was little more than a year old. He was raised by his mother and his maternal grandfather (a high school professor and the brother of Albert Schweitzer's father), and he was exposed to a range of academic subjects at an early age. He discovered philosophy when he was in his teens, and went to study the subject at the prestigious École Normale Supérieure in Paris, receiving his doctorate in 1929.

After two years in the French Army, Sartre spent the rest of the 1930s teaching and writing. In 1932, he received a grant to visit Berlin, where he studied under the philosophers Edmund Husserl and Martin Heidegger, and their influence can be detected in both his philosophy and his writing. His early psychological studies received little attention, but his first novel, *La Nausée* (*Nausea*, 1938), which was followed shortly afterwards by *Le Mur* (*The Wall*, 1939), attracted recognition. *Nausea* paints a bleak picture of the purposelessness, loneliness, and alienation of existence within the constraints of bourgeois society, and reveals Sartre's existentialist position.

Writing and Resistance

In 1939, at the start of World War II, Sartre was drafted into the army and served as a meteorologist. He was captured by the Germans in 1940 and held prisoner for a year. Released due to ill-health, he returned to occupied Paris where he became involved with the resistance and worked on what became his best known book, *L'Être et le Néant* (*Being and Nothingness*), published in 1943.

The book is an exposition of his existentialist stance, and in it he introduces concepts such as the "bad faith" or self-deception that occurs when we allow ourselves to be defined by cultural labels, or by other people's subjective perceptions of us, or when we are "moral"—which means accepting an external ethical order rather than taking responsibility for creating our own. The feelings of futility, aloneness, and meaninglessness to which the existentialist view of the world gives rise can be overcome by creating one's own values and meanings.

After the War

His writing spoke powerfully to the people of postwar France, to whom questions of responsibility and its denial were very real. *Being and Nothingness*, together with his philosophical essays and plays, brought him fame, and Sartre

abandoned teaching to devote all his time to writing.

He believed in the importance of engaging in the political dialog of the day, and he became a commentator on the big issues of the time. He wrote copious books, plays, literary reviews, and criticisms, and he and his partner Simone de Beauvoir founded and edited the intellectual magazine *Les Temps Modernes*. He condemned the Soviet invasion of Hungary, was opposed to French rule in Algeria, and supported the French students during the Paris riots. Politically he took a left-wing, and increasingly Marxist, position, which was evidenced in his *Critique of Dialectical Reason* (1960), a work that revealed a more optimistic form of existentialism, and he and de Beauvoir visited Castro in Cuba, where they also met with Che Guevara.

The most appealingly modern of writers, Jean-Paul Sartre retained his place at the forefront of intellectual society in France until his death in 1980. His ideas on existentialism, and on the continual struggle to find meaning in the modern age, struck a chord with contemporary thinkers, particularly in the context of growing consumerism and the dawn of a truly global era. Sartre died in Paris on 15 April, 1980.

#69

◀ *During an interview with journalists in 1947, Sartre denied that he had "founded" existentialism, insisting that it was the contemporary current of thought. It was undoubtedly influenced by philosophers such as Kierkegaard, Nietzsche, and Heidegger.*

"Once freedom has exploded in the soul of man, the gods no longer have any power over him."
Jean-Paul Sartre

HAILE SELASSIE (1892–1975)

Emperor of Ethiopia

Influential black African leader; international spokesman for postcolonial Africa; modernized the Ethiopian legal and educational systems, and infrastructure; helped to found the Organization of African Unity

- Politics & Leadership
- Science & Technology
- Popular Culture & the Arts
- Business & Commerce
- Writers & Thinkers

◀◀ REWRITING HISTORY

Since the 1930s, Haile Selassie (formerly Ras Tafari), who claimed to be descended from Solomon and the Queen of Sheba, has been the focus of a religious movement that originated in Jamaica. A symbol of Black Nationalism and Pan-Africanism, he is regarded as Jah, the Messiah, and an incarnation of God.

Haile Selassie was one of the most prominent black Africans of the twentieth century. A consummate politician, he ruled Ethiopia for more than 40 years and implemented a major modernization program. He made his presence felt on the international stage, meeting world leaders and raising the profile not only of his country but also of all African nations and their rights to self-rule.

Political Beginnings

The man who was to become Emperor of Ethiopia was born Tafari Makonnen, the son of the governor of the province of Harar, in southeast Ethiopia. A Coptic Christian, he was taught by a priest and then continued his education in the country's capital, Addis Ababa. Through his father's position as an adviser to Emperor Menelik II, the young boy was able to spend time at the imperial court where he gained his first political experience. He impressed the Emperor with his ability and intelligence and was made a provincial governor at the age of 17—a role that didn't bestow much responsibility, but nevertheless allowed him to continue his studies. When the Emperor died and his grandson succeeded him, Tafari led the opposition movement that overthrew him.

Taking Power

The late Emperor's daughter then became Empress, with Ras (Prince) Tafari as Regent and heir to the throne, and he soon gained a considerable degree of political power, introducing his supporters into the government, taking control of the army, and introducing a radical program of modernization for the country. He created law courts, overhauled the legal system, established a national newspaper, introduced electricity and telephones, and encouraged the import of cars. Arguably as importantly, he also raised the profile of Ethiopia on the world stage, successfully negotiating Ethiopia's entry into the League of Nations in 1923 and undertaking a tour of the Middle East and Europe in 1924. Sidestepping attempts by opponents to remove him from power, he was crowned as King in 1928 and then became Emperor on the death of the Empress in 1930 in a lavish ceremony befitting his title as "His Imperial Majesty Haile Selassie I, King of Kings, Lord of Lords, Conquering Lion of the Tribe of Judah, and Elect of God."

Exile and Return

He continued his program of modernization, introducing a written constitution in 1931 that paid lip service to democracy while consolidating his power as sole ruler, but he was brought to a halt by the expansionist ambitions of Benito Mussolini. Italian Fascist forces invaded Ethiopia in 1935, and after leading his own army in battle and being defeated, Haile Selassie fled to Europe, where he made an impressive, impassioned, but ultimately ineffective speech to the United Nations calling on fellow members to support his country. Haile Selassie spent the next five years in exile in England, before returning to Ethiopia in 1941 after the defeat of the Italians by combined Ethiopian and British forces. His constitutional reforms and program of modernization continued, but at a more cautious pace, making him less popular with younger Ethiopians whose expectations for change were high. In 1960 an attempted coup was put down by his faithful army and police force, but it was an intimation that his hold on power might not be absolute. However, his stature internationally, and

especially within Africa, was growing, and in 1963 he took a leading role in the formation of the Organization of African Unity and the establishment of its headquarters in Addis Ababa. Throughout the late 1960s and '70s, a growing wave of student unrest and Marxism, combined with soaring commodity prices and the Emperor's apparent disregard for a severe famine that was killing tens of thousands of Ethiopians, led to an uprising, and in 1974 he was deposed. He died under house arrest the following year, but he remains a prominent figure of the twentieth century—a modernizing black African leader who had powerful Western allies with whom he dealt on equal terms, and yet who was willing to speak out in support of fellow African countries in their quest for independence from colonial rule.

▲
Seen here in his study at the palace in Addis Ababa, Emperor Haile Selassie was an eloquent defender of his country's freedom, appealing directly to the League of Nations when Ethiopia became the target of Italy's aggressive expansionism.

INDIRA GANDHI (1917–1984)

Indian Prime Minister

Masterful statesperson; President of the Indian National Congress; Finance Minister; Minister for External Affairs; supported the secession of East Bengal from Pakistan; instituted major social and economic reform

 Politics & Leadership

■ Science & Technology

■ Popular Culture & the Arts

■ Business & Commerce

■ Writers & Thinkers

◀◀ REWRITING HISTORY

Indira Gandhi has been accused of promoting eugenics through the implementation of a program of enforced sterilization. Aimed at men with two or more children, it is thought that involuntary vasectomy was meted out to unmarried young men as well as political opponents. The program brought the vital issue of population control in India into disrepute.

Indira Gandhi had a major impact on one of the world's most populous countries over a period of more than 20 years. Paradoxically, while her reforms increased participation in national democracy and improved conditions for many, and her hard-line approach to secession held the country together, she sought to exercise autocratic power and widened India's religious divisions.

Political Youth

Born in Allahabad, northern India, Indira Priyadarshini Nehru Gandhi was the only child of Jawaharlal Nehru, a leading figure in the Indian nationalist movement and later first Prime Minister of independent India (1947–64). Her home life gave Indira an apprenticeship in politics at a very early age, and she herself was active in the Indian Independence Movement as a teenager, founding the children's wing of the Indian National Congress. After the death of her mother in 1936, she spent more time with her father and became more deeply involved in the politics of the country. After attending Visva-Bharati University in West Bengal, she studied at Somerville College, Oxford University, and soon after her return to India in 1941 she joined the Indian National Congress. The following year she married Feroze Gandhi (no relation to Mahatma Gandhi), and they had two sons, Rajiv and Sanjay. She was elected to the Congress Working Committee in 1955 and became president of the Indian National Congress party in 1959.

First Term as PM

Her father was opposed to nepotism, and she did not stand as a candidate in the 1962 elections, but after his death in 1964 she was elected to parliament and appointed Minister for Information and Broadcasting, a role in which she soon showed her ability to make the most of media attention. Upon the death of Lal Bahadur Shastri in 1966, Gandhi was chosen by the Congress

Party to replace him as Prime Minister, and she led the party to victory in the 1967 elections. However, India was suffering food shortages and deepening unemployment, and the Congress Party was losing its dominant position. Gandhi attempted to redress the situation by reorganizing the party structure and introducing more socialist policies aimed at broadening social justice. This move to the left, and particularly her nationalization of the banks, caused a split in the Congress Party, but her New Congress Party won a resounding victory in midterm elections in 1971.

Later that year she sent troops into East Pakistan against Pakistani forces, leading to the creation of Bangladesh and making her more popular than ever. However, in 1975, when she was found guilty of violating election laws, Gandhi responded by declaring a State of Emergency, suspending the constitution, arresting thousands of political opponents, and abrogating civil rights. Believing, mistakenly, that she had debilitated the opposition, she lifted the State of Emergency in 1977 and called elections, in which she suffered a spectacular defeat.

Second and Final Term

Indira Gandhi returned to power in 1980 (the year in which her younger son Sanjay died in an airplane crash), and introduced a highly autocratic style of leadership, crushing dissent within her own party and overruling opposition-led state governments. Her dismissal of the Sikh government of Punjab state, in an attempt to curry favor among Hindus, sparked a state-wide call for Punjabi secession and led to civil unrest. Having blocked attempts at a negotiated settlement, in June 1984 she sent troops into the holy Golden Temple of Amritsar to remove Sikh militants. "Operation Blue Star" resulted in the deaths of more than 400 Sikhs and earned her the hatred of the Sikh community. At the end of October she was shot and killed by two of her Sikh bodyguards, an act that led to riots and the massacre of some 3,000 Sikhs by Hindus. Indira Gandhi was succeeded by her elder son Rajiv, who was later killed by a Tamil Tiger suicide bomb.

#67

The Golden Temple of Amritsar is the cultural and spiritual center of the Sikh religion. Indira Gandhi's decision to send in the troops to deal with Sikh militants in this sensitive location led directly to her assassination.
▼

BENAZIR BHUTTO (1953–2007)

Former Prime Minister of Pakistan

The first Asian woman to become President of the Oxford Union; elected the first female head of a modern Muslim country; twice elected Prime Minister of Pakistan; Bhutto campaigned for a democratic Pakistan

- Politics & Leadership
- Science & Technology
- Popular Culture & the Arts
- Business & Commerce
- Writers & Thinkers

◀◀ REWRITING HISTORY

Benazir Bhutto wed Asif Ali Zardari in a traditionally arranged marriage. Had her family made another choice for her, Bhutto's political career may well have turned out differently. Nicknamed "Mr. 10 percent" by opponents for his supposed tendency to take backhanders, Zardari has long been a controversial and often unpopular figure in Pakistani politics.

Twice elected Prime Minister of Pakistan, Benazir Bhutto was the first female leader of a Muslim country. Her terms in office were disrupted by corruption charges, and she endured many spells in prison or exile. She died at the hands of an assassin while campaigning for the 2008 Pakistan general election.

Daughter of the East

Benazir Bhutto was born in Karachi, Pakistan, in 1953, the daughter of Begum Nusrat Ispahani and Zulfikar Ali Bhutto. She completed her early education in Pakistan before attending Radcliffe College in Cambridge, Massachusetts, where she obtained a BA degree *cum laude* in comparative government. Between 1973 and 1977, Bhutto read politics, philosophy, and economics at Lady Margaret Hall, Oxford University, England. In 1976, she was elected president of the Oxford Union debating society, becoming the first Asian woman to hold the post. She returned to Pakistan after her studies, intending to pursue a career in the Foreign Service. However, Bhutto soon found herself mired in Pakistani politics. In 1973, Benazir's father, who had founded the Pakistan Peoples' Party (PPP), was elected Prime Minister of Pakistan. A coup led by General Muhammad Zia-ul-Haq removed him from power in 1977, and Bhutto was placed under arrest on charges of conspiracy to murder. Despite widespread doubt that the charge was genuine and appeals for clemency from around the world, Zulfikar Ali Bhutto was hanged in 1979. Benazir Bhutto had been put under house arrest during her father's imprisonment and remained in detention after his execution. In 1984, she was permitted to go to the UK, where she became leader in exile of the PPP, leading the pro-democracy movement against Zia-ul-Haq's military regime.

Taking over Her Father's Legacy

In 1986, Bhutto was allowed to return home to Pakistan. The following year she married Asif Ali Zardari and the couple were to have three children. In August 1988, General Zia died in a plane crash, paving the way for democratic elections. The PPP won the largest number of seats at the subsequent elections, and the 35-year-old Benazir Bhutto became prime minister of a coalition government on December 2, 1988. Mindful that she had to keep the army on her side, and hemmed in by the need to appease all parties in the coalition, Bhutto did not succeed in pushing through as many liberal and secular reforms as she had wished, though she did manage to restore basic human rights. In August 1990, the Bhutto government was dismissed by President Ghulam Ishaq Khan and Bhutto was charged with corruption and misuse of power, though she was never tried. Bhutto returned to power after the 1993 elections, and her husband Zardari became a government minister. In late 1996, Bhutto's government was again dismissed, and Bhutto was accused of corruption and placed under house arrest. Zardari was arrested in connection with the 1996 assassination of his wife's brother Murtaza Bhutto, who had been an outspoken critic of Benazir and her husband, and remained in jail until 2004. In 1997, the Pakistan Muslim

League inflicted a heavy defeat on the PPP, and Bhutto's political career seemed over. She left the country with her children and went to live in Dubai, the United Arab Emirates. In 1999, she was convicted of

taking bribes from a Swiss company and sentenced in absentia to five years in prison.

Exile and Final Return to Pakistan

In 2002 Pakistani President Musharraf passed an amendment to Pakistan's constitution that limited a Prime Minister's number of terms of office to two, effectively disqualifying Bhutto from ever holding the post again. However, Pakistan's deteriorating political situation in 2007 forced Musharraf to seek a deal with Bhutto and the PPP. They agreed on a power sharing deal involving Musharraf staying on as President, with Bhutto as Prime Minister. In October 2007, Bhutto was granted an amnesty from all corruption charges and on October 18 she returned to Karachi, ready to take part in the 2008 elections. Two suicide bombing attacks shortly after she landed at the airport killed over 130 people, though Bhutto herself was unhurt. Two months later, she was not so fortunate. On December 27, 2007, Bhutto was assassinated as she returned from a campaign rally at Liaquat National Bagh.

◄ *During her period in power, Benazir Bhutto travelled the world as the first female head of a Muslim state. Here she is seen speaking to the US press as she arrives at St Andrews Air Force base in Washington DC for a state visit in 1988.*

KIM II-SUNG (1912–1994)

Head of the Korean Workers' Party and President of the Democratic People's Republic of Korea

Fought in a guerilla war against the Japanese in Manchuria; assumed power in North Korea after the Korean peninsula was divided; became head of the Korean Workers' Party; led North Korea in the Korean War

- Politics & Leadership
- Science & Technology
- Popular Culture & the Arts
- Business & Commerce
- Writers & Thinkers

 REWRITING HISTORY

Kim II-sung's official biography differs considerably from contemporary reports of his life. It elevates many of his relations, including his parents, uncles, grandparents, and even a great grandparent, to revolutionary hero status. According to the official version, his father was a leader of an anti-Japanese movement, whereas contemporary accounts say that his opposition amounted only to general grievances.

Kim II-sung was a communist Korean leader who first came to prominence as a guerilla fighter against the Japanese during the 1930s. After the Korean peninsula was split into two separate countries in 1948, Kim seized power in North Korea. For the next 46 years, Kim exercised autocratic power as the country's "Great Leader."

The Creation of the Democratic People's Republic of Korea

Kim II-sung was born Kim Song-ju in 1912 in Pyongan-namdo, a northeastern province of Korea, then under Japanese occupation. In the 1920s, Kim's family fled to Manchuria to escape oppressive Japanese rule. Kim attended school in Jilin, where he became interested in communist ideology. Jailed briefly for communist activity, Kim joined a guerilla movement and fought against the Japanese. During this period Kim took the name Kim II-sung, which means "of the sun". In 1940, Kim was forced to flee to the Soviet Union, where he undertook further military and political training at the Soviet Khabarovsk camp. He served in the Red Army until the end of World War II. At the end of the war, Korea was divided at the 38th parallel, with the Soviet Union administering the northern portion. In return for his loyalty to the Soviets, Kim was installed as head of the Provisional People's Committee in 1945. When any hopes of reunification ended in 1948, Kim became Prime Minister of the newly created Democratic People's Republic of Korea. He also assumed the chairmanship of the Workers Party of Korea (WPK).

Kim II-sung's Rule

Kim's early years as leader were marked by continued border scuffles with South Korea. These disputes erupted into civil war after North Korean forces crossed the border into South Korea in June 1950. More than 3.5 million Koreans died in the conflict, which ended in 1953 with the borders re-established in their approximate prewar positions. In the postwar period, Kim maintained relations with both the Soviets and the Chinese, though North Korea became increasingly isolated from the rest of the world.

Kim succeeded in purging any opposition to his rule and concentration camps were established to house dissidents. Others faced summary execution. Kim gradually began to stamp his personality cult on every aspect of Korean life and he became an absolute, despotic ruler. In 1972, the country's new constitution appointed Kim as President. By the time of his death in 1994, the country was virtually bankrupt, crippled by high armament expenditure and reduced international trade. His death was met by hysterical outpourings of grief around the country and his embalmed body, placed in a glass coffin, is now on public view at the Kumsusan Memorial Palace.

Juche and the Cult of Personality

Official North Korean historical accounts base the entire account of the country's modern history on Kim's revolutionary activities and political ideology. During his 46 years in power, Kim established an extreme, omnipresent personality cult that has been passed down to his son and successor Kim Jong-iI. Kim also established a political philosophy, known as Juche, which remains the official state ideology of North Korea. Meaning "self-reliance," Juche teaches that "man is the master of everything and decides everything" and that the Korean revolution was entirely due to the revolutionary zeal of the North Korean people. According to Kim, the three fundamental principles of Juche are independence in politics, self-sustenance in the economy, and the capacity for self-defense, all of which require absolute loyalty to the party and leader on the part of the people. The political

system that Kim set up is still very much in evidence in North Korea. The country continues to be a one-party state with the result that North Koreans are subject to severe social, political, and economic restrictions, and human rights abuses are widespread. Kim's personality cult remains in place and he is officially revered as the nation's "Eternal President," a title bestowed on him in 1998 by his son.

#65

◄ *Kim II-sung's embalmed body lies on public display at the Kumsusan Memorial Palace in Pyongyang. The palace was formerly the official residence for Kim II-sung but his son and successor Kim Jong-il transformed the building into a lasting memorial for his father.*

President of the Soviet Union

General Secretary of the Communist Party of the Soviet Union (1985–91); President (1988–91); helped bring about an end to the Cold War; introduced reforms in domestic and foreign policy; winner of the Nobel Peace Prize

- Politics & Leadership
- Science & Technology
- Popular Culture & the Arts
- Business &·Commerce
- Writers & Thinkers

REWRITING HISTORY

The nuclear disaster that occurred at Chernobyl during Gorbachev's second year in office proved to be the spark that ignited glasnost. In traditional Soviet style, the authorities attempted to cover up what had happened, but the scale of the tragedy was so vast that it proved impossible, and the flood of information that followed led to an open appraisal of much that was wrong with the way the Soviet Union was being run.

A relatively young man when he became leader of the Soviet Union, Gorbachev was a consummate politician and a radical reformer. His liberalizing policies undermined Communist authority in the Soviet Union, which disintegrated as a result, and led to greater freedom throughout Eastern Europe and improved relations between his nation and the rest of the world.

Early Potential

Mikhail Sergeyevich Gorbachev was born into a collective farmer family in the agricultural Stavropol region of Russia, east of the Black Sea. While he was still at school, he worked on the collective farm and then at the Stavropol machine-and-tractor station, which brought him into contact with the realities of agriculture, economics, and political administration. In 1950, Gorbachev enrolled in the law department of the Moscow State University, and there he became a member of the Young Communist League. He joined the Communist Party in 1952, and met and married Raisa Titorenko in 1953, the year in which Stalin died and a period of political and intellectual change began in the Soviet Union. A hard-working student, he proved adept at establishing useful contacts, and when he returned to Stavropol after graduating in 1955 he began to climb the Young Communist League ladder.

Climbing the Ranks

During the 1960s he rose steadily through the ranks of the territorial Communist Party administration, being appointed first secretary (effectively the mayor) of Stavropol City by Leonid Brezhnev in 1966. He then completed a degree course in agrarian economics at Stavropol Agricultural Institute, and was made first secretary for the Stavropol Territorial Party Committee in 1970 (equivalent to State Governor). Later that year Gorbachev was elected to the Supreme Soviet, and in 1971 he was made a member of the Central Committee. In 1978, Gorbachev was called to Moscow to serve as party secretary in charge of agricultural administration, and when his patron, Yuri Andropov, took over as party leader after the death of Leonid Brezhnev in 1980, Gorbachev joined the ruling Politburo, its youngest full member. In 1985, he was made General Secretary of the Communist Party—the leader of the Soviet Union—at the age of just 54.

Perestroika and Glasnost

Gorbachev quickly made changes of personnel throughout the Communist bureaucracy and took steps to encourage the development of a market economy and move toward democracy—a policy that became known as perestroika (restructuring). It was accompanied by glasnost (openness), encouraging free speech and eventually abolishing state censorship. On the international stage, Gorbachev improved relations with Europe and the US, meeting repeatedly with President Ronald Reagan and signing a nuclear arms limitation treaty in 1987. He also pulled Soviet forces out of Afghanistan, recognized the electoral victory of Solidarity in Poland, and supported the fall of Communist power in East Germany and other Eastern European countries. He was awarded the Nobel Peace Prize for his efforts in 1990.

At home, electoral reform went ahead, but the economy was worsening, and Gorbachev soon found himself in the crossfire between conservative forces, fearing the loss of their own power amid the breakup of the Soviet Union, and a popular demand to speed up and deepen the process of perestroika, for which Boris Yeltsin was a vociferous spokesman. With the erosion of Communist Party power, the constituent republics of the Soviet Union aspired to ever more autonomy, with some seeking independence. His one-time ally Boris Yeltsin was elected President of Russia and, after a failed coup in 1991, Gorbachev resigned as President of the Soviet Union when the republics voted it out of existence.

Following Mikhail Gorbachev's announcement that he was willing to pursue significant arms agreements, he and President Reagan signed the Intermediate-Range Nuclear Forces (INF) Treaty at the White House in 1987, eliminating an entire class of nuclear weapons.
▼

Mikhail Gorbachev was at the helm of the Soviet Union during a period of immense change. His openly conciliatory approach helped to achieve progress on a number of fronts, including a greater degree of democracy in the USSR, a significant reduction in nuclear armaments, and even greater political engagement with one-time enemies in the West. In conjunction with his American and European counterparts, he brought about an end to an ideological war that had dominated and divided the world for almost 50 years.

MOTHER TERESA (1910–1997)

Missionary and Charity Worker

Founded the Missionaries of Charity to help India's poor; awarded the Nobel Prize for Peace; beatified by Pope John Paul II

Mother Teresa was a Roman Catholic missionary, famous for her work among the homeless and poor in the slums of Calcutta, India. She founded the Missionaries of Charity, which now has branches in more than 100 cities worldwide. Although tiny in stature, Mother Teresa held her own in the company of the world's most powerful political figures, including presidents and princesses.

The Call of God

Mother Teresa was born Agnes Goxha Bojaxhiu in Skopje, Macedonia, then part of the Ottoman Empire, in 1910. Her grocer parents were of Albanian descent. When she was very young, Agnes showed a fascination with the stories of the saints and by the age of 12, she had decided that she wished to devote her life to God. At 18, she left the family home to join a community of Irish nuns, the Sisters of Loreto, who worked in India. After a few months learning the English language in Ireland, Agnes was sent to Darjeeling, India, to begin her preparation for a life devoted to God. She took her first religious vows as a nun in 1931, taking the name of Teresa after Thérèse de Lisieux, the patron saint of missionaries. In 1937, she took her solemn vows. Between 1931 and 1948, Teresa worked at St Mary's High School for girls in Calcutta. The school lay near to the slums of Calcutta, and Teresa became increasingly drawn to helping the poor. In 1946, she experienced "the call within the call," which told her to leave the school and go out to live and work among the poor. In 1948, she took out Indian citizenship and swapped her Loreto habit for the simple white sari with a blue border that was to become her mission's dress. Although she had no funding, Teresa opened a school for the slum children, quickly expanding her work to helping the hungry and destitute. She soon attracted the help of other volunteers and also received financial support from sympathizers.

Missionaries of Charity

In 1950, Mother Teresa received official permission from the Vatican to begin the order that would become the Missionaries of Charity. As well as taking

◀◀ REWRITING HISTORY

Not everyone approved of Mother Teresa's work. She has come under fire for her attitude toward suffering, which she believed brought people closer to Jesus, and has been accused of secretly baptizing the dying. She also faced criticism for taking donations from dubious sources, including the Duvalier family in Haiti, and for the poor and ignorant medical care administered to the sick and dying in her homes.

the three traditional vows of poverty, chastity, and obedience, the order's members took a fourth vow promising to serve the poor. Before beginning her work, Mother Teresa underwent an intensive medical training course with the American Medical Missionary in Patna, India. The Missionaries of Charity started out by teaching uneducated children from the Calcutta slums but their work soon evolved into ministering to the dying, the work for which Mother Teresa has become so famous. In 1952, Mother Teresa opened the first Home for the Dying in a former Hindu temple, and three years later she opened an orphanage. She also established leprosy clinics throughout the city and also increased the number of educational facilities. Increased funding allowed Mother Teresa to expand her work outside of Calcutta, and before long she had established missions in more than 22 Indian cities. She also helped to establish foundations in other countries including Sri Lanka, Tanzania, and Venezuela. In 1969, Mother Teresa sanctioned the establishment of a lay order, the International Association of Co-Workers of Mother Teresa, to

further her work with the poor. At the time of her death in 1997, the Missionaries of Charity had grown from an initial 12 members to some 4,000 nuns and 100,000 lay volunteers working in more than a hundred countries. Mother Teresa herself achieved worldwide recognition and financial support for her work, including the first Pope John XXIII Peace Prize in 1971 and the Nobel Prize for Peace in 1979.

The Saintly Nun

Much of the Missionaries of Charity's growth can be attributed directly to the personality of Mother Teresa. She dedicated her whole life to working for those who could not help themselves, and did so with an aura of sanctity and love that could melt the most cynical of world leaders, including Fidel Castro who allowed her to establish a mission in communist Cuba. She may have been just 5 feet tall (1.5 m), but Mother Teresa commanded attention wherever she went, imbued as she was with an energy and radiance that shone through the darkest of places. It was no surprise that in the aftermath of her death, there were immediate moves to canonize her. In 2003, she was beatified by Pope John Paul II, placing her one step from sainthood. She is now known as the Blessed Mother Teresa of Kolkata.

#63

◄ *For more than half a century, Mother Teresa worked among the poor on the streets of Calcutta, a familiar sight in her simple blue and white sari. Despite her diminutive stature, the Polish-born nun commanded attention on the world stage, earning respect across the globe.*

DWIGHT D. EISENHOWER (1890–1969)

Supreme Commander of Allied forces in Europe during World War II

President of Columbia University; Supreme Commander of NATO; 34th President of the United States (1953–61)

- Politics & Leadership
- Science & Technology
- Popular Culture & the Arts
- Business & Commerce
- Writers & Thinkers

◀◀ REWRITING HISTORY

Although it was not new, the term "military-industrial complex" entered common parlance when Eisenhower issued a largely unheeded warning in his farewell speech, saying "we must guard against the acquisition of unwarranted influence, whether sought or unsought, by the military-industrial complex. The potential for the disastrous rise of misplaced power exists and will persist."

Dwight Eisenhower was the right man in the right place at the right time. As the United States' military leader in Europe in World War II, he displayed an intuitive understanding of military strategy and the strength, resolution, and diplomatic ability to work with the Allied powers to achieve the defeat of Nazi Germany.

A Life in the Military

David Dwight "Ike" Eisenhower, born in Denison, Texas, was the third of seven sons born to poor Swiss-German Protestant parents. The family moved to Abilene, Kansas, when Dwight, as he was known, was two years old. After graduating from high school he attended West Point Military Academy, graduating in 1915, and then trained tank battalions at Camp Colt in Pennsylvania during World War I. After the war he attended the Command and General Staff School at Fort Leavenworth, Kansas, graduating first in his class. He then held several staff positions, including Aide to General Douglas MacArthur in the Philippines, before returning to the US to take up the position of Chief of Staff of the Third Army in 1941. By the end of that year, Army Chief of Staff General George C. Marshall—who had been impressed by Eisenhower's grasp of military strategy—appointed him as head of the War Plans Division. The US entered the war at the end of that year, and in 1942 Eisenhower was chosen to command US forces in Europe, a choice that some criticized, given his complete lack of combat leadership. He was then made Supreme Commander of the Allied Expeditionary Force, a task that demanded both diplomatic and strategic skills, and one in which he proved that the choice had been a wise one.

Five-Star General

Eisenhower played a key role in planning and then leading the Allied invasion of North Africa, Sicily, and Italy in November of 1942, for which he was rewarded by promotion to four-star general. Eisenhower was also in charge of preparations for Operation Overlord, the invasion of western Europe by Canadian, British, and US troops that began with the Normandy landings on D-Day, 6 June 1944. Promoted to five-star general, the highest rank in the American military, he led the Allied forces in a sweep across France that ultimately led to the defeat of the Nazis. By the end of the war, General "Ike" Eisenhower, now Army Chief of Staff, was a household name across large parts of Europe and throughout the United States.

Back Home

On his return to the US he avoided being drawn into politics and served instead as an unlikely president of Columbia University, but in 1951 he returned to the military to direct a multinational force, this time as Supreme Commander of the recently formed North Atlantic Treaty Organization (NATO). A man with no strong partisan leanings, he was approached by both parties to stand as presidential candidate, and in 1952 he stood as the Republican candidate, winning with a strong majority over Democrat Adlai Stevenson, whom he again defeated convincingly four years later. As the United States' 34th president, Eisenhower showed the consensual style and diplomatic skills that characterized his wartime leadership, choosing able deputies to whom he could reliably delegate responsibilities. Overseas, he brought an end to the war in Korea and made a number of decisions in keeping with the policy of containing the spread of Communism laid down by his predecessor Harry S. Truman. These included sending US advisers to support the anti-Communist regime in South Vietnam and adopting a strong stance toward Castro's Cuba, both of which were to blow up under his successor, President Kennedy.

At home he signed the 1957 Civil Rights Act and sent troops to Little Rock, Arkansas, to enforce the Supreme Court's 1954 schools desegregation ruling. He also expanded the Social Security program, raised the minimum wage, and instigated the creation of the Interstate Highways system. He cut the military budget, but was coerced into increasing spending on missiles and creating NASA, largely in response to the Soviet launch of Sputnik I.

Eisenhower's crucial role in the planning and execution of the later stages of World War II has secured his place in history. The political ability he demonstrated during the war served him well in peacetime, as an able and admired president of postwar America.

#62

"Every gun that is made, every warship launched, every rocket fired, signifies in the final sense a theft from those who hunger and are not fed, those who are cold and are not clothed."
Dwight D. Eisenhower

◀ *Despite being arguably the most powerful man in the world at the time of the D-Day landings, Dwight Eisenhower had the common touch and a famous ability to make his fellow soldiers feel at ease in his company.*

ROBERT OPPENHEIMER (1904–1967)

American Nuclear Physicist

Scientific director of the Manhattan Project, which developed the world's first atomic bomb; fought to impose controls on the development of nuclear energy and weapons; Fellow of the Royal Society; cofounder of The World Academy of Art and Science

- Politics & Leadership
- **Science & Technology**
- Popular Culture & the Arts
- Business & Commerce
- Writers & Thinkers

◀◀ REWRITING HISTORY

Oppenheimer's fall from grace owed as much to academic and political rivalries occasioned by his high-profile career as they did to the politics of left and right. In 1963 he gained a degree of rehabilitation when President John F. Kennedy awarded him the Enrico Fermi Award for lifetime achievement in the field of energy.

A highly intellectual and multifaceted individual, Oppenheimer was first and foremost a brilliant scientist, whose academic achievements covered many theoretical fields. As leader of the team that developed the first nuclear bomb, he became one of the best-known scientists of his generation, and one of the first to have to face the moral implications of his work.

A Social Conscience

J. Robert Oppenheimer (there is uncertainty about what, if anything, the "J" stood for) was born in New York City, the son of a wealthy German textile merchant. Educated at Harvard and Cambridge, he completed his PhD studies at the University of Göttingen in Germany in 1927 and then went to teach at the University of California, where he spent the next 13 years, making significant contributions to theoretical astronomy, general relativity, nuclear physics, and quantum physics. He became a guiding light in theoretical physics, and was instrumental in making the US an international leader in the field. This was a period of intense political debate among intellectuals in the US, and Oppenheimer, an extremely intelligent and cultured man with interests in philosophy and Indian religion, gave his support—and financial assistance—to various left-wing movements calling for social reform at the time. Although he was never officially recognized as a Communist, many of his friends were.

The Manhattan Project

At the start of World War II, Oppenheimer became involved in nuclear weapon research being conducted at Berkeley, California, focusing on the chain reaction that would be at the heart of such a weapon. When the Army took control of the bomb-making effort that became the Manhattan Project, its director, General Leslie R. Groves, chose Oppenheimer as scientific director, a surprising choice given that Oppenheimer was hardly an ally of the conservative military and his left-wing activities has already been flagged as a potential security risk. It was Oppenheimer who chose the site for the research center at Los Alamos in the desert of New Mexico, and under his leadership the first nuclear test explosion—which he named "Trinity"—took place on July 16, 1945. It marked the dawn of the Atomic Age, and Oppenheimer later said that as he watched the giant fireball mushroom into the sky he was reminded of words in the Hindu holy book, the Bhagavad-Gita: "Now I am become Death, the destroyer of worlds." Within a month, on the orders of President Harry S. Truman, the Little Boy and Fat Man nuclear bombs were dropped on Hiroshima and Nagasaki, killing in excess of 200,000 people.

A Period of Disgrace

As governments around the world started to take in the military and political implications of nuclear physics, Oppenheimer emerged as the symbolic head of this new science. When the US Atomic Energy Commission was created in 1946, Oppenheimer was made head of its General Advisory Committee, which soon called for the creation of a supranational Atomic Development Authority to control the development of this awesome source of energy solely for peaceful purposes. It was soon clear that a nuclear arms race was inevitable, which persuaded Oppenheimer to lobby against going ahead with the development of the hydrogen bomb. He later changed his position on this, but his political past came back to haunt him and in 1953, in the fever of the McCarthy era, his opposition to the H-bomb was attributed to his having Communist sympathies. Despite support from many colleagues at formal hearings, he was stripped of his security clearance and forced out of all political roles. He continued to be director of the Institute of Advanced Studies at Princeton, eventually holding the position of senior professor of theoretical physics once held by Albert Einstein.

Debate still continues about the extent to which the two atomic bombs dropped on Japan helped to bring the war to an end, and controversy inevitably surrounds America's decision to use them. Perhaps unfairly, Robert J. Oppenheimer came to symbolise the destructive potential of nuclear physics. His subsequent—unsuccessful—campaign against the ensuing arms race demonstrates the limited capacity of scientists to control the consequences of their own work.

Nicknamed "Jumbo," the world's first atomic explosive device is moved into position prior to the Trinity test. Oppenheimer was later to doubt the wisdom of developing nuclear energy for anything other than peaceful purposes.
▼

FRED ASTAIRE (1899–1987)

Screen and Stage Dancer, Choreographer, Singer, and Actor

Starred in many Broadway and London stage musicals with his sister Adele; moved into Hollywood movies in the 1930s; established the silver screen's most famous dancing partnership with Ginger Rogers; awarded an Honorary Academy Award and nominated for Best Supporting Actor

REWRITING HISTORY

Fred Astaire's move into show business was precipitated by the temperance movement. Fred's father lost his job at the Nebraska Storz Brewing Company when the brewery shut down, and he made the radical decision to move the family to New York so that his children could have a career in vaudeville.

With an elegance never before witnessed on the silver screen, dancer and singer Fred Astaire charmed moviegoers in a total of 31 Hollywood musicals. His most celebrated dancing partner was Ginger Rogers, but he made any dancing partner look good. After hanging up his tap shoes, Astaire moved into dramatic acting, while still working as a recording artist.

Brother-and-Sister Act

Fred Astaire was born Frederick Austerlitz in Omaha, Nebraska, the son of an Austrian immigrant. Fred's elder sister Adele showed early talent as a dancer and Fred was persuaded to join her in dancing lessons. In 1904, the family moved to New York so that the children could pursue a career in show business. The brother-and-sister act made its professional debut on the vaudeville circuit in Keyport, New Jersey, in 1905; Fred was just six years old. They made their Broadway debut in 1917 in *Over the Top*. Other Broadway shows followed and in 1922 Fred and Adele earned top billing for *The Bunch and Judy*. Shortly afterward they were invited to appear on the London stage in *Stop Flirting* (1923). The musical was an instant hit and the Astaires were asked to record several numbers from the show for HMV Records. They returned to Broadway for the Gershwin musical *Lady, Be Good!* (1924), later taking the show to London. They also starred in another Gershwin hit, *Funny Face* (1927), on both sides of the Atlantic. In 1931, Fred and Adele made their final appearance together in *Band Wagon* and Adele retired to marry Lord Cavendish.

Fred and Ginger

Astaire's successful stage career attracted the attention of Hollywood moguls, and in 1933 RKO Pictures producer David O. Selznick invited him for a screen test. Fred was unimpressive; Selznick thought the test "wretched" and commented on the dancer's "enormous ears and bad chin line." Despite this inauspicious start, Fred was signed by RKO. RKO loaned him out to MGM and Fred's Hollywood debut came in the MGM movie *Dancing Lady* (1933) with Joan Crawford. For his first RKO movie, *Flying Down to Rio* (1933), Fred was paired with established actress Ginger Rogers and appeared fifth on the billing. The duo's dance sequence to the Carioca won over the public and heralded the birth of the most famous dance partnership in movie history. As Katherine Hepburn said, "He gives her class and she gives him sex." They appeared in nine more musicals together, including *The Gay Divorcee* (1934) and *Top Hat* (1935). The movies also provided Astaire with many recording hits, notably "Cheek to Cheek" and "Top Hat, White Tie and Tails." After his partnership with Ginger, Fred danced with a number of leading ladies, including Eleanor Powell and Rita Hayworth, and continued to enjoy great success. In 1946, Astaire announced his retirement to concentrate on his horse-racing interests and he also founded the Fred Astaire Dance Studios. Retirement was short lived, however—Astaire stepped in for the injured

Gene Kelly to make Irving Berlin's *Easter Parade* with Judy Garland. The movie's success quashed any further talk of retirement and Astaire carried on dancing until he was 70, both on the big screen and on television. In 1949, he received an Honorary Academy Award. Astaire later played a number of dramatic roles in movies such as *The Towering Inferno* (1974), for which he received an Academy Award nomination for Best Supporting Actor. His final movie was *Ghost Story* (1981).

The Astaire Legacy

Fred Astaire may have had unprepossessing looks, but when he danced there was no one to touch him. His sheer elegance made his dance routines look simple, yet they were far from that. He injected each routine with originality and grace, perfecting every movement through hours of practice and striving to get the best out of his dancing partner. Astaire choreographed most of his own dance routines, and had considerable say in the artistic content of his movies. Traditionally, dance scenes had played little role in the movie's plot and were for spectacle only, whereas Astaire made his dance routines tell a story. Fred Astaire's influence was not confined to Hollywood musicals; classical ballet star Rudolph Nureyev and pop star Michael Jackson are just two among many diverse twentieth-century dancers who have paid homage to Astaire.

◀ *Fred Astaire's first dance partner was his sister Adele. The brother-and-sister double act enjoyed stage success in the US and Europe before Adele retired from show business and Fred went on to Hollywood fame.*

LUDWIG WITTGENSTEIN (1889–1951)

Austrian-English Philosopher

Wrote two highly influential philosophical works—Tractatus Logico-Philosophicus *and* Philosophical Investigations; *demonstrated the application of modern logic, via language, to metaphysics; offered a fundamental critique of the role and inherent limits of philosophy*

- Politics & Leadership
- Science & Technology
- Popular Culture & the Arts
- Business & Commerce
- **Writers & Thinkers**

◄◄ **REWRITING HISTORY**

When Wittgenstein's father died in 1913, Ludwig and his siblings became some of the wealthiest people in Europe. When Hitler rose to power, the family used their wealth to persuade the German authorities to change their racial status from Jewish to part "Aryan," handing over 1.7 tons of gold, with a current value of some US$50 million.

One of the most important analytic philosophers of the twentieth century, Wittgenstein placed logic and language at the heart of his work. In two very different books, he investigated the relationship between language, knowledge, and the world, and brought about a fundamental reappraisal of philosophy.

Science to Philosophy

Ludwig Josef Johann Wittgenstein was the youngest of eight children born into an extremely wealthy industrialist family in Vienna, then in the Austro-Hungarian Empire. Educated at home, he showed a talent for mechanics, and at the age of 14 he was sent to school in Lintz to study mathematics and physical sciences. After taking a course in mechanical engineering in Berlin, Germany, he studied aeronautical engineering at the University of Manchester, England, where he became deeply interested in the philosophy of logic and mathematics, and in 1911 he went to study logic under Bertrand Russell at Cambridge University. After a year, he left academic life and sought solitude in a small hut in the Norwegian countryside, and there he began to formulate his own philosophical approach to the problems of logic and language.

Language and the Mind

At the outbreak of World War I he returned to Austria and joined the Army, serving on the Russian front, where he distinguished himself by his bravery, and in the Tyrol, where he was taken prisoner by the Italians. Throughout the war he wrote copious notes, and from the prisoner of war camp he was able to send Bertrand Russell the manuscript of the only one of his books that would be published in his lifetime. Considered one of the most important works of twentieth-century philosophy, the *Tractatus* explores the relationship between reality, the mind, and language. In it Wittgenstein proposes that the world is the sum of all that is the case, a set of facts, and that thoughts and propositions are "pictures" of these facts and the relations between them. There is a direct correspondence between language and reality because they share the same structure, or "logical form." It follows that there are things that cannot be said and statements that are either senseless or nonsensical (because they cannot be true or false). The propositions of the natural sciences are meaningful, but philosophy is not on the same level as these. Wittgenstein sees its role as being not to solve problems but to clarify thought and to determine what can meaningfully and truthfully be expressed in language, showing the limits of language, which to Wittgenstein are the limits of the world. As far as Wittgenstein was concerned, the *Tractatus* dealt with all the problems of philosophy, although, in keeping with his central tenet, he felt that much of the importance of his work lay in what he did not say—precisely because it could not be expressed in language—and this has left his work open to interpretation and sometimes confusion.

The Later Wittgenstein

Satisfied, Wittgenstein then spent several years in Austria teaching in a school, working as a gardener, and helping the architect Paul Engelmann design a town house in Vienna. In 1929 he was wooed back to Cambridge, where he was shocked to discover that he was a famous philosopher. Persuaded to submit the *Tractatus* as his doctoral thesis, he gained his PhD and took a teaching position in the University, and in 1938 he became a British citizen.

In the second phase of his career he developed a totally different approach to philosophy and language, which was published after his death as *Philosophical Investigations*. Revising his earlier emphasis on logic and his view that there was a strict representational relationship between language and reality, he proposed instead a much looser vision of language, with the meaning of a word residing in its everyday use. His work proved to be a critique of traditional philosophy, and it continues to influence numerous interrelated fields, including psychology, ethics, economics, anthropology, sociology, and linguistics.

#59

◀ *Working from preliminary plans drawn up by architect Paul Engelman, Ludwig Wittgenstein designed and built this house in Vienna for his sister Margaret. It has simple, clean lines inside and out, but Wittgenstein paid extraordinary attention to every detail of the finish.*

"I am not interested in erecting a building, but in [...] presenting to myself the foundations of all possible buildings."
Ludwig Wittgenstein

CHARLES LINDBERGH (1902–1974)

American Aviator and Author

The first person to fly single-handedly across the Atlantic; helped develop the first medical life support machine; recipient of the Congressional Medal of Honor; Pulitzer Prize winner

- Politics & Leadership
- **Science & Technology**
- Popular Culture & the Arts
- Business & Commerce
- Writers & Thinkers

REWRITING HISTORY

A degree of mystery and doubt still surrounds the kidnapping and murder of Lindbergh's son, and many unanswered questions remain about the evidence itself and the possibility that someone within the family may have been involved. There are those who still contend that Bruno Richard Hauptmann, who was executed by electric chair in 1936, was innocent.

By achieving the first nonstop solo flight from the US to the European mainland, Charles Augustus Lindbergh transformed the public's perception of long-distance flight from harebrained recklessness to a modern and supremely American form of transport. Passenger flights and then scheduled commercial flights followed within a few years.

The Desire to Fly

The son of a congressman from Minnesota, Charles Lindbergh was born in Detroit, Michigan, and went to school in Little Falls, MN, and in Washington DC. Fascinated by all things mechanical, he attended the University of Wisconsin to study mechanical engineering but he soon dropped out to fulfill his dream of flying. In April of 1922, he went to Lincoln and took flying lessons with the Nebraska Aircraft Corporation, but couldn't afford to post the bond that would allow him to fly solo. To raise money and gain experience, he spent the summer as part of a barnstorming flying team, where he wing-walked and parachute jumped. He also spent time servicing airplane engines. After a winter spent in Minnesota, he bought an army surplus biplane for $500 and, after just half an hour of dual flight, went solo in his own craft. After a period running his own barnstorming show he joined the US Air Service Reserve as a cadet, and after graduating in 1925 he took a job the following year as an airmail pilot flying between Chicago and St Louis.

Accepting the Challenge

The French-American New York hotel owner Raymond Orteig had offered a $25,000 prize for the first nonstop flight between New York and Paris. There had already been flights across the Atlantic, but no one had done it mainland to mainland with a solo flight in a fixed-wing aircraft, and Lindbergh believed he could do it. The challenge was a huge one given the unreliable nature of aero engines, the unpredictable weather over the Atlantic, and the problem of carrying enough fuel, and six experienced aviators had already lost their lives in the attempt. Backed by two businessmen from St Louis, Lindbergh commissioned the building of the Spirit of St Louis, and he soon set a record for crossing the States nonstop.

In May of 1927, Lindbergh and his plane were ready, and he took off from Roosevelt Field on Long Island. More than two and a half thousand miles and 33 hours later he landed at Le Bourget airport in Paris to international acclaim. He was an instant hero, receiving honors from France, Belgium, and Britain as well as his home country, where he was awarded the Congressional Medal of Honor and the Distinguished Flying Cross, and was promoted to colonel in the Air Corps Reserve. On a tour of the US, funded by the Daniel Guggenheim Foundation for the Promotion of Aeronautics, he was given a tumultuous reception in 75 cities. Lindbergh's heroic Atlantic crossing made aviation the flavor of the times in the US. Flight wasn't just exciting—it was patriotic, it was safe, and it was the transport of the future. Airplane manufacturers found investors ready and willing to invest money, and Lindbergh's success ultimately opened the door to the speedy development of long-distance commercial flights.

After the Event

The public attention led to tragedy for the Lindbergh family when, in 1932, his young son was kidnapped and later found dead. A German immigrant was found guilty and executed for what was described as "the crime of the century." To regain his privacy, Lindbergh moved to Germany in the 1930s, and his knowledge of that country's air power led him to advise the US against entry into the war in 1939, saying that Germany was unbeatable. This earned him a reputation as a Nazi sympathizer, which prompted him to resign his commission, but once the US was committed to the war he rejoined the Air Force and flew sorties against the Japanese. In his later years, Lindbergh devoted himself to writing (winning the Pulitzer Prize for his autobiography *The Spirit of St Louis*), inventing, and environmentalism.

#58

◄ *Lindbergh's monoplane, Spirit of St Louis, was custom-built by Ryan Airlines in San Diego, California. The design was based on their mailplane but with an increased range. Named in honor of the town in which Lindbergh and his backers lived, the plane can now be seen at the Smithsonian Institution's National Air and Space Museum in Washington D.C.*

◀◀ REWRITING HISTORY

Although a confidante of many US Presidents, Graham enjoyed a particularly warm relationship with Richard Nixon. He spent the first night of Nixon's presidency at the White House, and was offered the ambassadorship to Israel by Nixon (he turned it down), though relations soured in the post-Watergate period.

BILLY GRAHAM (b. 1918)

Evangelical Preacher and Broadcaster

Rose to national prominence after William Randolph Hearst publicized his Los Angeles revival meetings; established the Billy Graham Evangelistic Association

Often referred to as "America's Pastor," Billy Graham has spent his entire life delivering the Gospel. An emotional and charismatic speaker, Graham has taken part in more than 400 rallies in over 180 countries, bringing a new level of sophistication to the evangelical movement. He has also acted as spiritual counselor to nine US Presidents, and remains the most popular minister in the US.

Receiving the Calling

William (Billy) Franklin Graham was born on the family dairy farm near Charlotte, North Carolina, the son of Morrow Coffey and William Franklin Graham. The family belonged to the Associate Reformed Presbyterian Church, and Billy was raised in a strict and pious household. His father enforced strong moral principles upon Billy and his sister Katherine, even forcing them to drink alcohol until they vomited, an event that gave the siblings a lifelong aversion to liquor. At the age of 16, Graham underwent a religious conversion after attending a revival meeting held by evangelist Mordecai Ham. After graduating from school, Graham went to the Bob Jones College in Cleveland, Tennessee, before transferring to the Florida Bible Institute (now Trinity College, Florida), near Tampa, where, according to Graham, he received his calling from God. In 1939, he was ordained by a church in the Southern Baptist Convention, and began to develop the persuasive preaching style that was to make him famous. In 1943, he graduated from Wheaton College, Illinois, with a degree in anthropology. Also that year, he married fellow student Ruth McCue Bell, whose parents were missionaries in China. He spent a brief period as pastor of the First Baptist Church in Western Springs, Illinois, but the remainder of his ministry has been nondenominational. During his time in Western Springs, Graham also took over a religious radio program called *Songs in the Night*.

Evangelical Career

In 1946, Graham became the first full-time evangelist for Youth for Christ International and began to preach throughout the United States. A skilled orator, Graham rose to national fame after a series of meetings held in Los Angeles in 1949. Preaching in a circus tent, Graham gained the attention of newspaper magnate William Randolph Hearst, who ordered his editors to "puff Graham." After receiving increased media exposure, Graham found himself preaching to an audience of ten thousand or so, and his three-week schedule of meetings was extended to eight. More tours—which were referred to as his "crusades"— followed, including a 12-week stint in London in 1954 and a 1957 stay in New York City that filled Madison Square Garden for four months. He had founded the Billy Graham Evangelistic Association (BGEA), in Minneapolis, Minnesota, in 1950, which was followed by the broadcasting of his Sunday radio program *Hour of Decision*. The BGEA went from strength to strength, increasing its audience through the publication of *Decision* magazine and prime-time television specials. Graham has also written many best-selling books including *Angels: God's Secret Agents* (1975) and *How to Be Born Again* (1977).

Graham's Audience

Since he began his crusades, it is estimated that Graham has preached to live audiences of more than 200 million people, with more than two million reported converts. Millions more have been reached through Graham's television and radio programs. Graham's appeal lies in his ability to reach his audience with a simple homespun philosophy that asks his followers to repent and invite Christ into their lives in order to reach salvation. Graham has traveled widely in his career, visiting around 185 countries. He was the first prominent evangelist to preach behind the Iron Curtain during the Cold War era and has also visited China and North Korea. Graham was also at the forefront of the desegregation movement in the US, personally paying Dr. Martin Luther King's bail money on one occasion and also inviting the Civil Rights leader to join him in the pulpit. He also refused to speak to segregated audiences in apartheid South Africa, demanding that blacks and whites sit together. Graham has acted as spiritual adviser to every president from Harry S. Truman through to Barack Obama, with the exception of the Roman Catholic J. F. Kennedy. Richard Nixon even offered Graham the ambassadorship to Israel, though Graham turned down the offer. Considered a liberal among the fundamentalists, Graham remains the more respectable face of American evangelicalism, displaying integrity, piety, and an ethical stance free from the sex and money scandals that have befallen other television preachers.

#57

Billy Graham's "crusades" took him across the globe. Here he is pictured in Usumbura (now Bujumbura), in Burundi, in 1960.
▼

BENITO MUSSOLINI (1883–1945)

Italian Dictator

Founded the National Fascist Party; transformed Italy into a totalitarian state; attempted to revive an Italian "Empire"; brought Italy into World War II on the side of Germany

- Politics & Leadership
- Science & Technology
- Popular Culture & the Arts
- Business & Commerce
- Writers & Thinkers

◀◀ REWRITING HISTORY

After Mussolini's death, his body was buried in Milan's Musoco Cemetery, but several months later his remains were placed in a small trunk by loyal Fascists and hidden first in a convent and then in a monastery in Pavia. The local Chief of Police then confiscated it and hid it. In 1957 it was finally buried in Mussolini's home town of Predappio.

As dictator of Italy from 1922 to 1943, Benito Mussolini implemented a homespun political philosophy that he called Fascism—the domination of all aspects of national and personal life by a totalitarian government. His rule caused untold suffering and brought Italy to its knees.

A Volatile Temperament

Benito Amilcare Andrea Mussolini was born in Dovia di Predappio, Italy. His mother was a teacher and his socialist father was a blacksmith. As a youth, Mussolini displayed an uncontrollable temper and was expelled twice for assaulting his fellow students with a penknife. He qualified as a teacher and taught locally before moving to Switzerland in 1902 to avoid conscription. An avid socialist, he read voraciously and pieced together an incoherent patchwork of political philosophy, which he expressed forcefully and publicly. His fervent views led to him being expelled from Switzerland, and then from Austria, where he worked as a journalist and trade unionist until 1909. Returning home, Mussolini was soon imprisoned for inciting a strike, gaining him yet further notoriety as one of Italy's leading young Socialists.

Opportunistic Politics

Mussolini soon founded his own paper, *The Class Struggle*, which was so successful that he was given the editorship of the official socialist organ *Avanti!* at the age of just 29. Following the party line, he opposed nationalism, imperialism, and the use of armed force, and spoke out strongly against Italy entering World War I—until he changed his mind. Convinced that war would lead to the desired revolution, he called for Italy to intervene. He had to resign from the paper, and was kicked out of the Socialist party. Siding with the Italian bourgeoisie, he soon found a pro-war publisher and became the founding editor of *Il Popolo d'Italia* (*The People of Italy*), in which he gave vent to his new-found nationalistic militarism, becoming a spokesman for the middle classes, espousing a new political program, and starting his own political movement—the Autonomous Fascists. When Italy did enter the war he signed up and went to fight, but was invalided out in 1917 after being wounded in a training exercise, and he returned to politics. He founded two more failed parties and stood unsuccessfully for election in 1919, but continued to gain support. In 1921 he was elected to Parliament, and he soon found himself as leader—Il Duce—of the National Fascist Party with more than quarter of a million members. With the support of influential groups within Italy, including the church and the military, with a vested interest in seeing a return to "law and order," he took power in 1922.

Totalitarian Rule

The period that followed was one of repression and bloodshed as Mussolini rode roughshod over the constitution, suppressing civil liberty, crushing all opposition (his henchmen even murdered the Socialist leader in 1924), and subjugating the working classes. By the start of the 1930s, those in economic power were reaping the benefits of his totalitarian rule, corruption was rife at all levels of government, the middle class was becoming disaffected, and the working class was barely subsisting. In 1935 Mussolini started to pursue his imperialist ambitions, first invading Ethiopia and later Albania, and in 1936 Italian troops entered the Spanish Civil War on the side of Franco, all of which entailed costs to Italy and little benefit.

The Final Years

Shunned by Italy's former allies, France and Britain, Mussolini entered into an ever deeper alliance with Hitler's Germany, and in 1940, once it was clear that France would fall to Germany, Mussolini brought Italy into World War II. Poorly supplied, badly organized, and spread too thin, the Italian military suffered defeat on all fronts, and when Allied forces landed in Sicily in 1943, Mussolini's own Fascist Grand Council decided to make peace with the Allies. They voted to hand power back to King Victor Emmanuel II, who had Mussolini arrested, but German commandos sprang him from the mountain-top prison and Hitler made him head of a puppet government in northern Italy. In April 1945, as Italian partisans and Allied forces moved northward, Mussolini tried to escape to Switzerland, but he was caught by partisans and summarily executed. His body was taken to Milan and hung by the heels in a public square. Mussolini's dictatorship lasted more than 20 years, and it undoubtedly transformed Italy from an ungovernable semi-feudal society into a modern nation state, but the costs in terms of human suffering and the loss of democratic freedoms and national pride were huge.

▲

With a bombastic style of oratory, Mussolini played on Italy's glorious past, with references to the Roman Empire, the country's great historical figures, and its archeological heritage.

Chairman of the People's Republic of China

Led the Communist Party of China to victory in the Chinese Civil War; the first Chairman of the People's Republic of China; launched sociopolitical programs such as the First Five-Year Plan and the Great Leap Forward; instigated the Cultural Revolution

- Politics & Leadership
- Science & Technology
- Popular Culture & the Arts
- Business & Commerce
- Writers & Thinkers

◀◀ REWRITING HISTORY

Chairman Mao was married three times (four if you count his first arranged and unconsummated marriage to a cousin). His first wife Yang Kaihui was the daughter of his former teacher Yang Changji. She was a communist like Mao, and in 1930 Yang was captured and executed by the Kuomintang. His other wives were fellow revolutionary He Zhizhe and the actress turned Gang of Four member Jiang Qing.

Mao Zedong was the most influential person in twentieth-century China. He masterminded the defeat of the Kuomintang in the Chinese Civil War and established communism in China. He initiated far-reaching sociopolitical reforms in the country, and unleashed the revolutionary zeal of the Red Guards during the Cultural Revolution. A cult figure during his lifetime, it became *de rigueur* to carry a copy of Mao's *Little Red Book* at all times.

The Chinese Communist Party

The son of a peasant farmer, Mao Zedong was born in Shaosan, Hunan province, in central China, in 1893. Mao served in the revolutionary army that toppled the Qing Dynasty in 1911. After the war, he enrolled at the Hunan First Normal School, where he came under the influence of the philosopher Yang Changji, who introduced him to socialist theories. In 1918, Mao started working at the University of Peking (Beijing) library, where he read the works of Marx and other communist writers. The Russian Revolution encouraged the spread of communist ideals and in 1921 Mao became a founding member of the Chinese Communist Party (CCP). Following orders from Moscow, the CCP joined forces with the ruling Kuomintang (KMT). Unlike many other leading members of the CCP, Mao did not choose to travel abroad to refine his political ideology but instead worked among the Chinese peasantry, whom he considered the most potent source of revolution.

The "Long March"

In 1927, the alliance between the CCP and the KMT broke down, and the KMT leader Chiang Kai-shek began a bloody purge of the communists, causing the outbreak of the Chinese Civil War. Mao led a failed uprising against the KMT and was forced to retreat to the mountains of Jiangxi Province. By October 1934, the KMT had succeeded in almost totally surrounding the communists. Mao made the decision to retreat. So began the "Long March." Mao led some 100,000 people in an 8,000-mile (12,500-

km) march across treacherous countryside to a new stronghold at Yunan in Shaanxi Province. During the year-long march, thousands perished and only about 20,000 reached the final destination, but Mao's strategy had succeeded and he became the undisputed leader of the communists. The Second Sino-Japanese War forced Mao and the KMT to collaborate, but as soon as the Japanese surrendered in 1946 civil war broke out once again. By 1949, the communists had gained control of the country and on October 1, the People's Republic of China was established, with Mao as its first head of state.

Sociopolitical Reforms

On taking power, Mao unleashed a campaign of mass repression against his critics. Hundreds of thousands, if not millions of people were executed and at least 1.5 million sent to labor camps during Mao's first few years in power. In 1953, Mao launched the First Five-Year Plan, aimed at boosting China's economy. The plan heralded a rapid collectivization of land. A second plan was initiated in 1958, which attempted to break away from the Soviet model of economic growth. Known as the Great Leap Forward, the plan established huge collective farms containing as many as 75,000 people. The plan was a great failure, however. Exacerbated by floods and poor harvests, an estimated 20–30 million people died in the resulting famine. Mao lost political prestige and his place as head of state was taken by Liu Shaoqi, though he remained chairman of the communist party. In 1966, Mao launched the Cultural Revolution, ostensibly to rid the country of its "bourgeois elements" but also to regain the power and prestige that he had lost. With his wife Jiang Qing, at his side, Mao organized his loyal students and workers as Red Guards to denounce the "revisionists" in the party. Liu and other top communists were removed from power, and Mao reasserted his party leadership. The Cultural Revolution ended with the death of Mao in 1976.

Mao Zedong's regime was characterized by the cult of personality, with images of the communist leader appearing everywhere. His portrait is seen here at the entrance to the Forbidden City in Beijing.
▼

Mao's Legacy

Mao remains a controversial figure in China. While officially revered as a great revolutionary and as the leader of the Chinese Revolution, he is also held responsible for the economic disaster of the Great Leap Forward and the reign of terror associated with the Cultural Revolution, both of which cost millions of lives. He ruled China as a dictator, establishing the cult of Mao and forcing his image and *Little Red Book* upon the Chinese people. Nonetheless, Mao was the single most important figure in China during the twentieth century, responsible for transforming China into an economic and military world power.

FRANKLIN D. ROOSEVELT (1882–1945)

President of the United States

Elected President for a record four terms; architect of the "New Deal"; led the US during World War II

- Politics & Leadership
- Science & Technology
- Popular Culture & the Arts
- Business & Commerce
- Writers & Thinkers

◀◀ REWRITING HISTORY

Though he spent most of his adult life confined to a wheelchair, FDR fought continually to regain the use of his legs. In 1926, he bought the Warm Springs in Georgia, where he established a hydrotherapy treatment centre for polio victims. He later helped found the National Foundation for Infantile Paralysis, now known as the March of Dimes, one of the reasons why he is commemorated on the 10 cent piece.

Franklin D. Roosevelt was the 32nd President of the United States. He assumed the post during a period of worldwide economic crisis and led America during World War II. FDR, as he is commonly known, was in office from 1933 to 1945, and is the only US President to have served more than two terms.

Privileged Upbringing

Franklin Delano Roosevelt was born in Hyde Park, New York, in 1882, the only child of James and Sara Roosevelt. His parents were both from wealthy old New York families and FDR enjoyed a privileged childhood, traveling frequently to Europe and becoming versed in the etiquettes of high society. He attended Groton, a prestigious preparatory school in Massachusetts, where he enjoyed the guidance of the headmaster Endicott Peabody. From 1900 to 1903, FDR attended Harvard University, majoring in History and then moved on to Columbia University to study law, passing the bar examination in 1907. He practiced law for three years, before being elected to the New York State Senate in 1910 as a Democrat, despite representing a traditionally Republican-held district. After a successful spell as Assistant Secretary of the Navy under Woodrow Wilson, FDR was chosen as the running mate of Presidential Democratic nominee James M. Cox of Ohio in 1920. However, the Cox-Roosevelt ticket was decisively beaten by Republican Warren G. Harding in the election and FDR returned to practicing law. In the summer of 1921, FDR contracted polio and lost the use of his legs. Despite having to use a wheelchair for the remainder of his life, Roosevelt trained himself to walk short distances with the use of hip and leg braces. In 1928, he was elected Governor of New York. He went on to win a second term in the post in 1930, and began his campaign for the presidency.

The New Deal

The Great Depression formed a backdrop to the 1932 presidential election campaign. FDR campaigned hard to bring on board the poor: laborers, ethnic minorities, urbanites, and Southern whites—the so-called New

Deal coalition of supporters. Won over by his promise of "a new deal for the American people," FDR defeated the incumbent President Hoover in November 1932 by seven million votes. Faced with 13 million unemployed and the closure of almost every bank in America, FDR immediately implemented his New Deal program designed to bring about relief, recovery, and reform. To initiate recovery, he set up agencies such as the AAA (Agricultural Adjustment Administration) to support farm prices and the CCC (Civilian Conservation Corps), which employed 250,000 young men in rural projects. Other measures regulated the stock market, insured bank deposits, and subsidized home and farm mortgage payments. FDR authorized a federal spending spree to stimulate the economy, including the creation of the Tennessee Valley Authority, the largest government-owned industrial enterprise in US history. Roosevelt's New Deal legislation saved millions from starvation and stimulated economic recovery, though it did

come under fire for increasing government debt and for taking the nation off the Gold Standard. Senior voices, particularly within the finance sector, criticized the extent of state intervention. FDR responded in 1935 with a new wave of New Deal legislation, including the introduction of social security, work relief programs for the unemployed, higher taxes on the rich, and new controls over banks and public utilities. He was reelected by a landslide in 1936 and took it as a popular mandate to take on his critics, namely the Supreme Court, which had been invalidating various New Deal legislation. In 1937, he tried to inject new blood into the Supreme Court by adding new justices. Despite its defeat, the move prompted the Court to adopt a more conciliatory stance.

Famous Resolve

At the outbreak of World War II, FDR reaffirmed US neutrality, while at the same time pledging help to nations faced with Hitler's aggression. In preparation, the US began a program of rearmament, which Roosevelt pushed through despite strong opposition. Given his long-standing disability and increasing frailty, the resolve Roosevelt demonstrated in providing strong leadership at a time of international crisis has been rightly acclaimed. His achievements in dragging America out of the Great Depression and overseeing a victorious entry into World War II set the platform for a new era of American prosperity and preeminence.

#54

◀ *In 1945, Franklin D. Roosevelt attended the Yalta Conference alongside the heads of government of the UK and the Soviet Union—Winston Churchill and Joseph Stalin. The meeting had been convened to discuss the organization of postwar Europe.*

MARGARET THATCHER (b. 1925)

Prime Minister of the United Kingdom

Longest serving British Prime Minister of the twentieth century; led the British to victory in the Falklands war; introduced a massive privatization program; presided over the miners' strike; survived an assassination attempt; introduced the poll tax

- Politics & Leadership
- Science & Technology
- Popular Culture & the Arts
- Business & Commerce
- Writers & Thinkers

 REWRITING HISTORY

Margaret Thatcher was a hate-figure for the liberals, who decried her support of capital punishment and failure to implement sanctions against apartheid South Africa. However, she did support a House of Commons bill to decriminalize male homosexuality as well as one that legalized abortion.

Margaret Thatcher was the first, and so far only, female prime minister of the United Kingdom. She led the Conservative Party to three election victories and was the longest consecutive serving prime minister since 1827. Famous for her unbending opinions and hard-line right-wing conservatism, she earned the nickname "Iron Lady." She was eventually deposed as party leader over rows about the role of the European Community.

The Grocer's Daughter

Margaret Hilda Roberts was born in Grantham, England. Her grocer father was active in local politics. After attending the local grammar school, Roberts won a scholarship to read Natural Sciences at Somerville College, Oxford University, where she specialized in chemistry. She became President of the Oxford University Conservative Association in 1946, only the third woman to have been elected to the post. After graduating, Roberts worked as a research chemist. In 1951, she married wealthy divorced businessman Denis Thatcher. Margaret Thatcher retrained as a barrister, qualifying in 1953. That same year, she gave birth to twins. After several failed attempts, Thatcher was finally elected to Parliament in 1959 as the Conservative member for Finchley. Thatcher rapidly rose through the ranks, serving as a junior minister between 1961 and 1964, before becoming Secretary of State for Education and Science in Edward Heath's cabinet (1970–74). In 1975, she stood against Heath for the Conservative Party leadership, which she surprisingly won easily. Between 1975 and 1979, Thatcher was leader of the opposition, before leading the Conservatives to victory at the polls in 1979 to become the UK's first female Prime Minster.

The Thatcher Years

Thatcher's first two years in power were tough. When she arrived in Downing Street, Britain was enduring one of the worst recessions of the twentieth century. Thatcher immediately set about implementing her radical and often unpopular political and economic policies. She reduced government intervention and public expenditure, while at the same time encouraging entrepreneurialism and privatizing many government-owned enterprises. Unemployment continued to rise, and by late 1981 her approval rating had fallen to a record low of 25 percent. The Falklands War in 1982 did much to restore her reputation and the economy gradually improved. In 1983 she won a landslide victory at the election, giving her a mandate to continue her policies. Thatcher then took on the unions, culminating in the year-long miners' strike that began in 1984 and ended with total capitulation of the miners. That same year, Thatcher escaped unscathed when the Provisional Irish Republican Army (IRA) bombed the Brighton hotel where Conservative Party members had been gathering for a conference. Internationally, Thatcher was close to President Reagan and worked with him to end the Cold War, as well as supporting his decision to bomb Libya in 1986. She also established a good working relationship with Russian leader Mikhail Gorbachev. In 1987 she won an unprecedented third term by a majority of 102 seats. Her final term in office was tarnished by the unpopular poll tax and increasing friction over the role of the European Community. In November 1990, once loyal Cabinet members turned against Thatcher, forcing a leadership election and her subsequent resignation, and Thatcher retreated to the backbenches. In 1992, she became Baroness Thatcher of Kesteven in the County of Lincolnshire, a title that permitted her to sit in the House of Lords, from where she continued to voice her still forcible opinions.

Thatcherism

Admired and detested in equal measure, Thatcher was one of the strongest leaders that Britain has ever seen. Never afraid to take on her opponents, and indeed her colleagues, Thatcher was abrasive and uncompromising— qualities epitomised by her famous expression, "The lady's not for turning." Thatcher was very much a figure of the '80s, epitomizing the individualistic "dog eat dog" attitude of that decade. Her legacy in British politics is formidable, and the term "Thatcherism" is still used to describe the form of laissez-faire political and economic policy that she followed during her time in office.

▲
Enjoying a significant rise in popularity as a result of victory in the Falklands War, Margaret Thatcher led the Conservative Party to an emphatic victory in the 1983 UK general election.

113

LE CORBUSIER (1887–1965)

Swiss Architect

Architect, urban planner, painter, writer, furniture designer, and theorist; a founder of the Modern Movement in European architecture

Le Corbusier stands as one of the key architects of the twentieth century, not only for the remarkable buildings that he created in many countries around the world, but for the new approach that he brought to the concept of living space. Influenced by such diverse factors as cubism, industrial production methods, and the availability of new materials, he changed the course of building design.

Early Guidance

Christened Charles-Edouard Jeanneret-Gris, Le Corbusier (who adopted this pseudonym in the early 1920s) was born in the small and prosperous town of La Chaux-de-Fonds, Switzerland, in 1887. At school he studied fine art and was strongly influenced by a decorative arts teacher, painter, and architect called Charles L'Eplattenier who encouraged his students to develop design styles that drew upon the local landscape of the Jura Mountains. It was L'Eplattenier who directed Le Corbusier's talents toward architecture, and at the age of 20 the young man designed and built his first villa. In 1908, he set out on a series of travels around Europe, visiting the famous buildings of Italy and Greece, and studying under leading architects in Vienna, Paris, and Berlin. Among these were Auguste Perret, a pioneer in the use of reinforced concrete, and Peter Behrens, an architect and industrial designer and a member of the Werkbund, a precursor of the German Bauhaus school of design. Le Corbusier returned to La Chaux-de-Fonds in 1911 with a head full of new ideas.

A New Approach

Setting up his own architectural practice, he proceeded to design and build a number of villas in his home town. The design of the first of these, La Maison Blanche, built in 1912 when he was just 25, was revolutionary. Not only is it asymmetrical, but the whole building is supported on four slender columns and has lightweight internal walls that can be moved if the owners wish to change the layout.

◀◀ REWRITING HISTORY

During the four years immediately following World War I, Le Corbusier turned to his earlier métier as a painter. He developed a style of cubism that he called "purism," breaking objects down into simple geometrical elements. This experimental artistic period was crucial to the development of his modular form of architecture.

In 1915 Le Corbusier took his ideas of geometry and modular design to the next stage with the Domino project, breaking house design down into elements that could be prefabricated and then assembled. In the 1920s, after a period spent painting, he returned to architecture with his concept of the home as a "machine for living"—a modern, precision-built, climatically controlled environment that meets human needs in a pure and simple form. He also introduced the "five points" of his architecture: the use of columns (or *piloti*) to raise the structure above the ground and create space and circulation beneath it; the separation of the load-bearing structure from the dividing walls, allowing for open plan design; the use of long sliding

windows; independence of the façade from the rest of the building; and a rooftop garden, effectively replacing the land lost to the building's footprint. He applied these principles to the design of small individual homes, extended the idea into large tenement blocks, and ultimately developed a total vision of urban planning, including plans for an entire new town of three million inhabitants. Few of his major projects were realized, but his concepts had a major influence on the rebuilding that took place after World War II and, although his grand vision was intended to cater for people's needs, many found the results dehumanizing.

A Monumental Legacy

After the war, Le Corbusier's own work moved away from mass-produced forms. He worked to create enormous, sculptural buildings using local materials as well as raw, unfaced concrete, giving rise to a style known as New Brutalism—one that proved popular with many European architects. One of the finest examples of his later architectural design is the chapel of Notre Dame du Haut in Ronchamp, France, completed in 1954. With its thick, sloping, rubble-filled walls, rough exterior, randomly placed windows of different sizes, and twisted billowing roof, it stands as a testament to Le Corbusier's talent for innovation in both form and materials. The legacy of his theories of urban planning, and of his conceptual genius, can still be seen in the work of architects in Europe, Britain, and the US today.

◀ *The roof terrace of Le Corbusier's* **Unité d'Habitation** *in Marseilles has a recreation center and a children's nursery, reclaiming the land lost to the building's footprint. Constructed between 1947 and 1952, the 12-story apartment block houses a total of 1,600 people.*

"His influence was universal and his works are invested with a permanent quality possessed by those of very few artists in our history."
President Lyndon B. Johnson

◄ Politics & Leadership

◄ Science & Technology

◄ Popular Culture & the Arts

◄ Business & Commerce

◄ Writers & Thinkers

JOHN MAYNARD KEYNES (1883–1946)

English Economist and Monetary Expert

Wrote the most influential economic work of the twentieth century; brought rigorous economic analysis into the realm of political decision-making; helped negotiate the terms of the America's wartime aid to Britain; instrumental in the creation of the World Bank

While remaining a firm believer in the capitalist market economy, John Maynard Keynes urged governments to use a degree of intervention and public spending to help even out fluctuations in national economic fortune. His theories have been implemented in many countries and have been credited with saving capitalism from itself. The recent international economic crisis has prompted a return to his policies.

A Family of Economists

Born into a respectable middle class family in Cambridge, England, the son of Cambridge University economist and logician John Neville Keynes, the young Keynes displayed a talent for mathematics at elementary school and won a scholarship to Eton, a prestigious private school. There he consistently came top of his class, displaying a precocious intellect and taking prizes in math, history, and English throughout his school career. In 1902 he went to King's College, Cambridge, becoming President of the Union, the University's renowned debating society. He was drawn to economics, and on graduating in 1906 he joined the civil service in the Revenue, Statistics and Commerce Department of the India Office, where he worked on problems of Indian currency but spent much of his time writing his own dissertation on the subject of probability. In 1908 he left the civil service and returned to King's College to complete his dissertation, which earned him a master's degree, and he was elected fellow of King's College, teaching economics there until 1915. He also became editor of the highly regarded journal of the Royal Economic Society and after sitting on the Royal Commission on Indian Currency and Finance he published his first book, *Indian Currency and Finance*, an incisive treaty on the gold exchange standard.

Speaking Out

During World War I, Keynes served with the British Treasury and played a key role in the management of finances between the Allies. At the end of the war Keynes assisted Lloyd George, the British prime minister, at the Paris Peace Conference, but he strongly disagreed with the terms of the war reparations set out in the Versailles Treaty, and he resigned over the issue. In 1919 he published his criticisms in *The Economic Consequences of the Peace*, claiming that the agreement would impoverish Europe and, with remarkable prescience, that it might lead to yet another war. He argued that all of Europe would benefit if the Allies helped rebuild the economies of Germany and Italy.

Keynesian Economics

Between the wars, Keynes elaborated on his central thesis, which flew in the face of the conventional wisdom that capitalism could and should be allowed to run itself. A firm believer in the capitalist market economy, he nonetheless disputed that private investment could be relied upon to keep a country's economy on an even keel, and believed that governments should use public investment (even if this meant running a deficit budget) as a tool to create employment, and in turn to increase spending power, consumption, production, and private investment. In the early 1930s, during the years of the Great Depression, he gave this advice to Franklin D. Roosevelt, but it went largely unheeded until the outbreak of World War II, when Keynesian economic management was found to work in precisely the way he said it would. During World War II he played a key role on behalf of the British Government in negotiating the terms of the Lend-Lease agreement with the US, and his writings and diligent work were central to the creation of the International Monetary Fund and the World Bank. Keynes' theories, expounded in several highly influential books, including *The General Theory of Employment, Interest and Money* (1936), fundamentally changed economic theory and affected the lives of millions of people as his ideas—including the introduction of welfare and unemployment benefits—were put into practice in the US and Europe.

#51

"*The ideas of economists and political philosophers, both when they are right and when they are wrong, are more powerful than is commonly understood. Indeed the world is ruled by little else.*"
John Maynard Keynes

◀ In July 1944, John Maynard Keynes was the UK delegate at a conference attended by 44 Allied nations to regulate international financial order at the end of World War II. The "Bretton Woods" conference led to the setting up of the International Monetary Fund.

IGOR STRAVINSKY (1882–1971)

Composer, Pianist, and Conductor

The first truly modern composer who revolutionized classical music; experimented with a variety of styles throughout his career, including neoclassical and serial musical forms

- Politics & Leadership
- Science & Technology
- **Popular Culture & the Arts**
- Business & Commerce
- Writers & Thinkers

◀◀ **REWRITING HISTORY**

Although Stravinsky became a naturalized US citizen, the country did not always welcome his musical contribution. In April, 1940, Stravinsky was arrested by the Boston police force for violating a federal law that prohibited the reharmonization of **The Star-Spangled Banner.** *Stravinsky's unconventional major seventh cord in the National Anthem had caused the offence.*

Igor Stravinsky was a Russian composer largely known for his original ballet scores and stage works. He is considered a revolutionary figure in the world of music, in large part due to the shocked reception that his seminal work, *The Rite of Spring*, received on its debut. His work spanned more than six decades in the twentieth century and is notable for its diversity of style.

Musical Roots

Stravinsky was born at Oranienbaum near St Petersburg, Russia. His father Fyodor Stravinsky was a professional opera singer, who sang bass at the Mariinsky Theater in St Petersburg. He learned the piano as a child and showed an early interest in musical theory and composition. By the age of 14, he could play Mendelssohn's *Piano Concerto in G minor*. Despite his early promise in music, his parents encouraged him to study law at university, and in 1901 Stravinsky enrolled at the University of St Petersburg. However, he showed little interest in the legal profession and did not complete his studies. A meeting with the Russian Romantic composer Nikolai Rimsky-Korsakov at the age of 20 changed the course of his life. Stravinsky began to study under Rimsky-Korsakov—an arrangement that remained until 1908—and his early compositions are clearly influenced by the folk-inspired melodies of his teacher.

Ballet Russes

When Stravinsky was in his mid-20s, he met Sergei Diaghilev, the impresario of the Ballet Russes, who had heard his composition *Fireworks* performed in St Petersburg. After undertaking some orchestration work for Diaghilev, Stravinsky composed a ballet score, *The Fire Bird* (1910), which signalled the beginning of a daring artistic collaboration between the two men. After *Petrushka* (1912), Stravinsky produced his most controversial composition, *The Rite of Spring* (1913), a work that marked him out as a revolutionary in the musical world. Premiered on May 29, 1913, at the Théâtre des Champs-Elysées in Paris, the ballet's subject matter—pagan fertility rites—and a dynamic new style of choreography by the famed dancer Vaslav Nijinsky caused a sensation. The start of the ballet featured the bassoon controversially played at the top of its register, which prompted audible dissent from the audience that grew into a near riot. The noise became so bad that the dancers could barely hear their cues and Nijinsky was forced to shout a count from the side of the stage. The chaotic scenes reflected the arrival of a provocative new movement in the arts—modernism had landed with a bang, and the classical music world would never be the same again.

Changing Styles

The outbreak of World War I led Stravinsky to take refuge in Switzerland, after which he returned to Paris. When war broke out in Europe again in 1939, Stravinsky moved to the US, becoming a citizen in 1946. Stravinsky continued composing almost up to the end of his life, and his music underwent remarkable changes during this time. From an early style rooted in Russian folk traditions, Stravinsky moved towards the neoclassical, drawing inspiration from eighteenth-century composers such as Mozart. Works from this period include *Pulcinella* (1920), *Oedipus Rex* (1927), the *Concerto in E-flat (Dumbarton Oaks)* (1937–8) *Apollon, Persephone* (1933) and *Orpheus* (1947). Stravinsky's neoclassical phase concluded in 1951 with the opera *The Rake's Progress*. From 1954 onward, Stravinsky used serial composition in his works, drawing on Austrian composer Arnold Schoenberg's 12-tone technique. Examples of this style include the ballet *Agon* (1957), and the religious pieces *Canticum Sacrum* (1955) and *The Flood* (1962).

Stravinsky's Legacy

Igor Stravinsky drew inspiration from and, reciprocally, influenced the leading artists of the time. He worked with Pablo Picasso on *Pulcinella*, and Jean Cocteau on *Oedipus Rex*, and performances of his music were attended by the highest society. He displayed a insatiable thirst for musical innovation and experimentation, yet his music retains a distinct identity across the many stages of its evolution. Stravinsky's dramatic and provocative use of rhythm and harmony gave his compositions a bold energy that inspired a new generation of young composers, redefining what was possible and challenging the conservative orthodoxies that had come to dominate the classical arts.

As well as being a composer of unrivalled brilliance and innovation, Stravinsky was also a noted pianist. Here he is pictured with German conductor Wilhelm Furtwängler.
▼

NELSON MANDELA (b. 1918)

President of South Africa

Lawyer; black South African rights activist and resistance leader; leader of the African National Congress party; figurehead of the anti-Apartheid movement; principal architect of post-Apartheid South African democracy; joint winner (with F.W. de Klerk) of the Nobel Peace Prize

- Politics & Leadership

- Science & Technology

- Popular Culture & the Arts

- Business & Commerce

- Writers & Thinkers

◄◄ REWRITING HISTORY

Nelson Mandela grew up with a personal understanding of what it means to be deprived of power. His branch of the family, although part of the ruling Thembu dynasty, was ineligible to succeed to the throne. His father served as a town chief, but the colonial authorities removed him from the position and relocated the family. The colloquial meaning of Mandela's given name, Rolihlahla, is "troublemaker."

The name of Nelson Mandela is synonymous with the struggle for black civil rights in South Africa. At once both a realist and a man of principle, he devoted his life to the goal of ending minority white rule and the oppression of the black majority, and he spent more than a quarter of a century in prison as a result, but he helped to make the dream that he shared with millions of black South Africans a reality.

Entering the Struggle

Nelson Rolihlahla Mandela was born in the Transkei, South Africa, the son of a tribal chief. Mandela attended University College of Fort Hare, but was asked to leave after organizing a student boycott. He later took a position as an articled clerk with a law firm, completed a BA at the University of South Africa by correspondence, and then gained a Law degree from the University of Witwatersrand. From the mid-1940s onward, he was an active member of the African National Congress (ANC), campaigning for black rights and advocating peaceful resistance to Apartheid (racial segregation), although their demonstrations frequently elicited a brutal response from the police, and in 1950 18 protestors were killed during a labor strike. In 1952, he and Oliver Tambo began South Africa's first black law firm, offering legal representation to poor blacks.

Challenging Authority

In 1956, the executive of the Congress Alliance, of which the ANC was a member, were arrested, and more than 150 people, including Mandela, were put on trial for treason. None was found guilty, but in the course of the trials Oliver Tambo left the country and began an international campaign to raise awareness of the ANC and the plight of black South Africans. In 1960, after the Sharpeville Massacre, in which 69 unarmed protesters were shot by police and public outrage led to further violence, the government banned the ANC. Accepting that peaceful protest could not end white supremacist rule, Mandela went underground and organized the ANC's military wing, which undertook acts of sabotage. In 1962 he was arrested, charged with organizing illegal demonstrations, and put on trial, where he presented his own defense. He was found guilty and sentenced to five years in jail, but in 1964 he was charged with treason and sabotage. As he had in his earlier trial, he took the opportunity to publicly challenge the legitimacy of the oppressive minority white government. Convicted and sentenced to life imprisonment, he was to spend the next 27 years of his life in prison. Throughout those years—many of them spent in solitary confinement—Mandela was the acknowledged leader of the ANC and a symbol of the ongoing struggle against apartheid. After 1984 he was repeatedly offered his freedom on certain conditions, but he staunchly refused, saying that the only condition he would accept was complete political freedom for all black South Africans.

A New Dawn

In 1989, the realistic reformer F. W. de Klerk replaced hardliner P. W. Botha as president. He legalized many of the banned organizations, including the ANC, and started to release some of the imprisoned black leaders. In 1990 Nelson Mandela was released without conditions, an event that inspired hope and jubilation in South Africa and around the world. As deputy president and then president of the ANC, he called for an end to the armed struggle that had been tearing the country apart, and he devoted his efforts toward a negotiated end to apartheid and the implementation of a nonracial democracy. When South Africa's first multiracial elections took place in 1994, the ANC received almost two-thirds of the votes cast, and its leader, Nelson Mandela, became President. His coalition "government of national unity" faced the monumental task of reconciling bitterly opposed elements and reconstructing a shattered society and economy, while at the same time appeasing a people who, having waited so long, wanted everything to change immediately. Mandela proved up to the task, and when he resigned in 1999, the transformation of South Africa was well underway.

◄ *Nelson Mandela spent 27 years in prison, 18 of them here in cell number 7 on Robben Island. He was forced to endure difficult conditions (for many of those years he had no bed), poor rations, isolation, and highly censored communication with the outside world.*

"Only free men can negotiate. Prisoners cannot enter into contracts."
Nelson Mandela

STEVEN SPIELBERG (b. 1946)

American Director, Producer, and Screenwriter

Broke box office records with three of his movies; Academy Award winner on three occasions; cofounder of the DreamWorks Studio.

- Politics & Leadership
- Science & Technology
- **Popular Culture & the Arts**
- Business & Commerce
- Writers & Thinkers

◄◄ REWRITING HISTORY

Steven Spielberg was himself a target of anti-Semitic abuse. "I was always aware I stood out because of my Jewishness. In high school, I got smacked and kicked around." With some of the profits from his holocaust movie **Schindler's List,** *Spielberg founded the USC Shoah Foundation Institute of Visual History and Education. The Foundation's aim is to record the testimonies of Holocaust survivors.*

One of the most successful movie moguls in silver screen history, Steven Spielberg has directed many of the top grossing movies in Hollywood, including *Jaws, E.T. the Extra-Terrestrial*, and *Jurassic Park*. Ignored by the Academy for many years, Spielberg eventually won Oscars for Best Director and Best Picture for *Schindler's List* in 1994, and another as director of *Saving Private Ryan* in 1998.

First Camera Work

Steven Spielberg was born in 1946 in Cincinnati, Ohio, the son of Jewish parents. His father worked as a computer engineer and his mother was a former concert pianist. Spielberg was fascinated by movies from an early age, and began making 8mm movies with the family's home movie camera. At the age of 13, Spielberg made a 40-minute war movie *Escape to Nowhere*, and three years later completed a 140-minute-long science fiction feature called *Firelight*. His poor grades, however, failed to get him accepted into film studies at the University of Southern California, prompting him to enroll at California State University instead. Spielberg continued to pursue his dream as a moviemaker, though, and in 1968, secured the finances to make the short movie *Amblin'* (1968), which won him a contract with Universal Studios as its youngest ever director. Spielberg dropped out of university to take up the position.

Hollywood Career

Spielberg made his professional debut in television, directing Joan Crawford in the pilot for *Night Gallery* and working on episodes for the TV series *Columbo* and *MarcusWelby, M.D.*. He graduated to movies for TV, including the much acclaimed *Duel* (1971), which secured his reputation both at home and abroad as a rising star. In 1974, Spielberg moved into theatrical movies with *The Sugarland Express*. It was his next project, though, that propelled Spielberg to international stardom. In 1975, Spielberg's version of the Peter Benchley novel *Jaws* broke box office records and won three Academy Awards. Two years later, Spielberg both wrote and directed *Close Encounters of the Third Kind*. The UFO movie earned Spielberg his first Best Director Academy Award nomination. His next movie, the 1979 war comedy *1941* was not a major success but Spielberg returned to form with *Raiders of the Lost Ark* (1981), the first of the immensely popular Indiana Jones movies. Spielberg received another Academy Award nomination for the adventure movie, but again did not win. Spielberg's *E.T. The Extra-Terrestrial* (1982) was an instant classic, becoming the top grossing movie of all time and cementing Spielberg's reputation as a favorite with moviegoers. Other successes in the 1980s included *Poltergeist* (1982), *Indiana Jones and the Temple of Doom* (1984), and *The Color Purple* (1985). In 1993, Spielberg made the dinosaur theme park movie *Jurassic Park*. Enhanced by stunning special effects provided by George Lucas, the movie again broke box office records, amassing $914.7 million worldwide. His next movie, the holocaust movie *Schindler's List*, finally won Spielberg his first Academy Award for Best Director as well as for Best Picture. In 1994, Spielberg took a break from direction to set up the DreamWorks studio with partners Jeffrey Katzenburg and David Geffen. Spielberg has continued to enjoy mainstream success, winning a second Oscar for Best Director in 1998 for the war movie *Saving Private Ryan*.

Spielberg's Legacy

Spielberg's reputation as one of the most successful and productive directors in the latter part of the twentieth century is without doubt. He directed some of the most popular blockbusters in Hollywood history, including three movies that went on to break box office records at the time. Both *Close Encounters of a Third Kind* and *Jurassic Park* are considered as milestones in movie making, both movies breaking new ground in terms of their state-of-the-art special effects.

One of Spielberg's most successful movies, **Saving Private Ryan,** *was renowned for its ultra-realistic depiction of the D-Day landing on Omaha Beach, Normandy, during World War II. The movie won Spielberg an Academy Award for Best Director.*
▼

- Politics & Leadership
- Science & Technology
- **Popular Culture & the Arts**
- Business & Commerce
- Writers & Thinkers

◀◀ REWRITING HISTORY

Before he was even born, Wright's mother declared that her child would build beautiful buildings, and she put images of English cathedrals on his nursery walls. When he was nine she bought him a set of variously shaped geometrical blocks designed as an educational tool for children, and young Frank spent many hours building three-dimensional structures with these.

FRANK LLOYD WRIGHT (1867–1959)

American Architect and Interior Designer

The best-known American architect; father of "organic architecture"; hailed as "the greatest American architect of all time" by the American Institute of Architects; designed more than 1,100 projects

The architecture of Frank Lloyd Wright, although instantly recognizable, is not so much a style as an approach. Wright believed that buildings should integrate with the landscape as well as with the people that inhabit them, and to achieve this he developed a wholly new kind of architecture, using natural materials in innovative ways.

Designs on Success

Frank Lincoln Wright (he changed his middle name to Lloyd, his mother's maiden name, after his parents' divorce) was born in the farming town of Richland Center, Wisconsin, in 1867. His father was a music teacher, speaker, and Unitarian minister, and his mother was a school teacher. The family moved to Massachusetts in 1870, and Frank spent his early childhood in Weymouth, although he spent his vacations at his uncle's farm in Wisconsin. Owing to financial difficulties, the family later moved back to Wisconsin and he attended high school in Madison. His parents divorced when he was in his mid-teens, and he became the bread winner for the family. After leaving school (there is no record that he graduated), he attended part-time classes in civil engineering at the University of Wisconsin-Madison for a year and then moved to Chicago, where he joined an architectural practice. In 1888 he was taken on by the architectural firm of Adler and Sullivan, and was apprenticed to Sullivan, whose maxim "form follows function" became a central tenet of modern architecture and whom Wright later acknowledged as having strongly influenced him. By 1890, Wright was overseeing all residential designs, but he and Sullivan fell out three years later when Sullivan discovered that Wright had been supplementing his income by taking design commissions "on the side." Wright, who was by now married to the daughter of a successful businessman and was climbing the social ladder, left and set up his own practice at the home he had recently built in Oak Park, Illinois.

Inspired by Nature

Over most of the next two decades, Frank Lloyd Wright developed what has become known as the Prairie School of architecture, a style of residential building that was visually responsive to the landscape of the Midwest: clean, flat lines; rough, unfinished building materials; and open plan interiors that reflected the changing lifestyle of the times. His highly distinctive work drew on his experience of the Wisconsin farmlands and a desire to create an "organic" architecture—buildings that were not only in keeping with their surroundings but that were also themselves an organic whole, with all the internal elements of the home, such as windows, fireplaces, stairways, and even furniture, all in harmony with each other. Wright's designs also responded to the needs of people, and his homes and commercial buildings were both practical and comfortable.

#47

◀ *In 1889, Frank Lloyd Wright bought a plot of land in Oak Park, Illinois, and built this house for himself and his new bride. It was to be his home for the next 20 years, and from his studio here he developed his distinctive architectural style.*

Taking it Further

In the 1920s Frank Lloyd Wright worked on ever more ambitious designs, often in the form of houses for wealthy personal friends. Graycliff, built on a bluff overlooking Lake Erie and constructed using local stone and cedar, features cantilevered balconies and uses glass extensively in highly imaginative ways to link the interior with the striking landscape. Fallingwater in Pennsylvania, probably his best known project, takes integration with the landscape to an extreme, with a stream and waterfall flowing out beneath the house, which is built into a hillside. It is a masterpiece of engineering as well as aesthetics. Although his work has not generally been emulated, Frank Lloyd Wright's innovative designs had a profound effect on American architecture, freeing it from its devotion to earlier European styles. Wright even referred to his work in the 1930s—creating practical, elegant, suburban homes for the middle class—as "usonian."

"Architecture is the language of the human heart. I want space to come alive."
Frank Lloyd Wright

125

- **Politics & Leadership**
- Science & Technology
- Popular Culture & the Arts
- Business & Commerce
- Writers & Thinkers

EVA PERÓN (1919–1952)

First Lady of Argentina

Wife and political partner of President Juan Perón of Argentina; campaigned for female suffrage; established a foundation to help the poor

Although she never formally held political office, Eva Perón exerted great influence in Argentine political life in the 1940s and 1950s, especially in relation to organized labor and social security. Her work among the poor earned her saintly status and to them she is known simply as Evita.

From Poverty to Acting

Born in the village of Los Toldos in Buenos Aires Province in 1919, María Eva Duarte was the youngest of five children of a wealthy rancher and his mistress. Her father returned to his wife when Eva was one year old, leaving his illegitimate family to a life of poverty. From an early age, Eva dreamed of becoming a big movie star, and she left home at 15 to pursue her goal. Although she lacked any formal theatrical training, Eva successfully landed a few small roles in motion pictures. Her big break came when she moved into radio, gaining a part in a daily drama for Radio El Mundo in 1942. That same year, Eva signed a five-year contract with Radio Belgrano to work on their *Great Women of History* series, making her financially secure for the first time in her life.

Meeting the Colonel

In 1944, Eva met Colonel Juan Perón, then Secretary of Labor, at a fund-raising event. He was 48, she was 24. Eva soon became the widowed Perón's close confidante, both emotionally and politically, and they began to live together, risking a scandal in traditional Argentine society. As Perón's power within the government grew, he began to consider a possible bid for the presidency, and looked to Eva for help. She cleverly began to court the support of the masses through the radio, with her soap-opera dramatizations of Perón's achievements in a daily program called *Toward a Better Future*. Perón's popularity and power grew, causing fear and resentment in the incumbent President, who had him arrested on October 9, 1945. Six days later, a mass demonstration organized in front of the Presidential Palace secured his release, and later that month Eva and Juan Perón were married.

◀◀ REWRITING HISTORY

Eva has often been credited as the force behind the demonstration that freed Juan Perón in 1945, an idea reinforced by Madonna's portrayal of her in the Hollywood move **Evita.** *In fact, as a mistress and an actress to boot, Eva had very little political clout at that time and it is more probable that the demonstration was organized by the labor unions.*

In 1946, Eva defied Argentine convention by appearing at the side of her husband as he campaigned for the presidency.

The Perón Presidency

After Perón became president, Eva went on a tour of Europe, meeting with numerous head of states. She returned a more sophisticated woman, restyling her hair into a braided chignon and wearing more subtle and business-like clothing. Eva immediately immersed herself in political affairs, campaigning for female suffrage, which became law in 1947. She effectively took over the running of the Labor Ministry and began to influence organized labor, supporting their call for higher wages and social welfare benefits. Eva never forgot her childhood deprivations, and worked tirelessly for the poor and underprivileged. In 1947, she established the María Eva Duarte de Perón Welfare Foundation with 10,000 pesos from her own pocket. The foundation grew into a multimillion-dollar enterprise, financed by contributions from trade unions, businesses, and industrial firms. It distributed food, clothing, and medicine to those in need, and also built homes and hospitals. It is largely through her work with the foundation that Eva gained her saintly status. She spent long working days at the organization, and would touch and kiss the poor and sick. In 1951, Eva considered the possibility of running as vice president. She had massive popular support but she eventually declined, bowing to pressure from the military and Argentine upper class. By the time of her husband's second inauguration as President in June 1952, Eva was suffering from advanced cervical cancer. She was given the official title of "Spiritual Leader of the Nation" a few days later, but succumbed to the illness in the following month. She was only 33 years old.

▲

With Eva at his side, President Juan Perón enjoyed great popularity with the common Argentine people. Here the couple are seen enjoying a rapturous reception from their Buenos Aires audience.

Champion of the Poor

Eva Perón's rags to riches tale, which has been immortalized in Hollywood movies and musicals, touched the lives of the Argentine underprivileged. Her work through the Foundation had a real impact for the needy, her involvement with organized labor helped to improve working conditions, and she successfully campaigned to gain women the vote. She remains a popular icon among the poor but is detested by the Argentine upper classes, arguably because of her lowly social background and socialist activities.

MARLON BRANDO (1924–2004)

American Actor

Popularized the "method" style of acting; achieved star status for his role in the Broadway play A Streetcar Named Desire; *nominated for seven Academy Awards, winning two; first actor to be paid $1 million for a movie*

- Politics & Leadership
- Science & Technology
- **Popular Culture & the Arts**
- Business & Commerce
- Writers & Thinkers

◀◀ **REWRITING HISTORY**

Brando's older sister Jocelyn was also an actress. She had a theater, movie, and television career lasting over five decades. Her credits include an appearance on Broadway in 1948 with family friend Henry Fonda in **Mister Roberts** *and as Glenn Ford's wife in the gangster flick* **The Big Heat** *(1953).*

Considered one of the greatest actors of all time, Marlon Brando brought a brooding intensity and hitherto unseen depth to the craft of acting. His personal life was controversial and he often expressed a loathing for the cult of celebrity, though he used his fame to bring attention to a number of social issues including the rights of Native Americans.

Early Career

Marlon Brando was born in 1924, in Omaha, Nebraska, one of three children born to alcoholic parents. The young Brando frequently went down to the local jail to fetch his mother Dorothy home after she had spent the night in the slammer. His dysfunctional childhood gave Brando an intensity that he later brought to his movie work. His mother was an actress and director of the Omaha Community Playhouse, teaching, among others, the then unknown Henry Fonda. Brando was a rebellious teenager and was expelled from his high school for riding his motorcycle through the school. He was then sent to Shattuck Military Academy in Minnesota, where his theatrical talents came to the fore. However, once again, his attitude toward authority got him into trouble, and he was expelled before graduating. After work digging ditches, Brando moved to New York, where he studied the Stanislavsky method of acting under Stella Alder and later worked at the Actors' Studio under Lee Strasberg, where he became dedicated to "method" acting. Brando made his Broadway debut in *I Remember Mama* in 1944. Critics voted Brando as Broadway's Most Promising Actor for his performance in the 1946 production *Truckline Café*. The following year Brando stunned Broadway audiences with his portrayal of Stanley Kowalski in Tennessee Williams' *A Streetcar Named Desire*. He received offers from Hollywood for movie work, making his debut as a paraplegic veteran in *The Men* (1950). To prepare for the role, Brando spent a month in bed at a veteran's hospital.

The Hollywood Years

In 1951, Brando reprised his role as Kowalski for the big screen adaptation of *Streetcar*, for which he received an Academy Award nomination for Best

Actor. He went on to be nominated for the next three consecutive years, for *Viva Zapata!* (1952), *Julius Caesar* (1953), and *On the Waterfront* (1954), the latter earning him the award for his portrayal of washed up boxer Terry Malloy. During the filming, Brando insisted on improvising whenever he felt the scripted scene could be improved, including the famous "I coulda' been a contender" scene. Brando's appearance as the leather-clad biker in *The Wild One* (1954) established his reputation as an icon of rebel culture. Throughout the 1950s Brando remained a major box-office draw, stunning audiences in a variety of roles ranging from Sky Masterson in *Guys and Dolls* (1955), in which he sang and danced, to an Air Force officer in the 1957 hit *Sayonara* and a Nazi soldier in *The Young Lions* (1958). His career stalled in the 1960s, however, harmed by on-set tantrums and a reputation for taking movies over budget, notably the 1962 flop *Mutiny on the Bounty*. In 1972, Brando's career underwent a renaissance when he was offered the part of mafia boss Don Corleone in *The Godfather*. Director Francis Ford Coppola considered Brando perfect for the role but had to overcome the objections of Paramount executives, who were worried by Brando's reputation for being difficult. Brando's behavior during filming was exemplary and his performance was magnificent, winning him a second Academy Award, though he turned it down in protest at the mistreatment of Native Americans. The following year, Brando starred in the erotic and controversial movie *Last Tango in Paris*, again winning an Oscar nomination. Brando's movie career thereafter was largely motivated by money, and his roles were limited by his expanding waistline. On a personal level, he faced tragedy when his son Christian was found guilty of murdering the lover of Brando's pregnant daughter Cheyenne. Cheyenne later committed suicide. Brando's last screen appearance came in *The Score* (2001). He died suddenly of pulmonary fibrosis in 2004.

#45

Marlon Brando played the role of Stanley Kowalski in both the stage and screen version of Tennessee Williams' A Streetcar Named Desire. The role brought him fame and his first Academy Award nomination.
▼

Legacy

Rebellious by nature, Brando was the first of Hollywood's "anti-stars." Although lauded by Hollywood executives, Brando refused to play the studio game. He failed to dress glamorously and did not act according to the rules of decorum, earning him his "bad boy" reputation. His personal life was chaotic; he had nine natural children from three wives and a variety of lovers, and adopted three others. In his acting, Brando refused to learn his lines, frequently departing from the script and replacing it with his own improvised words. Nonetheless, Brando revolutionized acting, setting the bar so high that future actors would be judged against his performances. He popularized method acting, whereby actors brought their own emotions and experiences to a role, with the aim of replacing the wooden performances of yesteryear with a rawness and sensitivity that was far more realistic than anything previously seen in Hollywood.

PABLO PICASSO (1881–1973)

Spanish Artist

Painter, sculptor, draughtsman, and writer; broadly regarded as the greatest artist of the twentieth century; cocreator (with Georges Braques) of Cubism; a central figure in the development of abstract art

- Politics & Leadership
- Science & Technology
- **Popular Culture & the Arts**
- Business & Commerce
- Writers & Thinkers

 REWRITING HISTORY

Picasso's international fame was undoubtedly due primarily to his paintings, but another factor was at play. Picasso was probably the first artist to be made into a celebrity by the media, which he actively courted. Constantly photographed and filmed, noted for the playboy aspects of his wealthy lifestyle, he was frequently in the public eye and became one of the best-known faces of the art world.

The immediately recognizable work of Pablo Picasso represents more than just a new way of painting. Taking myriad influences from the full range of artistic genres, he demonstrated a new way of seeing the world and rendering it in two dimensions, effectively reinventing perspective. The most influential artist of the twentieth century, he laid the foundation on which modern and post-modern art is built.

A Natural Artist

Pablo Blasco (he took the surname of his mother, María Picasso y López, when he was 20) was born in Málaga, Spain, where his father, José Ruiz y Blasco, was a professor at the School of Arts and Crafts. When he was ten years old the family moved to La Coruña, and he was soon attending the School of Fine Art, where he was taught by his father. His draftsmanship and artistic ability were astounding, and when the family moved to Barcelona he immediately gained entrance to the School of Fine Art there at the age of just 15. When he was 16, and already an accomplished painter, he became an advanced student at Madrid's Royal Academy of San Fernando, but soon returned to the vibrant artistic life of Barcelona, Spain's cultural hub.

His study of art history and contemporary art led him inevitably to Paris, the international center that had nurtured so many new schools of painting. From 1900 to 1903 he divided his time between the two cities, eventually settling in Paris and setting up a studio in which he proceeded to experiment with all the recent painting styles, producing work that was truly revolutionary and attracting a coterie of artistic and literary colleagues and patrons. His paintings were not just innovative—they were also widely different from each other, revealing a rapidly developing creative talent and a unique ability to distil the essence of various contemporary artistic influences. These early years in Paris are referred to as his Blue and Pink periods, denoting the prevalent colors in his palette at that time.

The Birth of Cubism

He had already been working on ways of representing volume on the two-dimensional canvas, but in 1907 he showed a new form of expression in a work entitled *Les Demoiselles d'Avignon*, a jarring, fractured oil painting in which the subjects are seen from more than one angle simultaneously. Drawing on a range of influences that included tribal art and Spanish sculpture, this dramatic departure from conventional representation caused immediate controversy. It was the first intimation of Cubism, and it was to have a profound effect on twentieth-century art. For the next four years Picasso continued to investigate the possibilities, breaking reality down into ever smaller fragments on the canvas, like a shattered mirror reflecting the subject from all directions. It is generally agreed that his masterpiece in this genre was *The Three Musicians*, completed in 1921.

Multimedia

Cubism was Picasso's greatest contribution to art, but it was by no means his only one. He extended his creativity into many fields, including sculpture, ceramics, printmaking, and set design for the theatre and ballet. During the

1930s, Cubism gave way to Surrealism as the artistic flavor of the times, and although he himself never adopted Surrealism, his paintings at that time do reflect its influence. The combination of both genres, as well as many other influences, can be seen in what many consider to be his most powerful piece—*Guernica* (1937). Created in response to the bombing of the Spanish town of Guernica by German forces on the side of General Franco during the Spanish Civil War, the giant mural depicts the full horror and brutality of the event, and has been hailed as the greatest of all antiwar paintings. He continued to paint and draw up until the time of his death in 1973—a creative career lasting 80 years. His output in a wide range of chosen media was prodigious, exceeding that of any other modern artist, and his influence on other artists, especially painters, is immeasurable.

#44

◄ *Pablo Picasso described Gertrude Stein as his only woman friend. The Paris home of this eccentric American writer was frequented by Cubist and experimental artists and writers, and she became an important patron of Picasso's work.*

President of the United States

Elected to the US Senate from 1935–45; succeeded FDR as the America's 33rd President; authorized the dropping of atomic bombs on Japan; won support for the founding of the United Nations and NATO; took the US into the Korean War

- Politics & Leadership
- Science & Technology
- Popular Culture & the Arts
- Business & Commerce
- Writers & Thinkers

◀◀ REWRITING HISTORY

*During the 1948 presidential election campaign, Truman made an unprecedented 21,928-mile (35,290-km) whistle-stop tour of the nation, appealing in person to the electorate. Had he not done so, the **Chicago Tribune's** late night extra prematurely declaring a win for candidate Dewey might not have been the laughing stock that it became.*

Harry S. Truman led the United States during the latter part of World War II, and made the decision to drop two atomic bombs on Japan. In the postwar period, he helped to found NATO and set the tone for the Cold War. A son of the Midwest, Truman was famous for his honest homespun philosophy and haranguing of the US Senate.

Political Beginnings

Harry S. Truman was born in Lamar, Missouri, the son of a farmer and livestock dealer. After graduating from school, he was prevented from going on to further education by financial constraints and he pursued a number of clerical jobs before returning to work on the family farm. In 1917, Truman was called up for military service and he saw active combat service in France during World War I, where he exhibited leadership qualities. After the war, Truman returned to Missouri, where he set up a haberdashery store. After the store went bankrupt during the 1921 recession, Truman turned to the political arena. In 1922, he won election to the administrative post of district judge and four years later became chief judge of Jackson County. Backed by Democratic political boss Tom Pendergast, Truman won a senate seat in 1934, which he retained until 1945. He came to national prominence after chairing a Senate committee investigating defense spending, and in 1944 he was chosen as Franklin D. Roosevelt's running mate for the presidency. They won the election, and Truman was sworn in as Vice President in January 1945. Eight-two days later, he unexpectedly found himself President. He had no experience of the secret affairs of the state, having only met twice with Roosevelt before his death.

The Presidency

Although he had not even known about the existence of the Manhattan Project prior to becoming President, Truman found that one of his first decisions involved launching the atomic bomb attacks on Hiroshima and Nagasaki in August 1945. After the war ended, Truman worked hard to secure a lasting peace, which included supporting the creation of the United Nations.

In 1947, he won approval for the Truman Doctrine, which prescribed a policy of containment toward the Soviet Union. In 1948, he authorized the Berlin Airlift after the Soviet blockade of West Berlin. At home, Truman's success was more limited, especially after the Republicans gained control in Congress in 1946. His domestic program was disrupted by industrial action, including an unprecedented railroad strike in 1946, and he failed to prevent the passage of the Taft-Harley Act, which curbed union powers. Although he entered the 1948 presidential election as the underdog, Truman won on a "Fair Deal" agenda that included national health insurance and a civil rights program. Truman's second term in the White House was dominated by rising Cold War tensions and war in the Far East. After North Korean forces had crossed the 38th parallel in 1950, Truman succeeded in obtaining a United Nations sanction to send US troops to Korea. The following year, fearing escalation of the war, Truman refused General Douglas MacArthur's request to attack Chinese bases north of the Yalu River. Truman later removed the general from command after MacArthur publicly criticized his decision. It was a deeply unpopular move with the American public, and led to criticism that Truman was soft on communism. At home, an industrial dispute in 1952 threatened to disrupt steel production and Truman took control of the steel mills, though his actions were later declared unconstitutional. By then, Truman appeared to have tired of presidential affairs and declared that he would stand down at the next election. He retired to Independence, Missouri, to write his memoirs.

#43

◄ *Harry S. Truman took over from Franklin D. Roosevelt during the last stages of World War II. In the summer of 1945, he met with Clement Attlee and Josef Stalin, leaders of the United Kingdom and the Soviet Union, respectively, at the Potsdam Conference to discuss postwar organization and the punitive measures to be taken against Nazi Germany.*

Growing Appreciation

While in office, Truman endured spells of deep unpopularity, and his approval ranking at one point reached a miserable 22 percent. Governing at a time of deep paranoia over the perceived threat of communism, Truman was often accused of being too liberal. However, since his death, Truman has come to be admired for his simple, honest, and decisive style, and he is now considered one of the most able presidents in US history. He did not initially seek the ultimate office, but once thrust into the post, he took on the challenge of governing America in a calm and competent manner, putting in place some of the twentieth century's most enduring institutions such as the United Nations and NATO.

FRANCISCO FRANCO (1892–1975)

Military General and Ruler of Spain

Fought in the Rif War in Morocco; led the Nationalist forces during the Spanish Civil War; ruled Spain until his death

 REWRITING HISTORY

Franco's credentials as a monarchist had been established at his 1923 wedding to María del Carmen Polo y Martínez-Valdès. His padrino (best man) was none other than King Alfonso XIII, grandfather of the current King Juan Carlos.

Often referred to as Generalissimo, Francisco Franco was an army general and political leader in Spain. He led the victorious Nationalist movement against the loyalist Republicans during the Spanish Civil War (1936–39), and ruled Spain as a virtual dictator until his death. Franco's 40-year reign was strongly nationalist in character, as well as staunchly Catholic and anti-communist.

The Birth of the General

Francisco Franco Bahamonde was born in El Ferrol, northwest Spain, in 1892, the son of a naval paymaster. He joined the Spanish army in 1907, enrolling in the Toledo Military Academy. Early in his military career, Franco fought in Morocco during the Rif War, rising to the rank of major. He was posted to the Spanish mainland in 1917, where he remained until 1920. He returned to Africa that year as second-in-command of the newly founded Spanish Foreign Legion. In 1923, he was promoted to commander of the Legion, and in 1926 became Spain's youngest general. In 1928, Franco was appointed director of the General Military Academy in Zaragoza. Although he maintained an officially apolitical stance when the Spanish monarchy fell in 1931, Franco became increasingly associated with nationalist conservative politics. In 1933, the Spanish electorate returned a right-wing government, and Spain entered a turbulent political period. Opposition to the government grew, culminating in an anarchist-led insurgency the following year. Franco was sent to Asturias to put down an uprising led by the region's striking miners. He was branded the "hangman of Asturias" for his actions, which left more than a thousand dead. In 1935, Franco became chief of the general staff.

The Spanish Civil War

After the election of the left-wing Popular Front in 1936, the political situation in Spain deteriorated rapidly. Leftist militant violence against the Catholic clerics and the assassination of opposition leader José Calvo Sotelo culminated in an attempted coup by Franco and other military leaders, who feared the establishment of a communist regime in Spain. Launched from a base in Spanish Morocco, the coup initially failed but heralded the beginning of the Spanish Civil War. During the bloody conflict that ensued, Franco emerged as the leader of the Nationalist movement. Aided by military help from the fascists in Italy and later Nazi Germany, Franco's Nationalists emerged victorious against the Republicans. After the Republican surrender on April 1, 1939, Franco dissolved the Spanish Parliament and assumed leadership of Spain. Shortly afterward, war broke out in Europe. Although Franco officially maintained a position of neutrality during World War II, he did permit Spanish volunteers to fight with the Germans against the communist Russian forces.

Spain Under Franco

Ideologically conservative, Franco came to represent the interests of Spain's traditionalists—the Catholics and the military—and was a staunch enemy of the liberal, left-wing elements. His rule was authoritarian, and dissent was suppressed through the systematic implementation of censorship, torture, imprisonment in concentration camps, and the death penalty. In 1947, Franco proclaimed Spain a monarchy, though he did not name a king, instead establishing himself as *de facto* Regent. Shortly after the end of World War II, Franco moved to normalize relations with the Allied powers, and in 1950 he established diplomatic relations with UN member nations. During the subsequent Cold War period, his fervent anti-communist stance and permission to establish US military bases in Spain earned him both respect and economic aid from the US. From the late 1950s onward, Franco began to moderate his domestic policies, concentrating on technological and economic development within Spain. This resulted in an unprecedented economic boom in Spain, referred to as "The Spanish Miracle," and is often cited as the most positive outcome of the Franco regime. In 1969, Franco designated Bourbon prince Juan Carlos as his successor, though he continued to rule until his death in 1975.

Francisco Franco as painted by Paco Ibera in **La Guerra Ha Terminado.** *The title of the painting refers to Franco's final bulletin of the Spanish Civil War issued on April 1, 1939 in which he declares* **"Our victorious troops have achieved their final military objectives. The war is over."**
▼

MUHAMMAD ALI (b. 1942)

World Heavyweight Boxing Champion

Won Olympic Light Heavyweight Boxing Gold Medal; won world heavyweight title three times; fought in, and won, the "Rumble in the Jungle" and "Thrilla in Manila" boxing matches

- Politics & Leadership
- Science & Technology
- **Popular Culture & the Arts**
- Business & Commerce
- Writers & Thinkers

◄◄ **REWRITING HISTORY**

Although Clay returned to a rapturous welcome after his Olympic victory in 1960, he was still denied service at a local whites-only restaurant. Disgusted at the racism in his home country, Clay threw his gold medal into the Ohio River in protest. He was presented with a replica during the Atlanta 1996 Olympics.

Flamboyant boxing heavyweight champion Muhammad Ali is one of the most recognizable figures in sporting history. With his unorthodox style and razor-sharp wit, Muhammad "The Greatest" Ali injected color and glamor into boxing, bringing new fans to the sport and attracting large purses to his legendary bouts.

Amateur Career

Cassius Marcellus Clay Jr. was born in 1942 in Louisville, Kentucky, the son of a billboard painter and a maid. Ali's introduction to boxing came through the theft of his bike. After the incident, the angry 12-year-old Clay encountered Louisville police officer and amateur boxing coach Joe Martin and threatened to "whup" whoever had taken his bike. Martin told Clay that he'd "better learn to box first," and directed his anger toward the boxing ring. Clay became passionate about boxing, training hard and outworking all the other kids. Within weeks, Clay was in the ring winning his first bout. As an amateur, Clay worked under both Martin and African-American trainer Fred Stoner, taking part in more than 100 bouts and winning all bar five. Clay went on to win six Kentucky Golden Gloves titles, two national Golden Gloves titles, and two National Amateur Athletic Union titles. In 1960, just months after his 18th birthday, Clay won the Olympic Gold Medal in Rome, beating Poland's Zbigniew Pietrzykowski on a 5-0 decision.

Turning Pro and Controversy

After his Olympic win Clay turned professional and began training with Angelo Dundee. Clay quickly established himself as a contender for Sonny Liston's world heavyweight title, and in 1964 was given the opportunity. Although Liston was a clear favorite, Clay won when Liston retired before the start of the seventh round. The next day, Clay announced that he had joined the Nation of Islam, shortly afterward changing his name to Muhammad Ali. The following year Ali retained his world heavyweight title after a rematch with Liston, whom he knocked out with a stunning right-hand punch in the first round. Ali then successfully defended his heavyweight crown against

Floyd Patterson, George Chuvalo, Henry Cooper, Brian London, Karl Mildenberger, Cleveland William, and Ernie Terrell. In March 1967, Ali fought Zora Folley in what would turn out to be his last fight for three and a half years. With US involvement in Vietnam escalating, Ali was called up to join the Armed Forces. He refused on conscientious grounds, famously quoting, "I ain't got no quarrel with them Vietcong." As well as facing a prison term, Ali had his boxing license suspended and was stripped of his title. As the American public turned against the war, support for Ali grew, and in 1970 he was allowed to fight again. He made his comeback against Jerry Quarry. In March 1971, Ali took on the undefeated champion Joe Frazier at Madison Square Gardens. Billed as the "Fight of the Century," the fight lived up to the hype, with Frazier coming out victorious. Ali subsequently defeated Frazier in a non-title fight (Frazier had lost the title to George Foreman) in 1974. In between, Ali fought Ken Norton, losing once and winning once. In 1974, Ali got another shot at the world crown when he fought George Foreman. The fight, which guaranteed Ali and Foreman an unprecedented $10 million, took place in Zaire and came to be known as the "Rumble in the Jungle." Going into the fight, Ali was the clear underdog but he fought tenaciously, dealing Foreman a knockout blow in the eighth round. Ali took part in another legendary fight in 1975, when he fought Joe Frazier for a third time in the "Thrilla in Manila" bout. The fight lasted 14 rounds before Frazier retired and was, Ali confessed, one of the toughest of his career. In 1978, Ali lost the crown to Olympic champion Leon Spinks but regained it several months later in a rematch, becoming the only man in history at that time to win the title three times. Ali retired in 1981, with a career record of 56 wins and five defeats.

#41

Born Cassius Clay, Muhammad Ali received his new name from Elijah Muhammad, the head of the Nation of Islam. Here the boxer listens to an address given by the leader.
▼

The Ali Style

Ali brought show business to boxing. Speedy on his feet, he was also quick witted. Nicknamed the "Louisville Lip," Ali soon gained a reputation for fast talking and self promotion. At press conferences, Ali would provide original headline-grabbing sound bites ("Float like a butterfly, sting like a bee"), taunting his

opponents with predictions of their defeat, ("To prove I'm great, he will fall in eight!"). Ali introduced new techniques in the boxing ring. His "Ali Shuffle" was an innovation, foxing opponents with his fast and fancy footwork. Ali also adopted the "headhunter" approach, never throwing body shots. Good-looking and charismatic, Ali changed the public's perception of boxing. His body may now be a shadow of its former self, affected as he is with Parkinson's disease, but Ali is still one of the most legendary and popular faces of twentieth-century sport and his ongoing public appearances attract both money and prestige for the many humanitarian causes that he now promotes.

HOWARD HUGHES (1905–1976)

Aviator, Movie Producer and Director, Industrialist, Philanthropist

Produced and directed big budget Hollywood movies; discovered actress Jane Russell; designed and built the Hughes H-1 airplane; set transcontinental and round-the-world aviation records

Known for dating Hollywood starlets, Howard Hughes was a dashing industrialist and movie producer. He was also a pioneering aviator, building record-breaking planes. One of the wealthiest men in the world, Howard Hughes is probably most famous today for the eccentric and reclusive behavior that he displayed in the latter part of his life.

Building on his Inheritance

Howard Hughes was born in Houston, Texas, in 1905, the only child of Howard and Allene Hughes. He was educated at private schools in California and Massachusetts, though he never graduated from high school. His mother died in 1922 and his father had a fatal heart attack in 1924. Hughes inherited much of the family's Hughes Tool Company, including the patent for a drill bit commonly used in the oil and gas industry. Hughes left the Rice Institute in Houston where he was studying to manage the family business, and in 1925 the 20-year-old Hughes married socialite Ella Botts Rice and the couple moved to Los Angeles, where he had an uncle in the movie business.

Movie Career

In 1926, Hughes began using his new-found wealth to finance Hollywood movies. His first movie to be released was *Everybody's Acting* (1926), followed by *Two Arabian Nights* (1927), which won an Academy Award for best comedy screenplay. Hughes signed up Jean Harlow to star in his next project, the aviator movie *Hell's Angels* (1930). Made at a record cost of $3.8 million, the movie launched Hughes's career as a director. In 1932, Hughes produced the controversial gangster movie *Scarface*. Its release was delayed due to censorship problems over the level of violence in the movie but Hughes successfully won the battle to retain key explicit scenes. Hughes took a break from Hollywood to pursue his interests in aviation but returned to movies in 1940 after spotting the well-endowed Jane Russell. He signed Russell up for *The Outlaw*. Again, the movie's release was delayed by censorship rows, this time due to the apparent overexposure of Jane Russell's breasts. The movie finally went for general release in 1946. Between 1948 and 1955,

◀◀ REWRITING HISTORY

Ever the perfectionist, Hughes is said to have been dismayed that the seams of Jane Russell's bra were visible during filming of **The Outlaw.** *Keen to showcase her most valuable assets, Hughes devised a seamless bra for his star. Russell later recounted that Hughes' bra was "uncomfortable and ridiculous" and revealed that she wore her own bra padded with tissue paper. Hughes was none the wiser.*

Hughes owned the RKO movie studio. Divorced from his first wife in 1929, Hughes was linked with a number of leading Hollywood actresses including Ava Gardner, Olivia de Havilland, and Katherine Hepburn. In 1957 Hughes married actress Jean Peters (they divorced in 1971).

Hughes the Aviator

A licensed pilot since 1928, Hughes founded the Hughes Aircraft Company in 1932 to indulge his fantasy of building fast planes. He set a new speed record of 352 mph (566 km/h) in 1935 in the Hughes H-1 Racer, and in 1936 and 1937 Hughes set transcontinental flight records, followed by a record-breaking round-the-world trip in 1938. His achievement won him many awards, including a Congressional Gold Medal in 1941. During World War II, Hughes landed a contract to build a troop carrier. Nicknamed the "Spruce Goose," the plane was not completed until after the war, leading to later allegations that he had failed to meet his wartime contracts. Hughes' aviation company became a major defense contractor after World War II, and in 1946 Hughes suffered a near fatal accident while at the controls of an experimental military plane. In 1953, Hughes gave all his stock to the newly created Howard Hughes Medical Institute, though this was generally considered a tax dodge. Hughes also bought heavily into TWA stock, but was later forced to sell due to conflict of interest issues.

The Recluse

Beginning in the 1950s, Hughes' behavior became increasingly erratic, exacerbated by an obsessive-compulsive disorder. He lived largely in a variety of hotel penthouses and took extreme measures to avoid being seen in public. His only public contact came in 1976, when he made a phone call to denounce Clifford Irving's biography as fraudulent. He died in a private plane en route to hospital in 1976, his appearance so changed that he had to be identified by his fingerprints. Hughes left an estate worth $2 billion but no legal will was ever discovered.

◀ *By the time he died, Hughes's appearance had changed beyond recognition, a result of his exacerbating mental problems. He is buried in Glenwood Cemetery, Harris County, Texas.*

GABRIELLE "COCO" CHANEL (1883–1971)

Fashion and Fragrance Designer

Revolutionized women's fashion; dressed women in suits and bell bottoms; introduced the "little black dress"; created the world's first signature fragrance

Coco Chanel threw out all conventions when she began designing for women in the early twentieth century. Out went fussy long dresses and in came suits and short skirts. She took the Chanel name from humble beginnings to a multimillion dollar enterprise with a worldwide reputation for its costume jewelry and perfumes as well as Chanel's signature *haute couture*.

Beginning with a Hat

Gabrielle "Coco" Chanel was born out of wedlock in 1883 in Saumur, France, one of six siblings. Her mother died when she was young, and Chanel spent some years in an orphanage, where she learned the skills of a seamstress. After leaving the orphanage, Chanel worked at a tailoring store. She began an affair with French playboy and millionaire Étienne Balsan, who introduced her to the trappings and tastes of the wealthy. What she didn't like, however, were the ostrich-boa draped hats that were fashionable among the rich Parisian women of the time and Chanel decided to design hats to suit her tastes. In 1913, she opened up a millinery store in Paris, but it soon went out of business. Chanel's relationship with Balsan had ended, but new love Arthur "Boy" Capel helped her open up a second store, this time in Brittany. In 1913, Chanel branched out with a new boutique in Deauville, where she introduced a range of women's sportswear. Her simple designs soon attracted women of society, and Chanel's reputation spread.

Building the Chanel Empire

Until Chanel came along, women's clothes were uncomfortable to wear, encasing women in stiff fabrics, restricting movement, and drenching them in perspiration. Chanel worked with less ornate fabrics, such as jersey, which had hitherto been considered too lowly for *haute couture*. Chanel's clothes liberated women, and she has come to be associated with the 1920s "flapper" generation of young women who challenged social norms with their short haircuts and skirts, use of cosmetics, and active athletic pursuits. Chanel herself cut her hair and wore clothes considered "mannish," such as suits. The

◀◀ REWRITING HISTORY

Biographers have had a hard time sorting out fact from fiction concerning the early life of Coco Chanel. Chanel concocted an elaborate story to mask the stigma of her illegitimate birth and poverty-stricken childhood. She changed the year of her birth to 1893 and claimed that her father went to America after the death of her mother, in an attempt to get rich, and that she was raised by two cruel spinster aunts.

introduction of the chemise in the 1920s established the Chanel "little boy" look, and the Chanel empire began to expand. In 1922, Chanel created a perfume, named simply Chanel No. 5 after her lucky number. The fragrance was the first to be associated with a designer's name and it remains popular today. In 1925, Chanel introduced the cardigan jacket that has become one of her signature pieces, followed by the "little black dress" in 1926. In the 1930s, Chanel worked in Hollywood, dressing stars such as Katherine Hepburn, Elizabeth Taylor, and Grace Kelly, though many disliked her unfeminine designs. She also produced art-deco inspired costume jewelry during this period. A wartime love affair with a Nazi officer caused her popularity to fall and Chanel spent 15 years of her life living in self-imposed exile in Switzerland. In 1954, she made a comeback, and her designs enjoyed great popularity again. New looks included bell-bottom pants. In the '50s and '60s, she found herself in great demand from Hollywood, where she designed clothes for Audrey Hepburn and other stars, and also stage costumes. In 1969, Katherine Hepburn starred in the Broadway musical *Coco* based on her life, although Chanel considered her too old for the role (Hepburn was 60, Chanel was 86). Chanel worked right up to her death at the age of 87 in 1971.

The Chanel Look

The Chanel name alone defines an entire look, marrying casual elegance with impeccable taste and quality. Coco Chanel rescued women from the confines of the corset and dressed them in comfortable, yet stylish clothes. Her menswear-inspired suits and "little black dress" remain classics, changing little from decade to decade, and women all over the world spend thousands of dollars in pursuit of chic simplicity. As Chanel herself once said "simplicity is the keynote of all true elegance."

Coco Chanel moved among the literary and artistic circles of Paris. She is seen here with her friend, the French artist and writer Jean Cocteau, for whom she designed stage costumes.
▼

ALFRED HITCHCOCK (1899–1980)

Director and Producer

Began working in silent movies; made the first British "talkie" movie; directed over 50 movies in a 50-year career; knighted for his services to the movie industry

 REWRITING HISTORY

The "wrong man" theme that occurs in many of Hitchcock's movies had its roots in his difficult childhood. As a child, Hitchcock was sent to the local police station with a note from his father asking the police officer to lock the young Hitchcock in the cells for 10 minutes as a punishment, which he did. This incident left Hitchcock with a morbid fear of being wrongly accused or doing wrong.

Known as the "Master of Suspense," Alfred Hitchcock was a British movie director famous for his psychological thrillers. He worked with many of Hollywood's finest stars, including Grace Kelly, Cary Grant, James Stewart, and Ingrid Bergman, and created some of the most memorable movies in cinematic history.

British Movies

Alfred Hitchcock was born in Leytonstone, England, the youngest son of a greengrocer. After a short career as a draftsman, Hitchcock began to work as a title designer at Islington Studios for an American movie company, the Famous Players-Lasky. Hitchcock learned the business fast, rising to the position of Assistant Director in just three years. His first shot at directing came in 1923 when the director of *Always Tell Your Wife* became ill and Hitchcock was asked to finish the movie. He was offered the job of directing *Number 13*, but the studio ceased its British operation before the movie could be completed. He joined Gainsborough Pictures, working on several movies for the studio before landing the directing role for a British/German production *The Pleasure Garden* (1925). The following year, Hitchcock directed *The Lodger* (1927), now regarded as the first of the classic "Hitchcock" movies. Two years later, Hitchcock made *Blackmail* (1929), the first British all-talkie movie. Other successful movies followed, including *The 39 Steps* (1935), *The Lady Vanishes* (1938), and *Jamaica Inn* (1939), by which time Hitchcock had established a reputation as Britain's leading movie director.

Move to Hollywood

In 1949, US producer David O. Selznick offered Hitchcock a seven-year contract, which took Hitchcock to America. His first US movie was an adaptation of Daphne du Maurier's *Rebecca* (1940), which went on to win the Academy Award for Best Picture. Throughout the 1940s and '50s, Hitchcock was a prolific moviemaker, turning out more than a movie a year and working with many of the major stars of the time. Classics from this period include

Notorious (1946), *Strangers on a Train* (1951), *Rear Window* (1954), *Vertigo* (1958), and *North by Northwest* (1959). In the early '60s, Hitchcock made two of his most famous movies, *Psycho* (1960) and *The Birds* (1963). His last major success was *Frenzy* (1972).

Themes and Plots

Many of Hitchcock's classic movies share common themes and cinematic devices. Hitchcock cleverly builds tension by sharing important details with his audience that remain hidden to the movie's characters until the horrific consequences unfold. The movies often contain a device known as a "McGuffin"—an incident that interests the main characters and

precipitates the plot, but one that essentially has no real importance. Examples include the reference to "government secrets" in *North by Northwest*, described by Hitchcock as "his emptiest, most nonexistent McGuffin." Many of Hitchcock's central characters are drawn into the plot through a case of mistaken identity—for example, *The Wrong Man* (1956) and *North by Northwest*. With his suave appearance and charming manner, the Hitchcock villain (Barry Foster in *Frenzy*, Robert Walker in *Strangers on a Train*, Claude Rains in *Notorious*) represented a departure from the Hollywood norm. Hitchcock's leading females, too, are often flawed characters; Janet Leigh in *Psycho* stole money from her employer to run away with her boyfriend and Tippi Hedren in *Marnie* (1964) is a serial thief with psychological problems. Hitchcock's actresses were generally blonde, in the Grace Kelly mold. Recurring images in Hitchcock's movies include trains, domineering or crazed mothers, and staircases. Hitchcock also had a habit of using famous landmarks, such as the British Museum and Mount Rushmore, as backdrops for suspense sequences.

The Hitchcock Legacy

Hitchcock's career spanned five decades and he made 53 feature-length movies. His direction was meticulous—typically planned down to the smallest detail—and he fought hard for directors to be given more artistic control. Despite never winning an Academy Award for Best Director, Hitchcock is hailed as one of the greatest directors of all time.

◄ *Cary Grant starred in the Hitchcock classic* **North by Northwest,** *considered by many to be one of the director's most accomplished movies. The suave movie star appeared in three other Hitchcock movies—***Suspicion, Notorious,** *and* **To Catch a Thief.**

REWRITING HISTORY

Ho Chi Minh died on September 2, 1969, on the 25th anniversary of his proclamation of the foundation of the Democratic Republic of Vietnam. The news of his death was delayed for 48 hours, so that the nation's anniversary could pass without disruption.

HO CHI MINH (1890–1969)

President of the Democratic Republic of Vietnam

Helped to found the French Communist Party; leader of the Viet Minh; became the first President of the Democratic Republic of Vietnam; led the clandestine operations against the French colonial forces, finally defeating them at Dien Bien Phu; organized the Vietcong guerilla movement

Ho Chi Minh was a revolutionary communist leader who led the Viet Minh independence movement in Vietnam. He established the communist-governed Democratic Republic of Vietnam in 1945 and rid the country of French colonial powers eight years later. Ho organized the Vietcong guerilla forces and laid the groundwork for the reunification of Vietnam under Communist rule.

Rebelling Against Imperialism

Ho Chi Minh was born Nguyen Sinh Cung in 1890 in a village in central Vietnam during the time of French colonial rule. His father was a Confucian scholar and teacher, who originally worked as an imperial magistrate but was dismissed for anti-French sentiments. Although he was educated at a French school, Cung grew up to be a committed nationalist. After completing his studies, Cung worked first as a teacher and then as a seaman. In 1911, Cung traveled Europe, spending some time in London before settling in France in 1919, where he embraced communism and helped to found the French Communist Party. In 1923, Cung went to Moscow to further his revolutionary studies. The following year, he moved to China, where he married a Chinese woman. During the 1920s and 1930s, Cung worked to spread communism throughout Asia, founding the Indo-Chinese Communist Party in 1930. In 1941, Cung returned to Vietnam, where he led the League for the Independence of Vietnam, known as the Viet Minh. During World War II, Cung, with American support, led successful guerilla campaigns against the Japanese occupation of Vietnam from his base near the Chinese border. In 1942, he was jailed in China by the Chiang Kai-shek led nationalists. After his release the following year, Cung returned to Vietnam. During this period, he became known as Ho Chi Minh, which means "He Who Enlightens."

The Democratic Republic of Vietnam

After the Japanese surrender to the Allies in August 1945, the Viet Minh was able to take control of Vietnam and Emperor Bao-Dao was forced to abdicate. On September 2, 1945, Ho proclaimed himself president of the newly independent Democratic Republic of Vietnam. However, the country did not receive official recognition internationally, and France tried to wrestle back control of its colony, forcing Ho and his supporters to retreat to their communist stronghold near the Chinese border. For the next eight years, Ho and his followers waged a guerilla war against the French. In May 1954, the Viet Minh inflicted a defeat against the French colonial forces at the Battle of Dien Bien Phu, and the French surrendered. Under the cease-fire agreement, Vietnam was to be temporarily divided at the 17th parallel until elections could be held for the whole of Vietnam. North Vietnam was to be ruled as a single party Communist state by Ho Chi Minh and South Vietnam came under the control of the anti-communist Ngo Dinh Diem. Ho almost immediately began a Maoist-inspired program of land reform, in which thousands of former landlords faced imprisonment or execution. When it became apparent that Ngo Dinh Diem had no intention of holding elections, Ho came under pressure to turn to armed resistance. Although he initially resisted, preferring to take a more moderate stance, Ho eventually authorized the supply of arms and training to various guerilla movements in the south. These movements morphed into the Vietcong, the scourge of US combat forces. In 1960, failing health resulted in Ho ceding the party leadership to Le Duan, though he remained a figurehead President. Ho refused all negotiations with the US after their entry into the war, believing that American public opinion would cause their withdrawal. Ho died in 1969 in Hanoi from heart failure, six years before the reunification of Vietnam under the regime that he had done so much to create.

Ho's Legacy

Although Ho Chi Minh's economic policies may have been largely discarded, his image is nonetheless very much in the forefront of present day life in Vietnam. He is still the focus of a personality cult and is revered as an almost divine figure in the country, where he is affectionately referred to as "Uncle Ho." His image appears everywhere, including on the nation's currency, and the city of Saigon has been renamed Ho Chi Minh City in his honor. Like Lenin, Ho Chi Minh's embalmed body is on public display in a mausoleum.

#37

Although Ho Chi Minh died before the end of the Vietnam War, he remained an inspiring figure in the communist fight for the reunification of Vietnam. Ho Chi Minh remains an object of affection in the hearts of the Vietnamese people and his image in the country is still very much in evidence.

▼

T. S. ELIOT (1888–1965)

American-born Poet, Playwright, Author, and Critic

Author of The Waste Land, *one of the most famous twentieth-century English-language poems and a leading example of modernist writing; Nobel Prize winner; directly influenced later playwrights such as Harold Pinter and Samuel Beckett*

Rich in its references to the classics and deeply connected to a range of literary and poetic traditions, the poetry of Thomas Stearns Eliot was also stark and new in its style. In the content and form of poems such as *The Waste Land*, he exposed the plight of Western culture and set English literature on a new path.

North and South

Born and raised in St Louis, Missouri, Thomas Eliot came from a well-educated family with a long history of involvement in Christian service, charity work, and education. His grandfather, a minister in the Unitarian Church, founded a university and several schools, and his father, the president and chairman of a brick company, was active in those institutions. Like his paternal grandparents, Eliot's mother was from New England, and the young Thomas spent many summer vacations there. Images and memories of both the US Southwest and New England were to surface later in his work. Eliot received a classical education at the Smith Academy in St Louis, a private school founded by his grandfather. His poetic talent was already evident and he read a valedictory poem at graduation.

Academic Years

After a year at Milton Academy in Massachusetts, he went to Harvard and received a Bachelor of Arts degree followed by a Master's degree. During his time there he continued to write poetry, some of which was published in the *Harvard Advocate* magazine. The *Advocate* was edited by the poet and critic Conrad Aitken, and he and Eliot became lifelong friends. While at Harvard, Eliot read Arthur Symons' *The Symbolist Movement in Literature*, which brought French Symbolism to his attention and deeply affected him, leading him to read the work of French poets such as Rimbaud and Verlaine. On leaving Harvard in 1910 he went to Paris for a year, studying at the Sorbonne and traveling in Europe. He returned to Harvard in 1911 as a PhD student, and spent three years studying the writings of the English idealist philosopher Francis Herbert Bradley, the subject of his thesis, as well as Buddhism and

REWRITING HISTORY

Just as the very different contexts of Missouri and New England informed his early writing, the combination of his American background and English perspective on World War I gave Eliot a unique perspective. Had he not received a scholarship to Oxford at the start of the war, the course of English literature in the twentieth century would have been significantly different.

Indian philosophy, before being awarded a scholarship to Merton College, Oxford, in 1914.

Eliot's Anglicization

Eliot stayed at Merton College for only a year, but during that time he met the young American poet Ezra Pound, who proved to be a vital element in his poetic development, and Vivienne Haigh-Wood, whom he married the following year. While teaching at a London school, Eliot completed and submitted his doctoral thesis on F. H. Bradley, but as he refused to go to Harvard to defend it, his PhD was never awarded. He then joined Lloyds bank, and in 1917 his first book of verse, *Prufrock and Other Observations*, was published. Its dramatically new and disjointed style, the use of internal monologue (later seen in the work of James Joyce), and its mood of disillusion and alienation created an immediate stir in literary circles. Taking a job as the literary editor of a feminist magazine, Eliot wrote several volumes of essays outlining the literary traditions that had influenced him and which he had brought to bear in his poetic commentary on the modern world. He was quickly accepted into London's literary society and soon became a leading member of the British intelligentsia. In 1921 he published a draft of *The Waste Land*, and it appeared in its final form, edited by Ezra Pound, the following year. The poem established his role as a leading figure in American and British literature. In 1925 he joined Faber and Faber as an editor, later becoming a director. In 1927 Eliot joined the Anglo-Catholic Church, also relinquishing his US citizenship and becoming a British Subject. Turning to drama, Eliot wrote *Murder in the Cathedral* in 1935, and then penned several plays intended for the commercial theater, including *The Family Reunion* (1939) and *The Cocktail Party* (1949). His book of children's verse, *Old Possum's Book of Practical Cats* (1939), formed the basis of the highly successful musical *Cats*. In 1948 Eliot received the Nobel Prize in Literature.

#36

"**This is the way the world ends / Not with a bang but a whimper.**"
Final lines of Hollow Men, *T. S. Eliot*

◀ *Eliot joined the publishing house Faber and Faber in 1925 and remained there for the rest of his working life. He is seen here (left) at a meeting of the board of directors in March 1944, discussing wartime paper rationing.*

DALAI LAMA (b. 1935)

Spiritual and Political Leader of Tibet

Formally recognized as the reincarnation of the 13th Dalai Lama; became the political leader of Tibet; became the leader in exile after fleeing Chinese-occupied Tibet; received the Nobel Prize for Peace

The 14th Dalai Lama is the current spiritual and political leader of Tibet. Although forced into exile in 1959, the Dalai Lama governs Tibetans in exile from his home in India, simultaneously maintaining Tibetan religious and cultural traditions. He is respected internationally for his tolerance, humility, and continual efforts for peace, both in Tibet and the wider world.

Finding the 14th Dalai Lama

The Dalai Lama was born Llamo Thondup in 1935 in Taktser, a village in northeastern Tibet. He was the fifth of 16 children of a peasant family. Llamo Thondup was recognized as the 14th Dalai Lama when he was two years old. According to Tibetan Buddhist tradition, the Dalai Lama is the earthly incarnation of Avalokitesvara, the Buddha of Compassion. When a Dalai Lama dies, his soul moves into the body of an infant. After the death of the 13th Dalai Lama in 1933, a search party of High Lamas was sent out to find his successor. Helped by a number of visions and omens, the High Lamas' four-year search ended when they found Llamo Thondup. They presented the young boy with a number of objects, some of which had belonged to the 13th Dalai Lama. He identified relics that had belonged to the Dalai Lama, claiming them as his own. Renamed Jetsun Jamphel Ngawang Lobsang Yeshe Tenzin Gyatso, the Dalai Lama is commonly referred to as Yishin Norbu (meaning Wish-Fulfilling Gem) by Tibetan Buddhists. At the age of four, he was taken to Lhasa and formally enthroned as the 14th Dalai Lama in 1940.

The Chinese Occupation

As well as being the spiritual leader of Tibet, the Dalai Lama is also traditionally the temporal leader of the country. In October 1950, the army of the People's Republic of China invaded Tibet. One month later, the 14th Dalai Lama was enthroned as Tibet's political head, leaving the 15-year-old with the daunting task of leading the country in its fight against its mighty neighbors. In 1951, the Dalai Lama reluctantly agreed to sign the Seventeen Point Agreement for the Peaceful Liberation of Tibet, which effectively gave

◀◀ REWRITING HISTORY

Without the presence and personal charisma of the 14th Dalai Lama as a religious figurehead and political spokesman to give cohesion to the Tibetan community, it is quite likely that Tibetan culture would have sunk without trace under Chinese domination.

China sovereignty over Tibet. Although the Dalai Lama tried to work with his communist rulers, even traveling to Beijing to meet with Chairman Mao, the political situation in Tibet remained tense. In 1959, the Tibetan people staged an uprising against their Chinese oppressors and the Dalai Lama was forced to flee to India in the resulting mayhem, fearful that the Chinese were planning to kill him. Since that time he has been the leader-in-exile of Tibet.

Leader in Exile

After fleeing Tibet, the Dalai Lama set up a government of Tibet in Exile in Dharamshala, India, commonly referred to as "Little Lhasa." Known officially as the Central Tibetan Administration (CTA) of His Holiness the Dalai Lama, the government claims to be the legitimate government of Tibet, though it does not receive official recognition by any country. It does, however, receive financial aid from many governments and is a founding member of the Unrepresented Nations and Peoples Organization (UNPO). Since the establishment of the CTA, the Dalai Lama has traveled extensively, lobbying for the Tibetan autonomy. His work has resulted in the United Nations General Assembly adopting resolutions calling on China to respect the human rights of Tibetans and their wish for self-determination. He has also established educational and monastic institutions in the area to ensure the continuation of Tibetan cultural identity. Although a practicing Buddhist, the Dalai Lama has expressed a tolerance for other religions and has worked tirelessly in the pursuit of peace. His humanitarian efforts have gained him worldwide recognition and in 1989 he was awarded the Nobel Peace Prize.

◀ *The 14th Dalai Lama has worked tirelessly to promote peace and interfaith harmony. Here he is seen taking part in a Hindu fire festival held on the sacred river Ganges.*

ANDY WARHOL (1928–1987)

American Illustrator and Painter, Printmaker, Sculptor, Moviemaker, Writer, and Music Producer

Merged commercial illustration and fine art; founding member of the pop art movement

Andy Warhol was one of the most influential artists of the late twentieth century, not only because he developed a unique and much-copied style of painting and illustration, but also because he took elements of popular culture and used art to turn them into icons, reflecting society's values back on itself.

Media Interests

Andy Warhol (christened Andrew Warhola) was born in Forest City, Pennsylvania, the third child of a Byzantine Catholic family. His father, who worked in the mines, had immigrated from Slovakia at the start of World War I and had been joined by his mother in the early '20s. Warhol had a somewhat isolated childhood, partly due to illness, and was very close to his mother. At an early age he developed an interest in radio, movies, and drawing, and on leaving high school in 1945 he went to study commercial art at Pittsburgh's Carnegie Institute of Technology (now Carnegie Mellon University), where he received a Bachelor of Fine Arts degree in Pictorial Design. In 1949, he moved to New York City and soon gained a reputation for his highly detailed illustrations for magazines and advertising, especially a series produced for the I. Miller Shoe Company in Times Square.

Art meets Popular Culture

At first, the commercial nature of his work caused galleries to shun his fine art, but whereas many commercial artists strove to keep these two aspects of their work separate, Warhol took the bold step of merging the two and making popular culture the overt subject of his art. He began to use mass-production means, such as silk screen printing, to create oversized and hyperreal images of celebrity figures and mass-market goods. His first one-man fine art exhibition, held in San Francisco in the summer of 1962, can be seen as the birth of west coast Pop Art, and a few months later his first New York exhibition, which included his now-famous images of Marilyn Monroe, Campbell's Soup cans, and Coca-Cola bottles, received ecstatic popular acclaim, despite criticism from an art world that was incensed at the intrusion of market culture.

REWRITING HISTORY

Andy Warhol's significant change in artistic direction at the end of the '60s has been attributed to an event that could have ended his life. In 1968, he received severe internal injuries and spent two months in hospital after being shot by a feminist member of the Factory group. News of his shooting was soon pushed off the front pages by the assassination of Robert F. Kennedy two days later.

The Pinup of Pop

Virtually overnight, he himself became a celebrity and a key figure in the psychedelic era, with a cult following that included bohemians, artists, musicians, and movie stars. Throughout the '60s, his studio on 47th Street (and later on Broadway), which he dubbed "The Factory," attracted a crowd of artists and admirers who collaborated with him on a range of paintings and sculptures. From 1963 onward, Warhol also took up cinematography, producing a host of idiosyncratic movies that ranged from an eight-hour study of the Empire State Building to heterosexual and gay pornography. At the start of the '70s, the style of his work moved suddenly toward a softer abstract expressionism, and much of his work consisted of commissioned portraits of high-profile personalities. In the eighties he turned to the mythical characters in cartoon strips and movies, as well as endangered wildlife, for his subject matter.

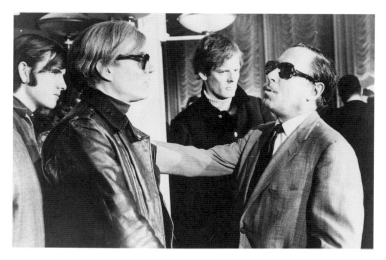

◀ *Both prominent members of the New York art scene during the '60s, Andy Warhol and Tennessee Williams are seen here talking aboard the giant cruise ship* S. S. France *in 1967. Warhol and his studio became a magnet for celebrity musicians, writers, artists, and actors.*

Mirror or Cynic?

By the time of his death in 1987 (of complications following gallbladder surgery), Warhol's place as a key figure in twentieth-century art was assured. Turning the products and personalities of American culture into art objects, he threw society's icons back at it under a spotlight, at the same time raising the question not only of what art is but also of whether anything is not art. Although some saw his work as cynicism or satire, he himself never judged the objects he depicted or the society that held them dear. His work is a reflection of the times in which he lived, a larger-than-life record of postwar American popular culture.

OPRAH WINFREY (b. 1954)

Talk Show Host, Actress, Producer, Publisher

First black news anchor; took The Oprah Winfrey Show *to the top of TV ratings; won Academy Award nomination for her role in* The Color Purple*; launched* O *magazine*

◄◄ REWRITING HISTORY

A victim of child abuse herself, Winfrey worked hard to get child protection legislation enacted. In December 1993, President Clinton signed the National Child Protection Act, also known as the "Oprah Bill," which established a national database of all indictments and convictions on child abuse and sex offense charges.

Oprah Winfrey is the epitome of the American Dream. She started life in poverty, rising through a mixture of charm and hard work to become the "Queen of Daytime TV," and the world's first black billionaire. Her empathy with her audience of more than 20 million Americans has made her one of the most powerful and influential African-American women in the world.

Troubled Teen

Oprah Gail Winfrey was born in 1954 in Kosciusko, Mississippi, to unmarried teenage parents Vernita Lee and Vernon Winfrey. She spent the first six years of her life living in extreme poverty with her grandmother on a farm that lacked running water and electricity. Her grandmother taught her to read and Winfrey did well at school, skipping two grades. She later moved to an inner-city neighborhood in Milwaukee, Wisconsin, to be with her mother who worked as a maid. Winfrey later revealed that she had been subjected to sexual abuse from the age of nine years at the hands of a cousin and others, and at the age of 14 she had a baby that died shortly after birth. She went to live with her father in Nashville, Tennessee, a move that Winfrey credits with saving her life. Vernon Winfrey provided a strict and disciplined environment, and encouraged Winfrey to read and get a good education. Winfrey became an honors student and a member of the high school's speech team, winning a full scholarship to the Tennessee State University. At the age of 17, Winfrey's public speaking skills helped her to win the title of the Miss Nashville Fire Prevention in a beauty and talent contest. Her win helped her to land a part-time job with a local black radio station, WVOL. At 19 years old and still a sophomore at college, Winfrey became the youngest, and the first black news anchor at Nashville's WTVF-TV. In 1976, she moved to Baltimore's WJZ-TV, where she worked first as a reporter, then coanchor for the six o'clock news. She then switched to cohosting WJZ's local talk show *People Are Talking*, which premiered in 1978. Despite being neither thin nor white, her audience warmed to her chatty, informal style and the show became an instant hit.

The Queen of Daytime TV

In early 1984 Oprah moved to Chicago to host a half-hour morning talk show *A.M. Chicago*, which aired at the same time as the talk show *Donahue*. Within weeks of taking the job, Oprah took the show from last place to the number one spot in the local ratings. In September 1986, the show was extended to an hour, renamed *The Oprah Winfrey Show*, and syndicated. It soon displaced Donahue as the nation's number one daytime talk show. Within a year, Winfrey's income had soared to $30 million. The show mixed celebrity interviews with discussions of social issues, and also featured home-decorating and gift-giving ideas as well as "Oprah's Book Club," which encouraged her audience to read. Winfrey has also worked as an actress. In 1985, she received an Academy Award nomination for Best Supporting Actress for her part in the Steven Spielberg's movie *The Color Purple* (1985). She also produced and starred in *Beloved* (1998). She founded Harpo (Oprah spelled backward) Productions as well as cofounding the women's cable television network Oxygen. In 2002, she launched the lifestyle magazine *O, The Oprah Magazine*. Winfrey donated ten percent of her income to charities, mostly in connection with young people and education.

The Winfrey Style

Winfrey brought a freshness and honesty to the world of television. Although rival host Phil Donahue pioneered the technique of moving among the audience, mic-in-hand, Winfrey's style was more intimate and confessional. She shared the tales of her poverty-stricken childhood, promiscuous adolescence, drug abuse, and weight problems with her audience, down to the most painful details. Listeners and guests related to her as a friend. Celebrity stars revealed details of their lives that had hitherto been kept secret, including Michael Jackson's tearful confession of abuse at the hands of his father. Her conversations with guests seemed real and unscripted, more akin to a proper talk between friends. Winfrey cried when stories moved her, and held hands with her guests.

#33

Oprah Winfrey has long been considered one of the most powerful and influential women in the US. Her early endorsement of the Democratic primary candidate Barack Obama in 2006 is widely held to have been influential in securing Obama the presidential nomination.

▼

REWRITING HISTORY

Without the focus and leadership provided by General de Gaulle following his 1940 radio announcement that "France has lost a battle, but France has not lost the war," the various French resistance forces might never have become as coordinated, organized, and effective as they did.

CHARLES DE GAULLE (1890–1970)

President of France

Soldier; author; politician; leader of the Free French resistance movement in World War II; founding father of the French Fifth Republic; a key player in the emergence of modern France

Fiercely patriotic and with a keen sense of his country's history, Charles de Gaulle rose to the occasion as a savior of France's honor during its occupation by Nazi Germany. In the postwar years, as its President for more than a decade, he showed his countrymen that they could again hold their heads high in Europe and internationally.

French Foremost

Charles André Joseph Marie de Gaulle was born in Lille, in northern France, into an aristocratic, Catholic, monarchist family. Many of his forebears had played roles in France's military history, and his father (a teacher of mathematics and philosophy) fought in the Franco-Prussian War, in which the French army was soundly defeated. The young de Gaulle was brought up to believe in the greatness of France and in the importance of restoring it to its rightful place as a leader among nations. After attending Catholic schools, in 1909 Charles de Gaulle entered the École Spéciale Militaire de Saint-Cyr, an elite officer training college, and he distinguished himself as a junior officer in World War I. Under the command of Marshal Philippe Pétain, whom de Gaulle deeply admired, he was wounded in the Battle of Verdun in 1916, taken prisoner and held in a German prisoner of war camp, from which he repeatedly escaped only to be recaptured.

Between the Wars

Charles de Gaulle studied the tactics and the organization of the German military both during and after the war, when he attended general-staff school, and he made a name for himself for his criticisms of static trench warfare and his advocacy of a more mobile military strategy using planes and armored vehicles. He gave lectures and wrote several books on this and other military subjects, including leadership qualities and the future of the French army. His opinions, which were contrary to those of the military mainstream, hindered his chances of promotion, and by the start of World War II he had risen only to the rank of colonel.

#32

Man of the Moment

In the summer of 1940, after de Gaulle's 4th Armored Division had launched one of the few French counterattacks against a German army whose "blitzkrieg" tactics, ironically, echoed those that he had advocated, he was promoted to Brigadier General. He was then brought into the War Cabinet by French Prime Minister Paul Reynaud, along with Marshal Pétain, in the hopes of revitalizing the morale of the French Army. However, defeat soon seemed inevitable. Pétain was made head of state and promptly signed an armistice with the Nazis that gave them control of most of France and established Pétain as puppet head of the Vichy Government. In disgust, de Gaulle escaped to London, and from there, with the support of Winston Churchill, he issued a now-famous rallying cry on BBC radio for the French to resist the German occupation, establishing him as leader of the resistance movement and placing him firmly on the political map.

◀ *Charles de Gaulle pictured with General Eisenhower. Despite leading the Free French forces during World War II, some within Allied command viewed de Gaulle with distrust. The sentiment was often reciprocated.*

President of the Fifth Republic

When the Germans were pushed out of France in 1944 and the Free French forces entered Paris, he was a natural choice to lead the country, and he presided over two interim governments in which he strove to prevent the allies taking control of France. However, he soon found himself at odds with the rest of France's political leaders and he resigned in early 1946. Not until 1958, with the collapse of the Fourth Republic, did he return to power. As head of the Fifth Republic of France for the next 11 years, with strong and newly created presidential powers, he did much to raise France's profile internationally and strengthen its economy. He "liberated" many of France's colonial territories, including Algeria, maintained a neutral (often seen as anti-American) position on Vietnam, opposed British influence in Europe, and actively distanced France from a range of alliances, such as NATO and the Atlantic Alliance. He was removed from power in 1969, in the wake of the previous year's labor and student uprising, but many positive aspects of France's role on the world stage today are due to the achievements of his presidency.

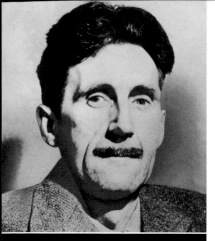

GEORGE ORWELL (1903–1950)

Novelist and Essayist

Used his experiences as a member of the Indian Imperial Police to write his first novel; took part in the Spanish Civil War; wrote two of the most popular satirical novels in the English language

- Politics & Leadership
- Science & Technology
- Popular Culture & the Arts
- Business & Commerce
- **Writers & Thinkers**

George Orwell is the pseudonym of novelist and essayist Eric Blair. His is most famous for his satirical works *Animal Farm* and *Nineteen Eighty-Four*, though he also wrote extensively as an essayist and periodical columnist. Most of Orwell's work is of a political nature, and attacks totalitarian regimes, middle-class attitudes, and imperialism.

The Colonial Experience

George Orwell was born Eric Arthur Blair in Motihari, Bengal, India, during the period of British rule in India. His father Richard Walmesley Blair worked in the opium department of the Indian Civil Service. His mother Ida Mabel Blair had been raised in Burma. When Orwell was four years old, his mother took the family back to live in England, where they settled in Henley-on-Thames. His father remained in India until 1912, and saw his son only briefly in the intervening years. Orwell was educated at St Cyprian's School, a private establishment in Eastbourne, Sussex. It was his experiences at this school that helped him to formulate many of his views on the English class system. He later wrote an essay about his unhappy time at the school, which was posthumously published as *Such, Such Were the Joys*. He won a scholarship to the prestigious Eton College, where he was an unexceptional student. After leaving school, Orwell joined the Indian Imperial Police and was posted to Burma. In 1927 he contracted dengue fever and was sent home to England to recuperate. While on leave, Orwell decided to resign from the Indian Imperial Police to become a writer, a career that had interested him from an early age. Orwell's Burma experiences became the basis for his novel *Burmese Days* (1934) and the essays "A Hanging" (1931) and "Shooting an Elephant" (1936).

From Down and Out to Published Author

Orwell wanted to write about people and places far removed from his own middle-class background, so he moved to London where he visited the poorer parts of the city, even dressing as a tramp for a period. Orwell used his experiences to write his first published essay "The Spike" (1931). In the

◀◀ REWRITING HISTORY

George Orwell is generally credited as being the first person to use the term "cold war" to denote the state of tension that existed between the Soviet Union and the Western powers in the postwar period. He used the term in an essay entitled "You and the Atomic Bomb," describing "a State which was at once unconquerable and in a permanent state of 'cold war' with its neighbors."

spring of 1928, Orwell moved to Paris, where he lived in a working-class district and took employment as a kitchen porter and dishwasher. He wrote two novels during his time, but both are lost. Toward the end of 1929, he became ill with pneumonia and returned to his parents' home in Suffolk, where he remained for the following five years. Orwell began teaching to earn a living, while still continuing to write.

In 1933, he had his first book published under the *nom de plume* George Orwell, which he took from the name of a river in Suffolk. *Down and Out in Paris and London* (1933), which drew on his experiences in the last years of the '20s, was well received and went on to be published in New York. Three more novels followed; *Burmese Days* (1934), *A Clergyman's Daughter* (1935) and *Keep the Aspidistra Flying* (1936). Orwell's *The Road to Wigan Pier* (1937)

established his reputation as a political writer. Commissioned by the Left Wing Book Club, the book is divided into two parts; the first part details the social conditions in parts of northern England; the second part is an essay on class and socialism. Orwell spent some months in the north of England researching material for the book, visiting people's homes and investigating the social conditions of poor working-class communities. In 1936, Orwell married teacher and journalist Eileen O'Shaughnessy, a marriage that was to have a major influence on his writings.

The Spanish Civil War

Shortly after his marriage, Orwell left to fight in the Spanish Civil War on the side of the Republicans. On the way to Spain, he stopped off in Paris where he dined with fellow writer Henry Miller. Orwell joined the militia of the Workers' Party of Marxist Unification (POUM), and later the British Independent Labour Party contingent (ILP) and fought on the Aragon Front. Eileen also traveled to Spain and worked as a volunteer in the offices of the ILP. In May 1937, Orwell was hit in the throat by a sniper, the bullet just missing his main artery. While he was recovering, the POUM was declared illegal by pro-Soviet communists, and Orwell and Eileen fled Spain. The infighting between various leftist factions had a profound effect on Orwell's writing and marked the beginning of his ascendancy as a revolutionary socialist and critique of the communist regime. On his return to England, Orwell wrote *Homage to Catalonia* (1938). He planned to travel to India

◀ *Orwell's gravestone is located in All Saints' Churchyard, Sutton Courtenay, Oxfordshire. His epitaph reads "Here lies Eric Arthur Blair, born 25 June 1903, died 21 January 1950", with no indication of his more famous pseudonym.*

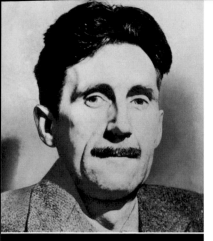

- Politics & Leadership

- Science & Technology

- Popular Culture & the Arts

- Business & Commerce

- **Writers & Thinkers**

▶ *George Orwell's most famous novel* **Nineteen Eighty-Four** *has twice been adapted for the cinema. This is a still from the 1956 movie, which starred Edmond O'Brien as Winston Smith. The more recent adaptation, made aptly enough in 1984, featured Richard Burton in the leading role.*

to take up work on a newspaper there but in March 1938 he fell ill with tuberculosis. He spent the summer months recuperating at a sanitarium before travelling to Morocco to escape the harsh British winter. He wrote *Coming Up for Air* (1939) while living in Casablanca.

World War II

When war broke out in Europe in 1939, Orwell's wife Eileen moved to London to work in the censorship department. Orwell volunteered for the war but was declared unfit for military service. He later served in the Home Guard. He continued writing essays, including "Inside the Whale" (1940), and also wrote reviews for plays, movies, and books for various periodicals including *The Listener*. London life suited Orwell and he had a wide variety of literary and political friends, primarily among left-wing circles. In August 1941, Orwell started working for the BBC's Eastern Service, which broadcast cultural programs to India. In 1942, he also started writing for the left-wing weekly *Tribune*, becoming literary editor the following year. In 1943 Orwell resigned from his job at the BBC to concentrate on writing his new book, *Animal Farm*, which was ready for publication in 1944. Its controversial political content, however, made it difficult for Orwell to find a publisher and he had his manuscript refused four times. In early 1945, Orwell was invited by David Astor to become a war correspondent for *The Observer*, a challenge he readily accepted. While he was on assignment in Europe, Orwell's wife died under anesthetic whilst undergoing a hysterectomy. In August the same year, *Animal Farm* was finally published by Secker and Warbury. The book was inspired by Orwell's experiences with communists during the Civil War and Orwell described the work as his novel "contre Stalin" and it can be seen to reflect Russian society in the period after the revolution. As such, the book is a satirical account of Stalinist totalitarianism, in which "all animals are equal but some animals are more equal than others." It tells the story of a dystopian society in which any hope of a better world through means of revolution is destroyed by the greed, corruption, and wickedness of its revolutionary leaders. It enjoyed worldwide acclaim and made Orwell a much sought-after writer.

The Masterwork

Orwell immersed himself in work, publishing over a hundred articles in the year following Eileen's death and beginning work on his magnum opus, *Nineteen Eighty-Four* (1949). Written shortly before he died, whilst living on the remote Scottish island of Jura in the Inner Hebrides, and despite being seriously ill with tuberculosis, *Nineteen Eighty-Four* tells the story of Winston Smith, a lowly civil servant working for "the Party"—a repressive totalitarian regime that seeks to control every aspect of the individual's life under the banner "War is Peace; Freedom is Slavery; Ignorance is Strength." Working in the Ministry of Truth, Smith's job involves censoring historical records in order to perpetuate the myth of the all-powerful Party. Set in a nightmare world in which three competing superpowers—Oceania, Eurasia, and Eastasia—wage continual war with one another, Smith becomes the victim of a society in which individual liberty is ruthlessly crushed under the pretext of protecting national security. Having attempted to break free from the suffocating constraints placed on him by the Party, Smith is eventually captured, tortured, and ultimately forced to renounce his personal beliefs in deference to the state ideology.

The enduring appeal of Orwell's masterpiece lies in its relevance to subsequent generations, who often hold *Nineteen Eighty-Four* up as a warning against the concentration of power in the hands of unaccountable elites. Concepts such as "Big Brother," "Doublethink," "Thought Police," and "Room 101" have entered into the English vernacular, as has the adjective "Orwellian," which is used to describe authoritarian tendencies. Although very much a product of the political climate in the postwar world, Orwell's novel retains its prescience today, whether in the context of widespread CCTV surveillance in countries such as England, or the growing corporate influence over mainstream media. Its ongoing success cements George Orwell's place as a preeminent social commentator of his time and one of the most influential writers of the twentieth century. He died in 1950, at the age of just 46, in University College Hospital, London.

#31

"Those who control the present control the past, and those who control the past control the future."
George Orwell

CHARLIE CHAPLIN (1889–1977)

Actor, Scriptwriter, Director, and Producer

Early career in vaudeville; toured with Stan Laurel in the US; made 30 movies for the Keystone Studio; established United Artists; awarded three Academy Awards; honored with a KBE

- Politics & Leadership
- Science & Technology
- **Popular Culture & the Arts**
- Business & Commerce
- Writers & Thinkers

 REWRITING HISTORY

Chaplin's mother suffered from mental illness and spent spells in an asylum. During these periods, Charlie and his brother Syd were forced to live in various paupers' institutions, an experience that would later inspire many of Chaplin's downtrodden characters. In 1921, Chaplin took his mother out of care and moved her to California, where she remained until her death seven years later.

One of the greatest stars of the silent-movie era, Charlie Chaplin had a career in the entertainment business that lasted more than 65 years. His "Little Tramp" character is one of the most recognizable figures in cinematic history, and continues to delight audiences today. He had a high-profile and often controversial life, falling out of favor after World War II, but later regaining the public acclaim that he so deserved.

Starting out in Vaudeville

Charlie Chaplin was born in 1889 in London, England, the son of music hall entertainers Charles and Hannah Chaplin. His father moved out when Chaplin was three years old, leaving him and his elder brother Syd in the care of their mother. Hannah attempted to continue her stage career but a problem with her larynx often caused her voice to break at unexpected moments. On one occasion, the five-year-old Chaplin was called to the stage to take her place, marking his entertainment debut. Three years later he had a part in a touring musical, *The Eight Lancashire Lads*. When he was 18, Chaplin began touring with Fred Karno's vaudeville troupe, and in 1910 he went to the US with the company. Chaplin shared a room with fellow troupe member Stan Laurel.

Hollywood Beckons

In 1913, Hollywood producer Mack Sennett saw Chaplin perform and offered him a contract at Keystone Studio. His first movie, *Making a Living*, was released in 1914. His next movie established Chaplin as a major comedy actor. For the movie, *Kid Auto Races at Venice*, Chaplin devised the little tramp character that was to become his trademark. His costume came courtesy of fellow actors; he took Fatty Arbuckle's oversized trousers and teamed them with Arbuckle's father-in-law's trilby, Ford Sterling's giant size-14 shoes, and Chester Conklin's tiny tailcoat. He made the mustache from crepe hair belonging to Mack Swain. Chaplin provided the cane himself. Chaplin made 35 movies for Keystone before moving to Essanay Company in 1915, where he made a further 15 movies. In 1916, he signed up with Mutual to make

12 of his most famous movies. In 1918, Chaplin signed with First National and opened his own studio. The following year, Chaplin collaborated with Douglas Fairbanks, Mary Pickford, and DW Griffin to form United Artists.

Disenchantment with America

In 1940, Chaplin made his first talkie, *The Great Dictator*, which poked fun at the Nazi regime. Although considered by many to be in poor taste, the movie grossed $5 million and was nominated for five Academy Awards. During World War II, Chaplin, who had not taken out US citizenship, found himself criticized by the British people for not supporting the war effort. He was later investigated by the FBI for supposed communist sentiments and denied re-entry to the States after an overseas visit in 1952. This, together with much-publicized controversy over his love life, resulted in Chaplin moving permanently to Switzerland. Twenty years later, Chaplin returned from exile to accept an Honorary Academy Award, for which he received a five-minute standing ovation. In 1975, his social rehabilitation was complete when he became a Knight of the British Empire.

Chaplin's Contribution to Cinema

Chaplin is considered one of the greatest comedians of all time, gracing his movies with a depth of meaning that contrasted vividly with the superficial slapstick comedy of his contemporaries. A master of pathos, Chaplin appealed to the masses during the difficult intervening war years, understanding the difficulties faced by the poor and destitute, while providing much needed comic relief. His movies were also subtly subversive; in Chaplin's pictures the underdog comes out on top when faced with the pompous bureaucrat. For the majority of his movies, Chaplin worked without a script, developing the story line from a vague idea that took on a life of its own, allowing Chaplin to improvise at will. A noted perfectionist, Chaplin would reshoot scenes constantly until he was completely satisfied, always working to get the very best out of his actors. The result is a body of work that includes such classics as *The Pawnshop* (1916), *The Gold Rush* (1925), the Academy Award winning *Modern Times* (1936), and *Limelight* (1952), in which he appeared with Buster Keaton.

Charlie Chaplin enjoyed a career that spanned more than 70 years. Success came early to the British-born comedian and, by the age of 30 years, he had starred in over 60 silent movies and had opened his own movie studio.
▼

BILL GATES (b. 1955)

Chairman of the Microsoft Corporation

One of the architects of the personal computing revolution; author of the operating systems for IBM-PCs; founder and former CEO and chief software architect of the Microsoft Corporation

- Politics & Leadership
- Science & Technology
- Popular Culture & the Arts
- **Business & Commerce**
- Writers & Thinkers

Bill Gates realized early that success in IT lay not in the manufacture of hardware but in the development of software. He coauthored the MS-DOS operating system for the IBM-PC, and has since monopolized the world's software market with Windows and other computer applications for the past three decades.

The Ultimate Computer Nerd

William Henry "Bill" Gates III, also know as "Trey," was born into a privileged family: his father was a lawyer and his mother, a banker. He discovered his interest in computing while attending the exclusive Lakeside School, where he showed a remarkable aptitude in programming the large mainframe computers of the day. As a teenager Gates was hired by the Computer Center Corporation to develop software, and he also wrote a class-scheduling program for Lakeside that ensured that he was placed in classes with a majority of female students. He graduated in 1973 with an almost 100 percent score on his Scholastic Aptitude Test, giving him an IQ of 170, and was enrolled at the US's most prestigious ivy league college, Harvard. At Harvard, Gates met his future business partners Steve Ballmer and Bill Allen and established links with Micro Instrumentation and Telemetry Systems (MITS), which was the manufacturer of one of the world's first microcomputer, the Altair 8800, the ancestor of the modern desktop PC.

Back to BASIC

In 1975, the 20-year-old Gates took a leave of absence from Harvard to work on a form of the programming language BASIC for the Altair 8800 that MITS was manufacturing in Albuquerque, New Mexico. Gates and collaborator Allen developed Altair BASIC, which was the first product of their newly formed partnership, "Micro-soft," which they registered as a trade name in November 1976 (minus the hyphen) as the now world-famous Microsoft. From then on, there was no turning back. Gates never returned to Harvard to complete his undergraduate degree, but his alma mater did award him an honorary doctorate in 2007, when he was listed as the richest man on earth, worth an estimated $55 billion dollars—not bad for a college dropout! Gates and Allen moved the fledgling Microsoft from Albuquerque to Bellevue, Washington, in January 1979, where he continued to develop software for several computer systems. Until then, software had been distributed free with the hardware, but Gates established the principle that software should be paid for, which earned him the enmity of many in the tight-knit world of hobby computing.

A Match Made in Silicon Heaven

The year 1980 witnessed Microsoft's big break. US computer giant IBM, then the world's largest manufacturer of mainframe computers, approached Gates to write BASIC software for its forthcoming first-generation personal computer, the IBM-PC. In the end, Gates produced the PC-DOS operating system for the new machine, but importantly he insisted that Microsoft keep the copyright because he was sure that other manufacturers would produce IBM-PC clones that would also need DOS. His hunch was correct, and the licensing and sales of MS-DOS made Microsoft one of the leading players in the software and operating system market. The first version of Microsoft Windows went on sale in 1985, and it remains the world's most widespread operating system. At the same time, Microsoft developed software applications, such as Word and Excel, which quickly became established as the industry cross-platform standard.

◀ The Microsoft brand is one of the most recognizable in the world, with its flagship operating system Windows used in computers across the globe.

The Gates Way

Bill Gates' management style and business practices have faced a fair amount of criticism and earned him several anti-trust lawsuits in the US and Europe. He has ruthlessly maintained Microsoft's position in the industry, brushing aside rivals such as Apple-Macintosh, whose OS many hold to be superior to Windows. Gates did not invent the personal computer, operating systems, or software applications—all of these developments would have occurred without him. His lasting contribution was to impose compatibility on millions of computers and computer networks worldwide through their shared Microsoft operating systems and applications. In the final analysis, what made Gates his billions has also made possible the astounding growth of personal computing and the World Wide Web in the past 20 years.

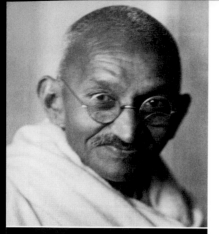

MOHANDAS GANDHI (1869–1948)

Political and Spiritual Leader of India

Pioneer of nonviolent civil disobedience movements; agitated for Indian civil rights in South Africa; led the "Quit India" movement against British rule

- **Politics & Leadership**
- ■ Science & Technology
- ■ Popular Culture & the Arts
- ■ Business & Commerce
- ■ Writers & Thinkers

◄◄ REWRITING HISTORY

Whenever we think of Gandhi, we picture a man dressed simply in a homespun yarn dhoti and shawl. Gandhi urged Indians from all castes, both men and women, to spend part of each day spinning. Their action, he said, would restore self-respect and help free India from dependence on foreign-made goods.

Popularly known as Mahatma ("Great Soul"), Mohandas Gandhi started a worldwide movement aimed at putting an end to colonialism. He began his campaign as a young lawyer in South Africa but returned to India where he spent the remainder of his life seeking to improve the lot of all Indians as well as working to end Raj rule.

Early Influences

Born in India during the time of the Raj, Mohandas Karamchand Gandhi grew up in Probander, in present-day Gujarat state. He left India in 1888 to study law in England, where he met members of the Theosophical Society, who introduced him to the Hindu classical scripture, the Bhagavad Gita—a work that was to have a profound effect on Gandhi. The epic poem calls upon the reader to undertake the battle of righteousness through selfless devotion to the service of fellow men. Gandhi returned to India in 1891, where he set up a law practice. The venture was largely unsuccessful, however, and in 1893 he accepted an offer from an Indian businessman, Dada Abdulla, to work as his legal adviser in the Colony of Natal, South Africa.

Satyagraha

Although he intended to remain in South Africa for a year only, Gandhi ended up staying there for over 20 years. During this time, he became aware at first hand of the racism that characterized colonial rule. Thrown off a train at Pietermaritzburg for refusing to move to a "colored" carriage, barred from hotels, and ordered to remove his turban in court by a Durban magistrate, these incidents opened Gandhi's eyes to the social injustices of British imperial rule. He resolved to fight these ills through the twin principles of what he called *satyagraha*, the force of truth and love, and the ancient Hindu ideal of *ahimsa*, or nonviolence, to all living things. In 1906, he called upon the Indian population of South Africa to stage nonviolent protest against a proposed Transvaal act that would enforce registration of every South African of Indian descent. He vowed that "Indians will stagger humanity without shedding a drop of blood."

Return to India

Gandhi returned to his homeland in 1915, where he became familiar with the injustices present in Indian society firstly through his contact with Congress Party leader Gopal Gokhale. In 1918, Gandhi became involved in the Champaran and Kheda struggles, when—with his help—Indian farmers successfully protested against the poor working conditions and high taxes imposed by their, primarily British, landlords. Gandhi's fame and reputation spread throughout the nation as a result. In 1919, the British Indian Army opened fire on a crowd of unarmed Indian protesters at Jallianwala Bagh in Amritsar, killing hundreds of innocent civilians. Gandhi responded with a resolution that criticized both the British Raj and the retaliatory actions of the Indians, and called for an end to violence by both sides. Gandhi assumed

leadership of the Indian National Congress in 1921 and began pushing his resolution of Swaraj, complete independence, both spiritual and political, from foreign domination. With this aim, Gandhi initiated the non-cooperation rule, which called upon Indians to boycott anything British, including schools, courts, jobs, honors, and goods. The movement came to an abrupt halt in 1922 after nationalists killed 23 policemen in Chauri Chaura, Uttar Pradesh. Gandhi was subsequently tried for sedition and imprisoned for six years. Released after only two years due to poor health, Gandhi went on to lead, in 1930, the Dandi Salt March in protest at a British law forbidding Indians from making their own salt. Deeply unsettled, the British responded by imprisoning over 60,000 people. Public opinion forced the British to negotiate with Gandhi, however, resulting in the signing of the Gandhi-Irwin Pact in 1931. In the 1930s, Gandhi worked hard to improve the lives of the Untouchables, those of the lowest castes whom he renamed *Harijan*, "Children of God." During World War II, Gandhi recognized the weak position of the Raj and in 1942 moved to endorse the "Quit India" campaign. The campaign quickly erupted into violence on an unprecedented scale, and Gandhi and the entire Congress Working Party were arrested. Gandhi remained in prison until May 1944. By the end of the war, it had become clear that Britain would relinquish control of India and Gandhi called off the campaign. India became independent on August 15, 1947 but the simultaneous creation of Pakistan marred the celebrations for Gandhi who believed that Muslims and Hindus could live side by side in peace. Gandhi was assassinated in 1948 by a Hindu extremist.

#28

◀ *After studying law in London, Mohandas Gandhi returned to India where he established a law practice. He enjoyed limited success, however, and soon left for a position in South Africa.*

JOSEPH STALIN (1878–1953)

General Secretary of the Communist Party, 1922–53

Created the Soviet Union's planned command economy; defeated Nazi Germany on the eastern front; built the "Iron Curtain" and triggered the Cold War and nuclear arms race

- **Politics & Leadership**

- **Science & Technology**

- **Popular Culture & the Arts**

- **Business & Commerce**

- **Writers & Thinkers**

REWRITING HISTORY

Had Joseph Stalin been born after the collapse of the Soviet Union, he would not even be Russian—he was a native of the republic of Georgia, which declared independence from its former master in 1991.

Lenin planned and carried out the Bolshevik revolution of 1917, and preserved the country from civil war and foreign invasion, but he died in 1924, his work barely begun. The man who was responsible for the creation of the USSR as the great rival of the US during the five decades of the Cold War was his successor, Joseph Stalin.

The Rise of "Uncle Joe"

Although his early life was marked by repeated hardships and personal tragedies, Stalin excelled at school. After graduation, the young Stalin became involved in revolutionary politics. Repeatedly arrested, imprisoned, and exiled by the secret police, he joined Lenin's Bolshevik faction in 1904, quickly rising through the ranks of the movement. After the tsar's overthrow in a democratic coup in February 1917, Lenin seized power in the Bolshevik revolution of November that same year. After a botched assassination attempt, Lenin's health began to fail, and he looked for a successor. He appointed Stalin as General Secretary of the Communist Party, a post that he would hold until his death in 1953. When Lenin finally died in 1924, Stalin was head of Russia's Politburo, but he was not yet a dictator. Within a decade, however, he had liquidated all his political rivals and had achieved absolute power.

Stalin's first task was to rebuild the Russian economy, shattered by a decade of war and revolution. He placed industry and business under state control and instituted a series of "Five Year Plans," setting strict targets for industrial production and growth. Despite early setbacks, Stalin's policies succeeded in modernizing Russia's backward economy in time to face the industrial might of Germany in World War II. Much less successful was his collectivization of agriculture in 1928, which led to famines that killed millions. On the political front, by the mid-1930s Stalin had achieved absolute power, and in 1936 he began a two-year reign of terror to eliminate his rivals and opponents. Historians estimate that during the "Great Purge" up to 700,000 people were executed and many more were deported to Siberian labor camps. Estimates of the total number of Stalin's victims during his 30-year rule range from six to ten million. Despite this staggering death toll, Stalin's rule also had beneficial effects. For the first time in history, Russian women were given equal rights to men, and free education and health care improved the lot of the general population. During his stewardship, the Russian economy grew, raising living standards for the Communist faithful at least.

Drawing the Iron Curtain

Stalin's greatest achievement in the eyes of many Russians, even today, was his defeat of Nazi Germany. Hitler's suicidal attack on Russia in 1941 diverted considerable manpower and hardware eastward and enabled the beleaguered British to hold on until the US entered the war. After the defeat of Germany in 1945, a new balance of power emerged, with the US-backed democratic Europe on one side and the Soviet-backed Eastern Bloc on the other. In

1945, British premier Winston Churchill coined the term "Iron Curtain" to describe the new geopolitical reality. Not content with his gains in Europe, Stalin challenged British and American hegemony in Asia, Africa, Latin America, and the Middle East, fomenting revolutionary movements and supporting the North Koreans in their war against the US-backed South.

◀ In November 1943, the leaders of the Soviet Union, the US, and the UK came together at the Tehran Conference in Iran. It was the first meeting of the Big Three during World War II. Here Joseph Stalin is seen with representatives from the other Allied powers outside the Russian Embassy in Tehran.

Living in Stalin's Shadow

Had Lenin not died after a botched assassination attempt, Russia might have taken a different political course—still Marxist-Leninist, no doubt, but not necessarily of the brutal totalitarian kind promoted by Stalin. Alternatively, if Hitler had stuck to his non-aggression pact, he might have succeeded in imposing a peace on Britain and the US, and the subsequent history of Western Europe and the world might now be very different, with three power blocs: Communist Russia, Fascist continental Europe, and democratic Anglo-America. Setting aside this intriguing alternate history, Stalin's actions indirectly dictated American domestic and foreign policy. The spectre of the "Red Menace" prompted US policy to lurch to the right, leading to the excesses of McCarthyism at home, and overseas, to the backing of repressive, undemocratic, right-wing dictatorships, including apartheid South Africa and Chile's murderous Pinochet Regime.

ERNESTO "CHE" GUEVARA (1928–1967)

Marxist Revolutionary, Guerilla Leader, and Politician

One of the primary leaders of the Cuban Revolution; served as a minister in Castro's government; led guerilla movements in the Congo and Bolivia; wrote a manual on the theories of guerilla warfare

- Politics & Leadership
- Science & Technology
- Popular Culture & the Arts
- Business & Commerce
- Writers & Thinkers

 REWRITING HISTORY

After his execution, Che Guevara's body was buried in a secret communal grave. In 1995, a former general in the Bolivian army revealed its whereabouts. Thirty years after his death, Che's remains were taken from their communal grave in Vallegrande and reinterred in a mausoleum in Santa Clara, Cuba, the site of his decisive victory over Batista forces in the Cuban Revolution.

Four decades after his death, Che Guevara remains a global symbol of revolution and counterculture. Alberto Korda's monochrome of Che is one of most famous images in the world, adorning posters and T-shirts, and inspiring revolutionary zeal the world over. Che remains a controversial figure, lauded by many as the ultimate *Guerrillero Heroico*, despised by others as a ruthless executioner.

Revolutionary Roots

Of Irish and Spanish descent, Ernesto Guevara was born in 1928 in Rosario, Argentina, the eldest of five children. Guevara was introduced to politics at an early age, both through reading the works of left-wing figures such as Karl Marx and poet Pablo Neruda and also through the Republican Spanish Civil War veterans who frequently visited the Guevara home. In 1948, Guevara enrolled at the University of Buenos Aires to study medicine. Three years later, he took a break from studying to travel through Latin America on a motorcycle. The poverty and social injustices that he encountered during his year-long journey had a major effect on the young Guevara, convincing him that he could do more for the world through revolutionary struggle than by becoming a doctor. Nonetheless, Guevara completed his studies, graduating in 1953. Later that same year, he travelled to Guatemala, witnessing the CIA-sponsored coup against Jacobo Arbenz's left-wing government in 1954, which cemented his hatred of the US.

Castro and the Cuban Revolution

Guevara moved to Mexico, where he met Fidel and Raul Castro, who were planning to overthrow the Batista government in Cuba. Guevara immediately joined their 26th of July Movement as a combat medic. The revolutionaries invaded Cuba in November 1956, but were attacked by Batista's army shortly after landing. The bloody battle that followed persuaded Guevara to abandon his medical kit in favor of the rifle. The surviving rebels made it to the Sierra Maestra mountains, where they became the nucleus of the guerilla army that would eventually topple the Batista regime. In the armed struggle

that followed, Guevara displayed such great bravery and skill that Castro
made him *Comandante*, the only one apart from Castro himself. Guevara
was a ruthless and feared disciplinarian during the campaign, unhesitatingly
shooting deserters and informers, but was also much admired for his moral
and intelligent leadership. Guevara played a pivotal role in the final battles
during the revolution, earning the appreciation of both allies and enemies
alike for his skillful deployment of guerilla tactics. Despite his men being
outnumbered ten to one, Guevara led the rebels to victory, taking over the
capital Havana in January 1959.

Continuing the Revolutionary Road

After the revolution, Guevara's first role in the Castro government was as
commander of La Cabaña Fortress, where he was responsible for issuing
death warrants for those considered war criminals or traitors, often without
a fair trial. He then served as president of the National Bank of Cuba and
later as Minister of Industry. He was instrumental in fostering Cuba's
close ties with the Soviet Union, and played a key part in the installation
of Soviet ballistic missiles, which precipitated the Cuban Missile Crisis in
1962. More importantly, he was one of Castro's closest confidantes, and did
much to influence the direction of Cuban affairs in the early postrevolution
phase, leading *Time* magazine to call him "Castro's Brain." More of an active
revolutionary figure than a government man, Guevara left Cuba in 1965
to direct a guerilla movement in the Congo and later in Bolivia. In 1967,
Guevara was captured and executed by the Bolivian army.

The Legacy of Che Guevara

Che Guevara fought and died for his beliefs, never straying
from the revolutionary path and never compromising his
ideals. As such, he remains a heroic figure and a role model for
revolutionary movements everywhere. He wrote extensively,
leaving behind a body of work that includes *Guerra de Guerillas*,
an instruction manual for guerilla warfare. He is still a national
hero in Cuba, where school children begin each day with the
pledge *Seremos como el Che* ("We will be like Che"). His death at
the age of 39 in the Bolivian jungle only further enhanced his
heroic stature, making him as potent in death as he was in life.

#26

*More than 40 years after
his death, the fatigue-
clad Che Guevara remains
an iconic figure for
revolutionary struggles
all over the world. The
guerilla leader has been
an inspiration to many
others in the fight for
social justice.*
▼

WOODROW WILSON (1856–1924)

President of the United States

President of Princeton University; elected Governor of New Jersey; became the 28th US President; took the US into World War I; introduced his 14 Points Peace Program; helped to establish the League of Nations; won the Nobel Prize for Peace

 Politics & Leadership

■ Science & Technology

■ Popular Culture & the Arts

■ Business & Commerce

■ Writers & Thinkers

REWRITING HISTORY

Had Wilson's 14 Points Peace Program been fully implemented in the Treaty of Versailles, the horrors of World War II may have been avoided. Many historians point to the harsh and punitive terms imposed on Germany as a leading cause for the rise of Adolf Hitler and the Nazi Party.

Woodrow Wilson served two terms as President of the United States. He was a leading proponent of progressive reform, establishing anti-trust laws and reorganizing the banking institutions. His second term in office was dominated by the entry of America into World War I. His peace proposals formed the basis of the Versailles Treaty and established the League of Nations.

The Road to the White House

Of Irish-Scots and Scots ancestry, Thomas Woodrow Wilson was born in 1856 in Staunton, Virginia, the son of a Presbyterian minister. His father served as a pastor in Augusta, Georgia, during the Civil War, and the young Wilson experienced the horrors of war at an early age. During Reconstruction, the Wilson family moved to Columbia, South Carolina, where Wilson's father worked as a professor at the Columbia Theological Seminary. Wilson could not read before the age of ten years, probably due to undiagnosed dyslexia, but self-discipline and hard work earned him a place at Davidson College in North Carolina. He transferred to Princeton University, graduating with a BA in 1879. He spent a year at Law School at the University of Virginia then took graduate studies at John Hopkins University, completing his PhD in history and political science in 1886 with his dissertation entitled "Congressional Government." Wilson lectured at Byn Mawr College and Wesleyan University before taking a post at Princeton in 1890 as Professor of Jurisprudence and Political Economy. Wilson served as President of Princeton between 1902 and 1910. He became a leading intellectual of the Progressive Era, working hard to reform education and making it less elitist. In 1910, Wilson successfully ran as Governor of New Jersey against a Republican candidate. As Governor, Wilson made wide-ranging progressive reforms, earning the attention and admiration of the nation. In 1912 he stood as the Democratic candidate for president, running a campaign based on his New Freedom reform program. He easily defeated William H. Taft and Theodore Roosevelt, who split the Republican vote, to become the nation's 28th president.

Presidency

Once in office, Wilson began implementing the reforms that he had outlined in his election campaign. He lowered tariffs and introduced graduated Federal income tax. He revised the banking system and established a Federal Trade Commission to prohibit unfair business practices. He introduced legislation to ban child labor and limit the working day of railroad workers to eight hours. When war broke out in Europe in 1914, Wilson determined to keep America out of the conflict, maintaining neutrality, even in the face of the sinking of US liner RMS Lusitania in 1915. In 1916, the "He Kept Us Out of War" slogan helped to win his reelection to the presidency. One year later, that all changed when the Germans began an unrestricted submarine campaign threatening US commercial shipping. In April 2, 1917, Wilson delivered a war message to Congress, formally asking for America's entry into the war. Wilson marshaled a massive war effort, which gradually tipped the scales in the favor of the Allies.

Wilson the Idealist

Wilson may have taken America into the war but he worked tirelessly to secure peace. On January 8, 1918, Wilson presented his 14 Points Peace Program to Congress. The first five points dealt with general principles, including arms reductions and freedom of the seas. Points 6 to 13 were specific to the ongoing territorial disputes. The last point specified that "a general association of nations must be formed under specific covenants for the purpose of affording mutual guarantees of political independence and territorial integrity to great and small states alike." Although the speech was met with objections by all parties concerned in the war, it formed the basis for the terms of the Armistice. During the Paris Peace Conference in 1919, Wilson was forced to compromise on many of his ideals and the Treaty of Versailles differed greatly, both in spirit and content, from his vision of "peace without victory." He did, however, score a major victory when the Conference adopted point 14 of his program to establish the League of Nations. Although Wilson failed to get America to join the League, he was rewarded for his peace efforts with the Nobel Prize for Peace in October 1919. However, while campaigning to persuade Americans to back the League, he suffered a stroke, from which he never fully recovered. Although Wilson may have failed to get his ideas fully implemented at Versailles, his idealism struck a chord that would resonate with future generations. His vision of an international organization working multilaterally to resolve global disputes laid the foundations from which the League of Nations and, latterly, the United Nations would rise.

▲
After the end of World War I, Woodrow Wilson campaigned for a lasting peace, winning a Nobel Peace Prize for his efforts. Here he is seen taking part in the procession for the burial of an Unknown Soldier on Armistice Day in 1921.

SADDAM HUSSEIN (1937–2006)

President of Iraq

Assumed the vice presidency of Iraq after a coup brought the Ba'ath party to power; became President of Iraq; instigated the eight-year-long Iran-Iraq war; invaded Kuwait, precipitating the Gulf War; his failure to comply with UN precipitated the 2003 invasion of Iraq by a US-led coalition

- Politics & Leadership
- Science & Technology
- Popular Culture & the Arts
- Business & Commerce
- Writers & Thinkers

REWRITING HISTORY

Saddam Hussein eventually met his death by the noose but he almost died much earlier. In 1959, he was sentenced to death for his part in the attempted US-sponsored assassination of Premier Qasim but escaped justice by fleeing first to Syria, and then to Egypt.

Saddam Hussein dominated Iraqi political life for more than 35 years, becoming one of the most reviled dictators in the world. He brought economic hardship to the country, as well as fear and instability. Backed by a ferocious state police force, Saddam chose to ignore sanctions brought against his regime by the international community. His luck ran out when an American-led coalition invaded Iraq in 2003.

Road to Power

The son of a peasant family, Saddam Hussein was born in 1937 in a village near Tikrit, north of Baghdad. He was raised by his maternal uncle Khairallah Talfah, a veteran of the 1941 Anglo-Iraqi war and a fervent Arab nationalist. In 1957, Saddam joined the Ba'ath Party, an Arab nationalist and socialist party originally founded in Syria. The following year, the Iraqi King Faisal II was overthrown in an army coup led by General Abdul Karim Qasim. The Ba'athists disapproved of the new government and Saddam took part in an unsuccessful assassination plot against Qasim. Forced into exile in Egypt, Saddam returned to Iraq in 1963 after a coup led by Ba'athist officers had removed Qasim. The Ba'athists did not remain in power long, and Saddam was imprisoned, although he later escaped. Saddam established himself as a leading Ba'ath party member, forming a close allegiance with fellow Tikriti Ahman Hassan al-Bakr. He played a major part in reorganizing the party for its second shot at power, ruthlessly liquidating rivals who stood in his way. In 1968, the Ba'ath Party came to power in a bloodless coup led by al-Bakr, who became president, with Saddam as his deputy. Although only second in command, Saddam was considered the driving force behind al-Bakr and no major decisions were made without his prior knowledge and approval. By 1979 Saddam had almost total control of Iraq, though he had yet to assume the highest office. He soon gained a reputation as a ruthless and shrewd manipulator, made invincible by the creation of a police state that tortured and murdered political opponents without hesitation.

Saddam as President

Saddam's power grew, and when ill-health forced the resignation of al-Bakr in July 1979, he assumed the presidency. Once he had gained the highest office, Saddam began establishing a personality cult. Giant Saddam images appeared throughout Iraq, on the sides of buildings, in stores and airports, and on the national currency. Keen to appeal to all walks of life, Saddam appeared in many different guises, as a Bedouin, a devout Muslim, in Western suits, and even in the garb of his Kurdish enemies. To consolidate his power, Saddam created an aura of fear that permeated every aspect of society. Nobody was free from the terror that Saddam imposed on Iraq, not even his own colleagues. Any government minister that showed the slightest hint of disloyalty would be arrested in public meetings, and often executed by a firing squad made up of former colleagues. Saddam, too, sanctioned the torture of children to obtain confessions from adult relatives. The use of such tactics institutionalized fear and permitted Saddam to gain absolute power. Once seized, he worked tirelessly to preserve his authority, displaying an energy and determination that even his enemies had to admire. The high prices fetched by oil in the 1970s gave Saddam the opportunity to embark upon an ambitious economic and social modernization program. Petrochemical, and iron and steel industries were constructed and education and medical facilities expanded. A literacy campaign was implemented and the position of women improved through legislation. The military capabilities of the nation also grew rapidly, giving Iraq the largest army in the Middle East. Internationally, Iraq grew politically closer to the Soviet

◀ *Saddam Hussein was a pervasive presence during his time in power and like many tyrants before, he worked hard to establish a cult of personality. His image appeared in every niche of Iraqi society, including on the national currency.*

Union, while isolating itself from the West, with the exception of France. Saddam took a hard line on Israel, leading Arab opposition to the Camp David Accords between Israel and Egypt. Saddam clashed, too, with the Kurdish tribal peoples in Iraq. Although he agreed in 1970 to give the Kurds some degree of autonomy, the agreement broke down and Saddam authorized military action against Kurdish villages, including those in Iran. Initially the Kurds had support from Iran, and Saddam found them a difficult enemy to defeat. However, he cleverly negotiated an agreement with the Shah of Iran, brokered by Algeria, in which Iran stopped helping the Kurds in return for border modifications between the two countries.

Bringing War to Iraq

After the Iranian Revolution brought Ayatollah Khomeini to power, relations between the two countries deteriorated, due in part to Iran encouraging the Iraqi Shi'ites to rebel against Saddam. In September 1980, Saddam's army crossed the Iranian border, beginning an eight-year war between the two countries. During the war, Saddam authorized the use of chemical weapons against both the Iranian army and the Kurdish civilians in the north of Iraq, killing and maiming thousands. Around a million people died in the long and bitter conflict. The war ended in a stalemate in August 1988; neither side had gained anything substantial and the economies of both countries were left in ruins. Faced with a $75-billion war debt, Saddam sought a bail-out from its wealthy Kuwaiti neighbor. When the emirate refused to help, Saddam took the foolhardy decision to invade the country in August 1990. He had, however, gravely miscalculated the reaction of the West. In January 1991, a US-led multinational force crushed the occupying Iraqi military, liberating Kuwait in the six-week Persian Gulf War. The coalition force did not, however, move to topple Saddam's regime, a decision that has been heavily debated ever since. Nor did it support subsequent Shi'a and Kurdish revolts against Saddam.

Sanctions and Downfall

In the postwar period, Saddam taunted the international community and seemed to get away with it, earning the admiration of many within the Arab community and the distaste of those in the West. He consistently refused to comply with UN resolutions that required the destruction of all nuclear, chemical, and biological weapons and research facilities. His belligerent behavior resulted in the continual enforcement of economic sanctions, leading to further hardship and suffering among the Iraqi peoples. The 9/11 attack on the Twin Towers in New York intensified simmering tensions between Saddam and the West. Though not directly linked to the attack, Saddam called it a heroic act, incurring the wrath of the Bush administration. Keen to finish off what his father had failed to do, George W. Bush placed Saddam high on his "War on Terrorism" target list. Unimpressed,

Saddam continued to play cat-and-mouse with the international community, eventually forcing the passage in November 2002 of Resolution 1441 by the UN. The resolution accused Iraq of violating a previous Security Council resolution regarding disarmament. Still Saddam refused to capitulate, and in March 2003, George W. Bush finally moved against Saddam, despite having no official mandate from the UN. Led by the US, the international coalition met surprisingly little opposition from the Iraqi army and Saddam was forced to flee. He remained in hiding until December that year, when he was discovered in a dug-out hole in a farmhouse near to Tikrit. Saddam was handed into Iraqi custody and was put on trial for crimes against humanity. Found guilty, he was executed by hanging in Baghdad on December 30, 2006.

Arab Strongman or Ruthless Dictator?

Saddam was a product of his time and place. Iraq was, and still is, a nation beset by ethnic and religious schisms. Democracy does not traditionally work well in such circumstances and Saddam showed sufficient strength and brutality in establishing a powerful regime. He brought prosperity and growth to the country, making it one of the most dynamic economies in the Arab world, though in the end he squandered it pursuing his own political agenda. Nonetheless, he is still considered a hero to many in the Arab world, especially among the Palestinians, who lauded him for standing up to the West. Iraq may now be governed by its first democratically elected government in its history, but many feel that once the international forces withdraw from Iraq another Saddam will rise up and take his place. The country is still bedeviled by unrest and terrorist attacks, and the climate of fear created during Saddam's long regime continues to haunt the nation. Iraq still seems a long way from its origins as the country that saw the birth of civilization.

Saddam Hussein had eight presidential compounds, the northernmost of which was Mosul Palace (seen here). The compounds comprised luxurious mansions, guest villas, and office complexes. Ostentatious in style, Hussein's palaces were lavishly adorned with marble walls and gold-plated faucets and bidets.
▼

RONALD REAGAN (1911–2004)

Actor, Governor, US President

Made more than 50 Hollywood B movies; elected President of the Screen Actors Guild; elected Governor of California for two terms; served two terms as US President; negotiated arms limitation treaty with Soviet Union; embroiled in the Iran-Contra affair.

- Politics & Leadership

- Science & Technology

- Popular Culture & the Arts

- Business & Commerce

- Writers & Thinkers

REWRITING HISTORY

Renowned for his conservative politics, Ronald Reagan showed a more liberal side as a young man. When he lived in Dixon, Illinois, during the 1920s, racial discrimination was extremely common and black people were refused rooms at the local inn. Reagan would often take them back to his house, where his mother would give them a room and a meal.

Actor-turned-politician Ronald Reagan was the oldest man ever to be elected President of the United States. Known as the "Great Communicator," Reagan was a charismatic public speaker, earning the affection of the American public. Widely credited for ending the Cold War and bringing prosperity to the US, Reagan also presided over a massive increase in US debt and illicit activities such as the Iran-Contra affair.

From Acting to Politics

Ronald Reagan was born in Tampico, Illinois, in 1911 to Nelle and John Reagan. He studied economics and sociology at Eureka College, Illinois, a church-based institution. He was an undistinguished scholar but a gifted athlete, especially in football, and a keen member of the drama society. After college, he worked as a sports radio commentator. In 1937, a screen test secured Reagan a Hollywood contract with Warner Brothers. He starred in over 50 B movies including *Knute Rockne, All American* (1940), from which he gained the nickname "The Gipper." His most notable movie was *Kings Row* (1942) in which he played an amputee who utters the line "Where's the rest of me?", which later became the title of his 1965 autobiography. His chance of major movie stardom was harmed by the entry of the US into World War II. His poor eyesight prevented an overseas posting and he spent the war years making training movies for the Army Air Corps. In 1940, Reagan married actress Jane Wyman. In 1947, Reagan became president of the Screen Actors Guild. During his terms in office (1947–52, and again in 1959), the previously liberal Reagan became more right-wing, providing the FBI with names of suspected communist sympathizers in the movie industry and appearing before the House Committee on Un-American Activities as a "friendly witness" in 1949.

Reagan's growing political stance caused the breakdown of his marriage to Wyman, leading to him becoming the only divorced US president so far in history. In 1952, he married actress Nancy Davis, the daughter of a staunch conservative physician. In the late '50s, Reagan worked mostly in television, including a stint as host of General Electric Theater. He also began making speeches to GE plant staff, often with a political message. He eventually became too controversial for GE and his contract was cancelled. A former Democrat, Reagan's political affiliation drifted toward the right, and he formally registered as a Republican in the early 1960s. Reagan's involvement in politics increased, and in 1964 he spoke in support of the presidential campaign of Barry Goldwater. His "Time of Choosing" speech attracted the support of prominent Californian conservatives, who persuaded him to run for the post of Governor. In 1967, after defeating the incumbent Pat Brown by a million votes, he was inaugurated as Governor of California.

As Governor of California

Faced by a cashflow crisis and a budget deficit, Reagan took immediate action to balance the figures. He froze government hiring and increased taxes. Following up on his campaign pledge to "clean up the mess at Berkeley,"

Reagan clashed with the anti-Vietnam student protesters, sending out state troopers to quell campus demonstrations, though he also increased spending on higher education. Re-elected as governor in 1970 with nearly 53 percent of the vote, Reagan made welfare reform a central part of his term, tightening eligibility requirements, while increasing aid to those truly in need, including the introduction of the Medi-Cal program to pay the medical bills of the poor. Although personally opposed to abortion, Reagan signed a bill to extend abortion rights, a decision that he later regretted. He also worked to reintroduce the death penalty, though only one execution was carried out during his governorship.

Although state spending increased massively during his two terms in office, Reagan succeeded in making California solvent once again, earning him a reputation for fiscal good management. Almost from the outset Reagan had his sights set on the presidency. He challenged Nixon for the Republican nomination in 1968 but was easily defeated. Eight years later, he stood as the conservative candidate against President Gerald Ford for the Republican nomination, losing by a narrow margin. In 1980, he ran again, securing the nomination. With George Bush as his running mate, Reagan crushed

◀ *President Ronald Reagan was known for his wacky sense of humor. In this picture taken at NASA's Mission Control center in Houston in 1981, Reagan is seen making a long-distance call to shuttle astronauts Joe Engle and Richard Truly, asking them to stop off in Washington and give him a lift to their California landing site.*

incumbent President Jimmy Carter, winning 489 electoral votes to Carter's 49 to become the nation's 40th president. He was reelected to the presidency in 1984.

Reaganomics

Reagan inherited an America beset by high inflation and unemployment and overshadowed by the hostage crisis in Iran. The start of his presidency could not have been better. As Reagan was delivering his inaugural address, news came in that the 52 hostages held by Iran for 444 days had been freed. Sixty-nine days later an assassination attempt on Reagan by John W. Hinckley gained him the sympathy of the American public and elevated his standing even more. To solve the nation's economic crisis, Reagan set in place his policy of "Reaganomics," which was based on the principle of supply-side economics. He cut income taxes in the hope of stimulating spending and production, while at the same time instituting large cuts in domestic spending. His policy enjoyed mixed results. Although inflation dropped, national debt doubled between 1981 and 1986, and the US went from being a creditor nation to one owing half a trillion dollars by the time Reagan left the White House. Nonetheless, under the Reagan administration, the US people experienced their longest recorded period of peacetime prosperity without recession or depression.

A Thaw in the Cold War

Reagan took a hard line against communism, calling the Soviet Union the "evil empire," and greatly increasing US military spending, seeking "peace through strength." As well as reversing Carter's decision to cancel the B-1 bomber, Reagan announced plans to deploy new medium-range Pershing nuclear-tipped missiles in Europe and asked for funding to develop the MX "Peacekeeper" missile. More importantly, Reagan spent billions of dollars researching an antiballistic missile defense system, popularly known as "Star Wars." In 1983, Reagan sent military aid to Grenada to help the Caribbean island put down a coup that had established a Marxist-Leninist government. In keeping with his "Reagan Doctrine," the president supported covert aid to anti-communist movements in Latin America, Africa, and Asian countries, including giving aid to the Mujahedeen forces fighting against the Soviets in Afghanistan. After Mikhail Gorbachev came to power, relations between the US and the Soviet Union improved, and in 1987 the two leaders negotiated a treaty to destroy medium-range nuclear weapons.

Reagan also waged a campaign against international terrorism, sending US bombers to Libya in retaliation for an attack on US soldiers in a German nightclub. During the Iran-Iraq war in 1987, Reagan controversially sent naval warships to the Persian Gulf to maintain oil supply. Reagan's last two years in office were marred by the Iran-Contra affair involving the secret sale of arms to Iran and the diversion of funds to the Nicaraguan rebels, violating a Congress agreement that banned supporting the "Contras." Despite denying any knowledge of the affair, Reagan's statements during congressional hearings revealed inconsistencies and his administration came under fire both at home and abroad. He left office in January 1989 and was succeeded by his vice president George H. W. Bush. In 1994, Reagan announced that he was suffering from Alzheimer's disease. He died in 2004, at the age of 93.

Reagan's Legacy

Although his term enjoyed many high-profile successes, including the ending

of the Cold War and an economic boom, the America that Reagan left behind was a nation heavily in debt. His lackadaisical management style led to illicit activities among his staff, including the internationally condemned Iran-Contra affair.

Although a popular public speaker, Reagan relied more on effect than substance. His grasp of international affairs often led to ridicule, and he was accused of warmongering and imperialistic tendencies. He appeared indifferent to minority civil rights and refused to impose sanctions on apartheid South Africa. His support of the pro-life movement and capital punishment earned him the disdain of liberals throughout the world. Nonetheless, he was politically charismatic and continues to enjoy one of the highest popularity rates for ex-presidents in history. His bravery in the face of a harsh and lingering illness only served to increase his standing.

#23

◄ *In the midst of the Iran-Contra scandal, Ronald Reagan gives his remarks on the final report of the President's Special Review Board. No conclusive evidence was found of direct involvement by the president.*

- Politics & Leadership

- Science & Technology

- Popular Culture & the Arts

- Business & Commerce

- Writers & Thinkers

REWRITING HISTORY

Despite electing him to the post of Secretary-General, Lenin quickly became critical of Stalin's authoritarian tendencies, encouraging his comrades "to consider a means of removing [him] from this post and appointing someone else who differs from [him] in one weighty respect: being more tolerant, more loyal, more polite, more considerate of his comrades." Unfortunately, they did not pay heed.

VLADIMIR ILYICH LENIN (1870–1924)

Leader of the Soviet Union

Russian revolutionary; leader of the Bolsheviks; masterminded the October Revolution; first leader of the Soviet Union

Vladimir I. Lenin was one of the most influential revolutionary leaders in history, whose political ideology changed the course of the twentieth century. In 1917, he led the Bolsheviks to victory in the Russian October Revolution, and established the first communist state in the world. His death at the age of 53 left the Soviet Union at the mercy of dictator Joseph Stalin.

Setting Out on the Revolutionary Track

Vladimir Ilyich Ulyanov—he adopted the pseudonym Lenin in 1901—was born in Simbirsk, Russia, in 1870, the son of a local schools inspector. From a young age, Lenin had been exposed to the revolutionary ideas of his elder brother Alexander. In 1887, Alexander was executed for his part in a plot to kill Tsar Alexander III. Alexander's execution had a profound effect on Lenin, who became increasingly involved in radical politics, leading to his expulsion from Kazan University. Lenin later completed a degree in law at the University of St Petersburg and practiced law in Samara for some years. In 1895, after moving to Moscow, Lenin helped to form the Union of Struggle for the Emancipation of the Working Class, an action that led to his arrest in 1896 and subsequent exile to Siberia. During his exile, Lenin wrote extensively, developing his socialist ideals, as well as marrying activist Nadezhda Krupskaya. After his exile ended in 1900, Lenin spent some years traveling in Europe, meeting with fellow revolutionaries. He helped found the Russian Social Democratic Labor Party (RSDLP) journal *Iska* (*Spark*) and wrote his influential revolutionary pamphlet "What Is to Be Done?", which called for the overthrow of the Russian imperial family. In 1903, internal agreements within the RSDLP led to a split between the "Bolshevik" (Majority) and "Menshevik" (Minority), with Lenin emerging as leader of the Bolsheviks.

Revolution in Russia

Lenin returned to Russia to support the 1905 Revolution but went back to Europe when the uprising failed to overthrow the Tsar. In 1909, he completed *Materialism and Empirio-criticism*, now a central tenet of Marxist-

Leninist ideology. Shortly after the outbreak of World War I, Lenin moved to neutral Switzerland, where he spoke out against those socialists who supported the war and denounced the war as an imperialist conflict. In support of his ideology, Lenin crafted his important work *Imperialism: the Highest Stage of Capitalism*. With news of the successful revolution, Lenin returned to his homeland in April 1917, where he published his "April Theses" criticizing fellow Bolsheviks for supporting the Provisional Government and calling on workers to rise up against the wealthy elites. In July, workers and soldiers took to the streets against government troops, forcing Lenin to flee to Finland in order to avoid arrest. Here he wrote *State and Revolution*, which outlined a new form of government based on workers' councils, or "soviets." In late-August, an abortive coup attempt by General Kornilov led Kerensky to ask for Bolshevik aid in protecting St Petersburg. Inspired by the promise of "peace, land, and bread," the masses rallied to the Bolsheviks and Kornilov was defeated. Lenin returned to St Petersburg and laid plans with Leon Trotsky to overthrow the Provisional Government. Lenin's call for "All Power to the Soviets!" inspired the storming of the Winter Palace in October by the Red Guards. The October Revolution marked the end of the Provisional Government and the start of Soviet rule.

Civil War and Repression

Lenin was elected chairman of the Soviet Council of People's Commissars by the All-Russian Congress of Soviets, where he began a process of land distribution and nationalization. Russia's withdrawal from World War I in 1918 was followed by civil war. Millions died in the fighting and from starvation, and both sides committed unspeakable atrocities. Lenin's War Communism policy, whereby the government had requisitioned food from the peasants for little or no pay in order to feed the army, had led to massive social unrest and a flagging economy. The ever-pragmatic Lenin introduced his New Economic Policy (NEP), which permitted a small degree of private enterprise, to quell the peasant uprisings and improve the economy.

An intense and utterly commited revolutionary, Lenin led the most influential revolutionary uprising of the twentieth century. His legacy has inevitably been overshadowed by the brutal dictatorship of Joseph Stalin, and it is indeed Stalinism that is synonymous with communist repression. Lenin's defining role was in winning the initial armed struggle, and creating a platform for communism to spread across the world.

#22

Lenin's position as the first leader of the Soviet Union was commemorated by the erection of statues of the revolutionary figure throughout Eastern Europe. In the post-Soviet era many of these statues were removed, though he remains an important historical figure in Russia.
▼

 REWRITING HISTORY

Fidel Castro is known for making very long and eloquent speeches. During his trial for the Moncada Barracks attack, Castro made a four-hour speech entitled "History Will Absolve Me." The speech later formed part of his 26th of July Movement manifesto and included five revolutionary laws that he wished to see implemented in Cuba.

FIDEL CASTRO (b. 1926)

Prime Minister and President of Cuba

Architect of the 1959 Cuban Revolution; Prime Minister of Cuba (1959–76); President of Cuba (1976–2008); repelled the Bay of Pigs invasion; precipitated the Cuban Missile Crisis

Bearded and dressed in military fatigues, Fidel Castro is the epitome of a revolutionary. The instigator of the Cuban Revolution, Castro ruled the Caribbean island from 1959 until ill-health forced his retirement in 2008. During this time, he introduced far-ranging social and political reforms, at the same time cracking down on opposition at home and making an international enemy of the United States.

The Seeds of Revolution

Fidel Alejandro Castro Ruz was born in Biran, Cuba, in 1926, the illegitimate son of a wealthy sugar plantation owner and a household servant (his parents later married). He was educated at a Jesuit boarding school, where he was a gifted student and athlete. In 1945, Castro entered law school at the University of Havana and immediately involved himself in student politics. He became increasingly disenchanted with the widespread inequality within Cuban society, which he felt was exacerbated by US influence in the country. In 1947, he joined the newly formed Cuban People's Party, a political party dedicated to social reform and economic independence from the US. Castro became a candidate for the party during the 1952 elections but a *coup d'état* led by former president General Fulgencio Batista ousted the incumbent president and forced the cancelation of constitutional elections. Convinced that armed revolution was the only means to gain power, Castro organized an underground movement to plot the overthrow of Batista. On July 26, 1953, Castro, his brother Raul, and a group of around 125 men and women attacked the Moncada Army Barracks. The attack was a disaster and most of the group were killed or captured. Castro was put on trial and sentenced to 15 years. He was released under a general amnesty after two years.

The Cuban Revolution

Castro went into exile in Mexico, where he founded the 26th of July Movement and began stockpiling weapons. In December 1956, Castro— together with Che Guevara and a group of around 80 rebels—landed in Cuba with the intention of establishing a stronghold in the Sierra Maestra

Mountains. Despite heavy losses, they succeeded in creating a platform from which to wage a guerilla war against the Batista government. Where the rebels gained control, they redistributed the land among the peasants, winning the support of the poor and gaining the respect of left-wing students and Catholic priests. Batista's use of torture and public execution further increased support for the rebel movement, even among the middle class. In 1958, Batista launched a massive offensive against Castro and his followers. Despite being heavily outnumbered, Castro's rebels inflicted great losses on Batista's troops, killing or capturing over 1,000 soldiers and persuading scores to desert. At the end of 1958, Castro left the mountains to march into the main towns. Batista fled to the Dominican Republic and on January 8, 1959, Castro's army marched into Havana. Castro became prime minister the following month.

Castro's Cuba

Castro's effect on Cuban social life was immediate and radical. Although he had vowed to hold elections, Castro reneged on his promise, saying "revolution first, elections later." He cut rental costs for low-paid workers by up to 50 percent, nationalized the US-owned telephone company and confiscated property owned by the Batista elite. Foreign ownership of land was forbidden, land holdings were limited to 993 acres (4 sq. km) per person, and peasants received confiscated land under a redistribution policy. Health and education became free for all—Cuba now has one of the highest literacy rates in the world and one of the lowest infant mortality rates. Castro's revolutionary social policies were popular with the poor but alienated many middle- and upper-class Cubans, resulting in over a million Cubans leaving for exile in the US. Foreign policy under Castro, too, underwent a major upheaval. Castro adopted a belligerent attitude toward the United States, mindful of the country's close association with the Batista regime, and in 1960 the US broke off diplomatic relations with Cuba. Castro turned to the Soviet Union and other Eastern European nations for economic and military aid, precipitating several CIA-sponsored attempts on his life and the US-backed Bay of Pigs invasion of Cuba in 1961. Although Castro initially denied being a communist, on December 2, 1961, Cuba was proclaimed a communist state. The US retaliated with a trade embargo, including a travel ban for US nationals. In 1962, Castro brought the world to the brink of nuclear war when he allowed the Soviet Union to build ballistic missile sites in Cuba. Castro's hold on Cuban society was absolute and he has been much criticized for human rights abuses. Nevertheless, many positive things came out of the Cuban Revolution, notably in the provision of health care and education for the poor.

In 1960, Fidel Castro spoke before a meeting of the United Nations General Assembly. His speech, which was a denunciation of US policy toward Cuba and its interference in Cuban internal affairs, lasted 4 hours and 29 minutes.
▼

JOHN LENNON (1940–1980)

Musician, Songwriter, Poet, and Peace Activist

Founded The Quarrymen, the forerunner of The Beatles; landed a recording contract with Parlophone Records; screaming fans greet The Beatles on their successful tour of North America; successful solo recording career; high-profile antiwar campaigner

- Politics & Leadership
- Science & Technology
- **Popular Culture & the Arts**
- Business & Commerce
- Writers & Thinkers

◀◀ REWRITING HISTORY

After The Beatles split up, relations between Lennon and McCartney grew increasingly acrimonious, and both men used their solo recordings to air their disagreements. Lennon's first post-Beatles album **John Lennon/Plastic Ono Band** *was inspired by Lennon's experience with primal scream therapy and deals with the pain of his split from The Beatles. The track "How Do You Sleep?" from the* **Imagine** *album is another dig at McCartney.*

John Lennon was a member of enormously successful pop and rock band The Beatles. With Paul McCartney, he wrote many of the pop world's most memorable songs. After The Beatles split in 1970, Lennon went on to have a successful solo career in the music business and also achieved fame as a peace activist, artist, and poet.

Growing Up in Liverpool

John Winston Lennon was born in 1940 in Liverpool during a German air raid over the northern English city. His father Alf was a seaman who deserted his wife Julia shortly after John's birth, and only entered John's life intermittently thereafter. Julia could not cope with the young baby by herself and John was raised in the home of his Aunt Mimi and Uncle George Smith. Lennon was introduced to music by his mother, who bought her son a banjo and later his first guitar. In 1958, Julia was knocked down and killed by a car driven by an off-duty policeman. Her early death had a profound effect on Lennon and cemented his close friendship with Paul McCartney, who also lost his mother early in life. After leaving Liverpool's Quarry Bank High School, Lennon went to the Liverpool College of Art, where he met his future wife Cynthia Powell. Lennon was a disruptive and rebellious student and dropped out of college before finishing his studies.

The Beatles

John Lennon idolized rock 'n' roll greats Elvis Presley and Chuck Berry, and in 1957 he formed his first band, The Quarrymen. A few months later, Lennon met Paul McCartney and invited him to join the band. Lennon and McCartney began writing songs together, the start of one of the world's most successful songwriting teams. George Harrison joined the band as lead guitarist, Lennon's fellow art student friend Stuart Sutcliffe became bassist, and Pete Best played the drums. The band went through several name changes until they decided upon The Beatles. The Beatles began playing gigs in Merseyside, often at the famous Cavern Club, and starting in 1960 they went on several tours to Hamburg, Germany, where they were received warmly in the clubs. After the first tour, Sutcliffe left the band and McCartney took over as bassist. The Beatles' big break came in late 1961 when music store owner Brian Epstein heard the band playing at the Cavern Club and offered to become their manager. In 1962, Epstein secured a recording deal with EMI's Parlophone label and the band released their first recording "Love Me Do," which reached number 17 in the British charts. At EMI's music producer George Martin's request, Pete Best left the band to be replaced by Rory Storm and the Hurricanes drummer Ringo Starr. Lennon married Cynthia Powell in 1962, and they had a son Julian. The Beatles' popularity soon spread and their first album *Please Please Me* also reached the top of the charts. After appearing on the *Ed Sullivan Show* in the States in 1964, The Beatles also conquered the North American market. Screaming fans greeted every Beatles appearance and the "Fab Four" gained a worldwide following. They

also starred in a number of movies, including *A Hard Day's Night* (1964) and *Help!* (1965). In 1965, Lennon and the other members of the band were awarded the MBE by Queen Elizabeth II. Lennon also took on a number of solo projects, publishing two books of his stories and drawings, *In His Own Write* and *A Spaniard in the Works*, as well as appearing in the Dick Lester comedy movie *How I Won the War*.

◄ *John Lennon grew up at the semi-detached home of Aunt Mimi and Uncle George Smith in Woolton, Liverpool. He did, however, have regular contact with his mother Julia, who bought him his first guitar. Julia tragically died after being hit by a car when Lennon was 17 years old.*

In March 1966, Lennon courted controversy when he declared that The Beatles were more popular than Jesus Christ. The statement caused a backlash among conservatives in the US Bible Belt regions and radio stations stopped playing The Beatles' music and concerts were cancelled. Lennon also began experimenting with LSD and other drugs around this time, and continued to produce some of the most creative work of his career, including *Sgt. Pepper's Lonely Hearts Club Band* (1967). He was arrested and charged with marijuana possession in 1968, a conviction that would have later repercussions when he moved to New York. His interests in 1960s counterculture grew and in 1966 he met Japanese avant-garde artist Yoko Ono at one of her art exhibitions in London. His subsequent relationship with her led to his divorce from Cynthia in 1968 on the grounds of Lennon's adultery. Lennon also dabbled in Indian spirituality, visiting the Maharishi Mahesh Yogi in India to study transcendental meditation. In 1968, Lennon released an experimental album with Ono entitled *Unfinished Music Number One: Two Virgins*. Featuring a naked Lennon and

▶ *When the Beatles arrived at John F. Kennedy Airport in New York in February 1964, they were greeted by a crowd of around 3,000 screaming fans. Their appearance on* **The Ed Sullivan Show** *two days later was watched by an audience of around 74 million. Beatle mania had arrived in North America.*

Ono, the album's cover was as controversial as the music. Lennon and Ono married in Gibraltar in March 1969. They turned their honeymoon into a political protest against the Vietnam War by allowing the media to photograph their "Bed-in for Peace" at the Amsterdam Hilton. They also recorded the anti-war anthem "Give Peace a Chance" during the "bed-in." Later that year, Lennon released two more albums with Ono, *Unfinished Music, No. 2: Life with the Lions* and *The Wedding Album*, which featured a recording of Lennon and Ono calling to each other over the sound of their heartbeats. In September 1969, Lennon performed live at the Toronto Rock and Roll festival with the Plastic Ono Band, which featured Ono and legendary guitarist Eric Clapton among others. Soon afterward, Lennon released the single "Cold Turkey," which told of his battle with heroin addiction. Ono's growing influence on Lennon caused friction with other members of The Beatles, and the band began to grow apart. In 1969, The Beatles released their final album *Abbey Road*, officially disbanding the following year.

John and Yoko

In 1971, Lennon moved to New York with Ono, releasing the successful album *Imagine* that same year. The title track, also called "Imagine", became one of the most enduringly popular songs of all time, and remains Lennon's signature tune and an anthem for world peace. The following year, Lennon and Ono, together with hippie band *Elephant's Memory*, recorded the double-album *Sometime in New York City*. The album, which contained somewhat simplistic political songs, was panned by critics. At the same time, Lennon found himself embroiled in a battle with US immigration due to his drugs conviction in 1968. His next album *Mind Games* (1973) was slightly better received but his personal life was on a downward spiral. In the fall of 1973,

he separated from Ono and moved to Los Angeles with his personal assistant May Pang where he began a year and a half of heavy partying with the likes of Keith Moon and Elton John. Lennon referred to this period as his "Lost Weekend", although he did improve his relationships with the other members of The Beatles during this time. Lennon and Ono reconciled after meeting at one of Elton John's concerts and they had a son Sean in 1975. Following Sean's birth, Lennon withdrew from public view to become a "househusband," and he did not return to the recording studio until 1980, when he and Ono released *Double Fantasy*, considered by many to be his finest post-Beatles work. It won Lennon a posthumous Grammy Award for Album of the Year in 1981. He also recorded enough material to be posthumously released as the *Milk and Honey* album (1984). On December 8, 1980, a schizophrenic fan, Mark David Chapman, shot Lennon dead on the steps of his Dakota apartment in Manhattan. Just two days previously, Lennon had said in a BBC interview with Andy Peebles that he felt he could go anywhere in New York and feel safe. Lennon's murder caused an outbreak of grief, the likes of which hadn't been seen since the assassination of J. F. Kennedy 27 years earlier, and on December 14, millions of fans worldwide held a ten-minute vigil for the murdered star.

Musical Influence

With over 150 songs to their name, the Lennon-McCartney collaboration produced some of the most memorable and innovative songs ever heard. Although they are always credited jointly, many of The Beatles songs were individually written. Lennon's influence on The Beatles tracks was darker and more bluesy and discordant than McCartney, who provided a lighter, more optimistic touch. Both musically and vocally, Lennon instilled the band's songs with an emotional rawness. The so-called "smart Beatle," Lennon also brought a hitherto unheard of degree of sophistication to rock 'n' roll. As well as producing beautiful and original melodies, he wrote intelligent, witty, and penetratingly mature lyrics that have stood the test of time. The most controversial and outspoken member of The Beatles, Lennon remains a symbol of 1960s counterculture, both for his work as a musician and as an activist for world peace. John Lennon's work continues to be honored even after his death. In 1992 he was awarded the Grammy's Lifetime Achievement Award and he has also been posthumously inducted into both the Songwriters Hall of Fame (1987) and the Rock and Roll Hall of Fame (1994).

JAMES JOYCE (1882–1941)

Novelist, Poet, Essayist

Stylistically one of the most influential writers of the twentieth century; developed an experimental use of language that rejected the traditional narrative model

- Politics & Leadership
- Science & Technology
- Popular Culture & the Arts
- Business & Commerce
- **Writers & Thinkers**

◀◀ REWRITING HISTORY

*The action in Joyce's great work **Ulysses** takes places on a single day—June 16, 1904. The date was chosen by Joyce in celebration of the very first date that he went on with Nora Barnacle. The two met in Dublin when the young Nora was working as a chambermaid in a local hotel.*

James Joyce was an Irish writer who lived most of his life in continental Europe, though his literary universe remained firmly entrenched in his home city of Dublin. Misunderstood and subjected to censorship during his lifetime, Joyce's works are now acknowledged classics, though they remain a challenging read for many.

The Dubliner

James Augustine Aloysius Joyce was born near Dublin, the eldest of ten surviving children of John and Mary Jane Joyce. Although witty and charming, John Joyce was a heavy drinker and he reduced the family fortunes from a state of bourgeois prosperity to near poverty. Joyce's mother was a devout Catholic and Joyce's later renunciation of the faith troubled her greatly. Joyce was educated by Jesuits, first at Clongowes Wood College, in Clane, and then at Belvedere College in Dublin. According to Joyce, he had the Jesuits to thank for teaching him how to think clearly, but he nevertheless rejected their religious teachings. In 1898, he enrolled at University College, Dublin, where he read modern languages. At this time, he became involved in Dublin's theatrical and literary circles. In 1900, his first published article, "Ibsen's New Drama," appeared in the *Fortnightly Review*, and he also began to write lyrical poems. After leaving university in 1903, Joyce turned his back on his family and Ireland and fled to Paris, ostensibly to study. He returned to Ireland within the year to see his mother before her death from cancer. In 1904, Joyce left for Europe once again, this time taking with him Nora Barnacle, whom he later married. Joyce spent most of the following ten years teaching English in Trieste, but also lived for short periods in Pola (now Pula, in Croatia) and Rome. Nora gave birth to two children, Giorgio and Lucia, during this time, and the family was further enlarged when several of Joyce's siblings also moved to Europe.

The Works

Joyce managed to scrape enough of a living to allow him to write. In 1907, he published *Chamber Music*, an anthology of poems. He returned to Ireland for brief spells, primarily to battle with publishers to get his collection of short stories *Dubliners* (1914) published. On one of his trips to Ireland, Joyce met with Ezra Pound, who was greatly impressed with the young novelist. Pound was working as editor of *The Egoist* and agreed to publish Joyce's semiautobiographical novel *A Portrait of the Artist as a Young Man* in serial form in the journal. It came out in book form in 1916. At the beginning of World War I, Joyce and his family moved to Zurich. At this time Joyce's eyesight began to fail, the start of a deterioration that would leave him nearly blind later in his life.

In 1920, Joyce moved to Paris, and here he completed his epic work *Ulysses* (1922). Although the book was published in France, it was banned elsewhere

on account of its perceived obscenity and it was not available in England or the US until the 1930s. Joyce's literary reputation grew throughout the 1920s and '30s, aided no doubt by the notoriety he gained from the censoring of *Ulysses*. In 1939, he published his final work, *Finnegans Wake*. His later years were marred by his daughter's schizophrenia (she received psychoanalysis from Carl Jung) and his blindness. Joyce died of a perforated ulcer in Zurich in 1941.

Style

Joyce is considered a giant among writers, but many regard his work as incomprehensible. His lack of plot, frequent use of internal monologues, and experimental use of language make great demands on the reader, and Joyce himself acknowledged that his work was difficult to fathom. "The only demand I make of my reader is that he should devote his whole life to reading my works," he once told a critic. His experimental writing broke the mold of traditional literature and opened the door to avant-garde writers such as Samuel Beckett and Jorge Luis Borges. Thinkers in other disciplines, such as psychology and philosophy, have used Joyce's work as a platform from which to explore their fields, and the allusive nature of his writing has ensured a lingering cult appeal.

◀ *James Joyce pictured in Zürich near the end of World War I. It was during his time in Switzerland that Joyce made the acquaintance of Harriet Shaw Weaver, a prominent editor who would become the main patron of his work.*

 REWRITING HISTORY

The son of an aristocrat and the beneficiary of a life of privilege, as an MP Churchill nonetheless fought to improve social conditions for the less fortunate, introducing minimum wages, creating Labor Exchanges to help the unemployed, and bringing in a budget that increased taxation of the wealthy to fund social welfare programs.

WINSTON CHURCHILL

Prime Minister of the United Kingdom

A long-standing Member of the British Parliament, Prime Minister, orator, wit, and author; led Britain to victory in World War II; represented the indomitable spirit of an island nation in the face of Nazi aggression

Winston Churchill was already in his sixties and nearing the end of an illustrious political career when he was given the role for which he is most famous—the leadership of the United Kingdom during World War II. With his stirring speeches and his distinctive bowler hat and cigar, he came to embody Britain's bulldog spirit.

The Young Churchill

Winston Leonard Spencer Churchill was born in Blenheim Palace, the home of family friends, in Oxfordshire, England. His parents were the statesman Lord Randolph Churchill and the society beauty Jenny Jerome, daughter of wealthy New York financier Leonard Jerome. Educated at Harrow private school, he attended the Royal Military College at Sandhurst before joining the 4th Hussars in 1895. Combining his writing ambitions with a military career, he fought in Cuba, on India's North-West Frontier, and in the Sudan, and wrote journalistic reports and a novel, as well as accounts of the military campaigns. After resigning his commission, he was sent to Africa by the *Morning Post* to cover the Boer War. His graphic account of his capture and subsequent escape from a South African prison brought him to the attention of the public.

Into Politics

In 1899 he stood, unsuccessfully, for election to the British House of Commons, but he was elected the following year. It was the beginning of a parliamentary career that was to last more than 60 years despite many political setbacks and electoral defeats. Although he was elected as a Conservative candidate, he soon switched allegiance to the Liberals, and served in a range of government posts under Prime Minister Campbell-Bannerman and subsequently under Herbert Asquith. In Britain at this time there was a growing fear that Britain might soon find itself at war with Germany, but Churchill held a different opinion and even advocated a reduction in Britain's military capability. It came as a surprise therefore, when in the fall of 1911 he was made First Lord of the Admiralty. Possibly galvanized by the Agadir Crisis, in which Germany had sent a gunboat into the Moroccan port of Agadir, Churchill took the German threat seriously and supervised an unprecedented expansion of the Royal Navy in preparation for World War I, basing a quarter of the navy in Gibraltar at the entrance to the Mediterranean. In 1915, however, he was demoted after championing a naval expedition to attack Germany's ally Turkey, which failed. In his new position as Minister of Munitions, he was instrumental in the introduction of tanks, in which he had long been interested.

After a period as Chancellor of the Exchequer, Churchill spent the ten years from 1929 to 1939 out of office, but he remained in the political spotlight and tried unsuccessfully to alert the nation to the threat posed by Nazi Germany. Although strongly critical of Neville Chamberlain's appeasement of Hitler, when war was declared he was appointed First Lord of the Admiralty. When Chamberlain resigned in 1940, Churchill was asked by King George VI to become Prime Minister of an all-party government.

His Finest Hour

Although in many ways Churchill's attitudes and politics harked back to an earlier age, wartime Britain had need of just such a man as its leader. The power of his oratory quickly quashed any thoughts that the British people may have had about a negotiated settlement with Nazi Germany, and prepared the country, and the British Empire, for a long and bitter conflict. Taking up the reins of government, Churchill also created—and filled—the post of Minister of Defense. He took steps to accelerate the production of munitions, and especially aircraft, and he applied his considerable skills as a military strategist. Churchill's strong relationship with Franklin D. Roosevelt was also of crucial importance in maintaining the supply of goods and armaments to Britain from America and led to the Lend-Lease agreement. Above all, with his relentless energy and dogged personal determination, through his speeches in public and on radio, Churchill kept up the spirits of the British people and the armed forces. After the war, Churchill and his party were defeated in the general election of 1945. He returned to power in 1951 but resigned as Prime Minister in 1955 due to ill-health. He died in 1965, and was given a state funeral.

#18

▲
Winston Churchill is seen here on June 18, 1940—the day of his famous "Finest Hour" speech rallying the nation before the Battle of Britain.

BOB DYLAN (b. 1941)

American Singer, Songwriter, Musician, Poet, and Artist

Became a spokesman for the protest movement in the 1960s; has influenced the music scene for almost 50 years; continues to top the charts

- Politics & Leadership
- Science & Technology
- **Popular Culture & the Arts**
- Business & Commerce
- Writers & Thinkers

REWRITING HISTORY

In late July 1966, Bob Dylan had a motorcycle accident that caused him to take a break from his relentless touring and recording schedule and reevaluate his life. Or so the story goes. More than 40 years later, speculation continues and theories abound, including the possibility that there was no accident and Dylan actually went to ground to kick a drug habit.

Through his songs and music, firmly rooted in the traditions of American folk music and yet new and original, Bob Dylan gave a voice to a disaffected generation in the 1960s. A philosopher-poet with a unique insight, he has continued to develop his music and his writing, and to occupy a special place in popular culture.

Musical Beginnings

Robert Allen Zimmerman was born in 1941 in Duluth, Minnesota, where his father worked for the Standard Oil Company. Six years later the family moved to the mining town of Hibbing, MN. By the age of ten, Bob was writing poetry, and while at high school he taught himself guitar and piano and formed several bands. Entering the University of Minnesota in 1959, he started playing folk music at clubs in Minneapolis and St Paul under the name of Bob Dylan, and eventually the music took priority and in 1960 he dropped out of college and headed for New York's Greenwich Village, one of the centers of the American folk music revival that had been gaining momentum since the 1950s. There he performed in folk clubs and coffee houses and he soon gained a reputation. Dylan had been strongly influenced by the American folk singer and songwriter Woody Guthrie, and he frequently visited his idol in Greystone Park Psychiatric Hospital, New Jersey, where Guthrie was suffering from Huntington's disease.

The Big Break

The individualistic singer attracted an avid following, and in late 1961 he signed a contract with Columbia records. The album *Bob Dylan*, released the following year, contained only two of his own songs, but his distinctive voice, steel string guitar and harmonica, and his blues and country treatment gave a new sound to a range of traditional folk and gospel songs. The album also established his trademark ability to counterpose humor and melancholy. The growing folk music wave of the '50s and early '60s had a political and humanitarian face, and was becoming increasingly allied with the Civil Rights and Freedom of Speech movements. Dylan's writing not only matched the mood of the times but also took the protest song to a new level. His 1963 album *The Freewheelin' Bob Dylan* contained only original songs, including several hard-hitting commentaries on contemporary issues such as black civil rights, the Cold War, and America's increasing interference in Vietnam. Songs such as "Blowin' in the Wind," "Masters of War," and "Oxford Town," which commemorated the campus riots that followed the enrolment of the first black student at Mississippi University, became anthems to an increasingly politically aware generation in an age of growing unrest in America. The title track of his next album, *The Times They Are a-Changin'*, eloquently demonstrated his position as both a commentator and, if unwillingly, a figurehead.

Still Singing

In a career of five decades, during which he has released more than 50 albums, Dylan has brought the traditional roots of American music—folk, gospel, country and western, blues—into partnership, and some would say, at times, collision, with modern musical styles, and in the process created new sounds. In the mid '60s, after touring and recording with Joan Baez, he "went electric" and gave profound impetus to the birth of folk-rock, alienating a sector of his stalwart folk fans but finding a broader appeal at the same time.

He subsequently went through periods of hard rock, country music, and Christian evangelism, as well as flirting with rap and movie scores. Bob Dylan

has received several Grammy Awards, he has five songs in the Rock and Roll Hall of Fame, and he has received many honors and inductions. His songs have been covered countless times, and his music has had a major influence on artists of every musical hue. In 2004, his 1965 song "Like a Rolling Stone" was hailed as The Greatest Song of All Time by *Rolling Stone* magazine, and he remains as popular as ever—his recent album *Together Through Life* (2009) topped the album charts in both the US and the UK.

#17

◀ *Seen here on stage at the American Film Industry's tribute to Michael Douglas in Culver City, California, in 2009, Bob Dylan continues to perform, release new albums, and involve himself in movie projects.*

MARIE CURIE (1867–1934)

Chemist and Physicist

Pioneer in the field of radioactivity; isolated radioactive isotopes; discovered two new elements—polonium and radium; directed the first studies into the treatment of neoplasms using radioactive isotopes; winner of two Nobel prizes

 Politics & Leadership

■ **Science & Technology**

■ Popular Culture & the Arts

■ Business & Commerce

■ Writers & Thinkers

◀◀ REWRITING HISTORY

The Nobel Foundation has continued to recognize the work of the Curie family. Irène Joliot-Curie, the daughter of Marie and Pierre, and her husband Frédéric Joliot-Curie were jointly awarded the Nobel Prize for Chemistry in 1935 for their discovery of artificial radioactivity. No other family in history can boast such an achievement.

Despite the educational restrictions that society placed upon her because of her gender, Marie Curie succeeded in conducting some of the most groundbreaking scientific research of the twentieth century—work that has led to the medical use of radioactive isotopes and saved countless lives. She remains one of only two people to have won Nobel prizes in two different categories: physics and chemistry.

Fighting for an Education

Marie Curie was born Maria Sklodowska in 1867 in Warsaw, then part of Poland under the control of the Russian Empire. Her father taught mathematics and physics, and her mother was also a teacher. After leaving school, she worked as a governess for a while, helping to finance her sister Bronisława's medical studies in Paris. She also attended the Floating University, a clandestine institute set up in Warsaw to enable both men and women to study free from the prohibitive restrictions imposed by Imperial Russia. In 1891, she joined her sister in Paris, changed her name to Marie, and enrolled at Sorbonne University. She obtained degrees in physics (1893) and mathematical science (1894), simultaneously working as a tutor to pay for her studies. During the course of her postgraduate studies into the magnetic property of steel, Marie met Pierre Curie, a professor in the School of Physics. They shared mutual academic interests and the two became good friends. Marie returned briefly to Poland where she hoped to continue her studies but returned to France after being denied entry to the University of Krakow on account of her gender. Marie married Pierre Curie in 1895.

Discovering Radioactivity

In 1896, Henri Becquerel discovered that uranium salts spontaneously emitted rays similar to X-rays. He had, in fact, discovered radioactivity. Marie decided to pursue his research for her doctoral studies. Using the Curie electrometer, a device developed by her husband and his brother to measure extremely low electrical currents, she found that the level of radiation from a sample of a uranium compound depended only on how much uranium it contained and not upon the chemical compounds that were present. This discovery—that the radiation emanated solely from the uranium atoms—was arguably her most significant. During her research into two uranium-rich minerals, pitchblende (uraninite) and chalcolite (torbernite), Marie discovered that pitchblende was four times more active, and chalcolite twice as active, as could be accounted for by the presence of the uranium. She concluded that these minerals must contain some substance more active than the uranium itself. Convinced that Marie was in the throes of discovering something scientifically major, Pierre suspended his own research to join forces with his wife. Finding the element proved difficult, as it formed only a tiny fraction of the ore. However, after processing tons of the ore, the Curies announced the discovery in 1898 of two new radioactive elements—polonium, named for Marie's country of birth, and radium. They also used the term "radioactivity" for the first time.

Scientific Accolades

Marie received her doctorate from the University of Paris in 1903. That same year, Marie, Pierre, and Henri Becquerel were awarded the Nobel Prize in Physics for their joint researches into the phenomenon of radiation. Marie was the first female recipient of a Nobel Prize. France duly rewarded the Curies. Pierre was given a professorship and Marie became director of research at Pierre's newly established laboratory. In the spring of 1906, Pierre was killed in a tragic accident on the streets of Paris when he was struck by a horse and carriage. The Sorbonne entrusted Marie with Pierre's academic post and she became the first female professor at the university. Grief-stricken, Marie immersed herself in work and by 1910 she had discovered a means to separate pure radium from the ore. In 1911, she became the first person to win a second Nobel Prize, this time in chemistry. Her work, however, failed to convince the French Academy of Sciences to elect her to membership, though her achievements did persuade the French government to fund the construction of the Radium Institute, now the Curie Institute, in 1914. During World War I, Marie actively promoted the use of mobile radiography units, known as *petites Curies* ("little Curies") to alleviate the injuries of wounded soldiers.

Marie Curie received international recognition in her lifetime—a 1929 tour of America resulted in a $50,000 gift to establish the Radium Institute in her native Warsaw—and she remained scientifically active throughout her life. She died from aplastic anemia in 1934, probably as a result of her work with radiation. In 1995, her remains, along with those of Pierre, were transferred to the Paris Panthéon, another female first.

#16

Marie Curie received many honors in her lifetime and continues to be a much lauded scientist. This statue of Marie Curie can be found at the Marie-Curie Sklodowska University in Poland.
▼

JAMES DEAN (1931–1955)

Movie Actor

Famous for his portrayal of the brooding adolescent; became an iconic figure for American youth

◄◄ REWRITING HISTORY

Had James Dean lived, Paul Newman may not have become the legend that he did. When Dean died, he was under contract to appear in **Somebody Up There Likes Me** *(1956) at MGM and* **The Left Handed Gun** *(1958) at Warner Bros. After his death, the roles went to Paul Newman, launching his career as a major Hollywood star.*

James Dean starred in only three major movie roles, the best known of which is *Rebel Without a Cause*. The movie earned Dean a cult following among American youth, who saw in him their own adolescent angst made real. Dean's untimely death at 24 guaranteed him a place as a tragic icon in the history of Hollywood.

The Road to Hollywood

Dean was born in Marion, Indiana, the only child of Winton and Mildred Wilson Dean. His farmer-turned-dental technician father moved the family to Santa Monica, California, when Dean was six years old. Three years later, Dean's mother died from cancer. Unable to care for his son, Dean's father sent the nine-year-old boy back to Indiana to be raised by his Quaker aunt and uncle on a farm in Fairmount. After graduating from high school in 1949, Dean returned to California, where he enrolled in Santa Monica City College, majoring in pre-law, while also taking classes in drama. Dean soon discovered that he was not cut out for the legal profession and transferred to UCLA to major in drama. Around this time, he met actor James Whitmore, who helped him land a small role in the TV drama *Hill Number One*. In early 1951, Dean dropped out of school to pursue acting full-time, landing bit-parts in the movies *Fixed Bayonets*, *Sailor Beware*, and *Has Anybody Seen My Gal?* In October 1951 Dean moved to New York where he worked as a tester for the *Beat the Clock* game show. He won a small part in the Broadway play *The Jaguar* and also landed roles in a number of television series. In 1953, Dean gained a place in the acclaimed Actors Studio, where he came under the guidance of legendary "Method" acting coach Lee Strasberg. His role as an Arab gigolo in *The Immoralist* in 1954 earned him the Daniel Blum Theater World Award for best newcomer, and Hollywood beckoned.

The Three Movies

Screenwriter Paul Osborn suggested Dean to director Elia Kazan for the role of Cal Trask in the adaptation of the John Steinbeck novel *East of Eden*. Kazan wanted a "Marlon Brando" type for the role—an actor who could give depth and intensity to the emotionally charged character. Dean met with Steinbeck, who thought Dean perfect for the part. In 1954, the relatively unknown Dean began filming for the role opposite Julie Harris, Raymond Massey, and Burl Ives. Dean's performance as Trask established him as the angst-ridden outcast, the prototypical loner and "angry young man." Dean improvised continually during filming; his dance in the bean field and his reaction when his father refused his money were unscripted but became classic scenes in the movie. Dean's second, and probably most famous, movie was *Rebel Without a Cause* (1955), costarring Natalie Wood. *Rebel Without a Cause* tells the story of Jim Stark, hell-raising adolescent who wants to be loved but courts only trouble. Half a century later, it remains the quintessential teenage-angst movie. His third and last movie was *Giant*, costarring Elizabeth Taylor and Rock Hudson, in which he played cowhand Jett Rink. Just as filming was coming to an end, Dean was driving his Porsche Spyder when he was involved in a head-on collision. He was pronounced Dead On Arrival at hospital. His funeral attracted three thousand fans.

The James Dean Cult

Less than a month after his death, *Rebel Without a Cause* opened to public acclaim, establishing Dean as the unofficial spokesman for American youth, trapped in a postwar society that didn't understand it and refused to listen. Elvis Presley apparently idolized Dean, and is said to have gone into acting as a means of emulating his hero. Dean continues to be a cult figure, immortalized in pop songs and adorning the bedroom walls of teenagers.

He was the first actor to be nominated for an Academy Award posthumously, and is so far the only actor in history to be nominated for two awards posthumously (for *East of Eden* and *Giant*), although he did not win either.

James Dean's portrayal of Jett Rink in the 1956 drama **Giant** *won him a second posthumous Academy Award nomination.*
▼

MICHAEL JACKSON (1958–2009)

Recording Artist

Member of one of the most successful all-boy bands; made the transition from child to adult star; transformed the music video; made the best-selling album of all time; founded the Heal the World Foundation

- Politics & Leadership
- Science & Technology
- **Popular Culture & the Arts**
- Business & Commerce
- Writers & Thinkers

◀◀ REWRITING HISTORY

Michael Jackson was a great humanitarian who donated millions to charity during his career. In 1992, he founded the Heal the World Foundation "to improve the conditions for children throughout the world." All profits from his Dangerous World Tour (1992–3) went to the foundation. Jackson also brought underprivileged children to his Neverland ranch to experience his theme park and zoo.

Anointed "King of Pop" by his loving fans, Michael Jackson had a career in the music industry that spanned four decades. With his eye-popping choreography and distinctive blend of soul, funk, and rock, Jackson was a consummate entertainer. As well as being a pop superstar, Jackson showed considerable business acumen, and he earned an estimated $700 million during his lifetime.

The Jackson Five

Michael Jackson was born in Gary, Indiana, the seventh of nine children. His father Joseph worked in a steel mill and also played in an R&B band. Jackson's musical career began at the age of five when he and his brother Marlon started to play the bongos and tambourine in the Jackson Brothers, a band formed by older brothers Jackie, Tito, and Jermaine. By the time he was eight, Jackson was sharing the lead vocals with Jermaine, and the band changed its name to the Jackson Five. The band played live in many clubs between 1966 and 1968 and Michael and his brothers began to attract the attention of established stars. Gladys Knight and Bobby Taylor recommended the all-boy band to Motown Records head Berry Gordy, who immediately signed the group. The Jackson Five's first four singles ("I Want You Back", "ABC", "The Love You Save", and "I'll Be There") all went to number one, a chart record. With his strong soulful voice and dynamic dancing, Michael soon began to outshine his older brothers, and in 1972 he released his first solo album, *Got to Be There*. A string of solo hits followed, including "Ben" and "Rockin' Robin." By the mid-'70s, however, the Jackson Five's popularity had begun to decline and, frustrated at not being in charge of their creative output, they left the Motown label in 1975. The band renamed itself The Jacksons and signed a new deal with CBS Records, releasing six albums between 1976 and 1984.

Reaching Superstardom

In 1978, Jackson met music producer Quincy Jones on the set of *The Wiz*, a version of *The Wizard of Oz* in which Jackson played the Scarecrow opposite

Diana Ross's Dorothy. Jones agreed to produce Jackson's next solo effort, *Off the Wall* (1979). Now a disco classic, *Off the Wall* was the first album to produce four top 10 hits in the US—the title track, "She's Out of My Life", "Don't Stop 'Til You Get Enough", and "Rock With You." It sold ten million copies and won Jackson a Grammy and three American Music Awards. Jackson's career reached its apex four years later with the release of pop masterpiece *Thriller*, a mix of disco, R&B, and funk. Seven of its nine tracks became hit singles, and *Thriller* went on to sell more than 65 million copies, making it the biggest-selling album of all time. In 1984, Jackson won a record eight Grammys. The album also launched Jackson as a showman of extraordinary talent and innovation. His extravagant *Thriller* 16-minute long video clip, in which Jackson is transformed into a werecat and zombie, is still regarded

as the best pop promo ever made. Directed by John Landis, the video featured the voice of veteran horror movie actor Vincent Price and cost $500,000 to make. Jackson soon recouped its cost though, as his lawyer had negotiated what was then the highest royalty rate in the history of the music industry, approximately $2 per album. In 1983, Jackson's "moonwalk" dance astonished the pop world when it debuted on a Motown television special and was seen by an estimated 47 million people. Jackson also teamed up with ex-Beatle Paul McCartney to record the hit duets "The Girl Is Mine" and "Say Say Say," and they appeared on each other's albums. The friendship waned in 1985 though, when Jackson outbid McCartney to buy the publishing rights to the Beatles' back catalogue for $47.5 million. That same year, Jackson co-wrote the charity single "We Are the World," which sold nearly 20 million copies.

◀ *Michael Jackson first found fame alongside his brothers as the youngest member of the Jackson Five. Signed to Motown Records, the Jackson Five were one of the most successful pop bands of the early 1970s.*

Wacko Jacko

In January 1984, Jackson was filming a Pepsi Cola commercial in Los Angeles when a pyrotechnic malfunction set fire to his hair causing second degree burns to his scalp. Jackson received an estimated $1.5 million in compensation in an out-of-court settlement, which he donated to a burns unit. The incident was the beginning of frenzied media attention about the pop superstar's changing appearance and eccentric behavior, earning Jackson the nickname "Wacko Jacko." Tales of nights spent in an oxygen tent and his close bond with Bubbles the chimpanzee did nothing to dispel speculation. In 1987, the release of the "Bad" video showed a lighter-skinned Jackson, leading to rumors of skin bleaching and plastic surgery. The album *Bad* (1987) was a critical success nonetheless, selling more than 30 million copies and leading to a year-long world tour, at the time the highest-grossing in history. As the tour came to a close, however, Jackson admitted that he was "one of the loneliest people in the world." During the promotion of his follow-up *Dangerous* album, Jackson agreed to be interviewed by Oprah Winfrey at his fantasy Neverland ranch. Jackson revealed a childhood of physical and emotional abuse at the hands of his father. He also admitted to having had plastic surgery but denied deliberately changing the color of his skin, attributing the problems instead to vitiligo, a disease that destroys its pigmentation. Jackson was himself accused of child abuse in 1993, but reached an out-of-court settlement with the family of 11-year-old Jordy Chandler. The following year, Jackson married Lisa Marie Presley, the daughter of Elvis, but the couple divorced just 19 months later.

The bad publicity began to take its toll, and Jackson's album *HIStory*, composed of old hits and new material, did not do well despite a massive promotional campaign. In 1996, Jackson's performance at the Brit Awards, where he appeared surrounded by children, was interrupted by an incensed Jarvis Cocker who stormed onto the stage. The following year saw Jackson inducted into the Rock and Roll Hall of Fame. He also married his second wife, nurse Debbie Rowe, who gave birth to his first child, Prince Michael. The couple also had a daughter, Paris Michael Katherine, before divorcing in 1999. Jackson's final album *Invincible*, released in 2001, lasted a mere six weeks in the charts, and Jackson's career was all but finished. He also faced criticism when he dangled his 11-month-old son Prince Michael II from a hotel balcony in full view of the press, and shocked the world with his TV documentary admission that he shared his bed with children. This admission was to haunt him when, in 2003, Jackson was charged with molesting a young boy. In June 2005, after a five-month trial, he was cleared of charges but the surrounding publicity forced Jackson to leave his beloved Neverland ranch for the Middle East. His last years were plagued by money troubles and in an effort to put his finances in order Jackson signed up in 2009 for a series of 50 comeback concerts in London marketed as the "This is It" tour.

The concerts were sold out within days, proving that the King of Pop had lost none of his iconic appeal. Sadly, it was not to be. On June 25, 2009, Jackson collapsed at his rented mansion in Los Angeles. Attempts to resuscitate the star by his personal physician failed and he died at the Ronald Reagan UCLA Medical Center that same day. His death was later ruled as homicide by the Los Angeles County coroner, due to the apparent administration of lethal levels of painkilling drugs including propofol and lorazepam. His premature death caused shock around the world and his life was celebrated in a memorial service held at the Staples Center in Los Angeles on July 7, 2009. A host of musical stars, including Stevie Wonder, Lionel Richie, and Mariah Carey performed at the event, which was watched by an estimated 31.1 million Americans on television, with up to a billion watching worldwide. The Reverend Al Sharpton spoke at the memorial, prompting a standing ovation when he told Jackson's children: "Wasn't nothing strange about your Daddy. It was strange what your Daddy had to deal with. But he dealt with it anyway." Jackson was later buried at the Forest Lawn Memorial Park in Glendale, California. A movie, *This Is It,* was later released featuring footage of Jackson as he prepared for the upcoming tour.

Legacy to Pop

Jackson's 40-year career had a major influence on the music industry, particularly his transformation of the pop video clip from mere promotional tool into a major art form. In so doing, he helped the fledgling MTV channel achieve fame and success in the US. He enjoyed a following among both black and white fans, breaking down racial barriers and raising the profile of African-American artists in mainstream entertainment. His musical influence can be seen in today's hip hop, pop, and R&B artists, including Justin Timberlake and Usher.

#14

Michael Jackson pictured on stage in California, in 1988. By the late '80s, Jackson's changing appearance was becoming increasingly apparent, although this did nothing to diminish his popularity. By 1989, his annual earnings were well in excess of US$100 million per year.
▼

MARILYN MONROE (1926–1962)

Model, Singer, and Actress

Cover girl model; Hollywood icon; formed Marilyn Monroe Productions; won Golden Globe for Best Actress for Some Like It Hot

- Politics & Leadership
- Science & Technology
- **Popular Culture & the Arts**
- Business & Commerce
- Writers & Thinkers

 REWRITING HISTORY

On May 19, 1962, Marilyn sang "Happy Birthday" to President J. F. Kennedy at Madison Square Garden for his 45th birthday celebration. For the occasion, Marilyn wore a flesh-colored beaded dress designed by Jean Louis. It was so tight-fitting that Marilyn had to be sewn into it. The dress was auctioned in 1999 at Christie's, New York, for $1,267,500, and appears in the Guinness World of Records as the most expensive dress sold at auction.

Vulnerable, yet incredibly sexy, Marilyn Monroe was the hottest property in Hollywood during the 1950s. Critics praised her acting, while men lusted after her beauty. She remains one of the most iconic figures in twentieth century popular culture and has been ranked as the sixth greatest female star of all time by the American Film Institute.

From Foster Care to Modeling

Baptized Norma Jeane Baker, Marilyn Monroe was born in Los Angeles in 1926. Her mother, Gladys, was a film cutter at RKO Studios, but she suffered from mental illness and Norma Jeane spent most of her childhood in foster care and orphanages. Norma Jeane's modeling career began in a munitions factory in Burbank, California, when *Yank* magazine photographer David Conover spotted her potential. She bleached her naturally brunette hair blonde and signed with the Blue Book modeling agency. Blessed with voluptuous curves and an alluring pout, she became one of their most successful models, appearing on several magazine covers. In 1946 she caught the attention of a 20th Century Fox studio executive who arranged a screen test for her. Offered a six-month contract at $125 per week, Norma Jeane took the stage name Marilyn Monroe.

Movie Career

Monroe's first screen appearance was a bit part in *The Shocking Miss Pilgrim* (1947), which eventually led to a six-month contract with Columbia Pictures, where she took acting lessons from the studio's head coach Natasha Lytess. She appeared in *Ladies of the Chorus* (1949), in which she sang two songs, but the movie was not a critical success, and once again, Monroe's contract was not renewed. However, a small role in the Marx Brothers' movie *Love Happy* (1949) brought her to the attention of agent Johnny Hyde. He landed her a part in John Huston's *The Asphalt Jungle* (1950), which earned her rave reviews and a role in *All About Eve* (1950). Although small, these parts established Monroe as a sex goddess and Fox re-signed her on a seven-year contract. Roles in *Niagara* (1953) and *Gentlemen Prefer Blondes*

(1953) launched her as a movie superstar, though not everyone fell in love with Monroe. Joan Crawford criticized her "vulgarity" and the publication of a nude photograph taken in her modeling days caused a major scandal. She also gained a reputation for continually arriving late on set, though actress Jane Russell put it down to stage fright, and she was suspended by Fox in late 1953. The blonde bombshell with the hourglass figure continued to attract interest, however, and her appearance in *The Seven Year Itch* (1955) contained one of the most iconic scenes in motion picture history—Monroe standing in a New York street as the air from a subway grating blows her white dress over her head. After *The Seven Year Itch*, Monroe worked hard to shift the "dumb blonde" label that had been applied to her early work, enrolling at the New York's Actors Studio, where she studied with director Lee Strasberg in a bid to land serious, dramatic roles. She also formed Marilyn Monroe Productions at this time so that she could choose her own roles and be free from the contract restrictions imposed by Fox. The first movie made under the new agreement was *Bus Stop* (1956), directed by Joshua Logan. Critics raved about her performance, which received a Golden Globe nomination. She went on to star with Laurence Olivier in *The Prince and the Showgirl* (1957) and despite clashing on set, Olivier commented that "Marilyn was quite wonderful, the best of all." Monroe's performance in the movie won her the David di Donatello award, the Italian equivalent of an Academy Award, and the French Crystal Star Award. In 1959, Monroe appeared with Jack Lemmon and Tony Curtis in the smash hit *Some Like it Hot*, for which she won a Golden Globe. Her behavior during filming, however, had been obstructive and Monroe's reputation for difficulty grew. Her mental health deteriorated—she began to see a psychiatrist and was prescribed a variety of drugs to help her cope. In 1960, she completed her last movie *The Misfits* (1961), written by her then husband Arthur Miller. In February 1961, she voluntarily entered a psychiatric clinic. In 1962, she began filming *Something's Got to Give* but was dismissed for not turning up to work. Four months later, Monroe was found dead at her Brentwood home in Los Angeles of a drug overdose, whether accidental or intentional remains subject to debate.

Marilyn's Fame

Marilyn Monroe's enduring appeal rests on the countless iconic images in which she features. Starting as a glamour model in magazines, she became one of the most marketable faces in the history of Hollywood. Her vulnerability, untimely death, and speculation surrounding her private life—Monroe was reportedly involved with JFK—have inevitably added to the allure of her legacy, and she is securely positioned in the pantheon of silver screen greats.

#13

In 1954, Marilyn Monroe traveled to Korea at the invitation of the United Service Organizations (USA) to entertain troops stationed there during the Korean War. Monroe later said that performing in front of 13,000 troops over the three-day period helped her to overcome stage fright.

▼

- Politics & Leadership
- Science & Technology
- Popular Culture & the Arts
- Business & Commerce
- Writers & Thinkers

SALVADOR DALÍ (1904–1989)

Artist, Painter, and Sculptor

The most famous surrealist artist of the twentieth century; a gifted draftsman; worked in a wide range of media, including oils and watercolors, sculpture, jewelry, film, photography and furniture; received the title of Marquis of Púbol from King Juan Carlos of Spain in 1982

Salvador Dalí, who once said "I am surrealism," brought his technical skills to a new form of artistic expression, one that combined masterly painting with psychoanalytic introspection and rich symbolism. Renowned for his flamboyant personality and trademark mustache, Dalí helped open the door to an art of the personal subconscious.

The Artist as a Young Man

Salvador Dalí was born in the small town of Figueras, Catalonia, in northeastern Spain in 1904, the son of a wealthy lawyer. He showed a prodigious talent for drawing at an early age, which his family encouraged, sending him to drawing school. His work was shown at a public exhibition in the local theater when he was 15. By the time he went to study fine art at the Academia de San Fernando in Madrid, in 1922, he had already discovered modern painting and was soon taking an interest in Cubism and the Dada movement. He also began to cultivate the ostentatious manner and foppish look for which he became known (his waxed and upturned moustache echoing that of the great 17th-century Spanish painter Diego Velázquez). At the student residence, his group of close friends included the poet Federico García Lorca and filmmaker Luis Buñuel, with whom he later collaborated. He held his first solo exhibition in Barcelona, in 1925, and left the Academy the following year, expelled before his final exams after declaring that no one there was qualified to judge his work.

Into the Limelight

Dalí's highly creative imagination, technical mastery of drawing and his painting skills won him a growing reputation, and his work caught the attention of Pablo Picasso, whom he met in Paris in 1926, and of the Surrealist painter Joan Miró. He drew upon many different styles of art in his work, but several of his early paintings show the strong influence of these two artists, and in the late 1920s he became increasingly drawn to the dreamlike illusionism of the Surrealist school.

REWRITING HISTORY

Dalí's forays into film included creating the dream sequence for Alfred Hitchcock's Spellbound *and the imagery for the short Disney cartoon* Destino, *begun in 1945 and finally released in 2003. Dalí also wrote a movie script for the Marx Brothers in 1937. Entitled* Giraffes on Horseback Salads, *the movie was turned down by MGM as being too surreal.*

Meaning "above and beyond reality," Surrealism juxtaposes seemingly unconnected random objects in fantastic scenery, giving expression to the subconscious mind through free association, unfettered by the "rational" or the "normal." Dalí himself was greatly influenced by the work of Sigmund Freud, whom he regarded as one of the most important figures of the twentieth century, and he developed what he called the paranoiac-critical method, giving free rein to the mind's propensity to make links between the seemingly unconnected. Dalí drew upon his dreams, daydreams, and what he believed to be his experiences in the womb, intentionally making himself the medium through which his subconscious and the painting could communicate, and many of his paintings feature explicitly sexual and fetishistic motifs.

One of a Kind

His work in the 1930s, beginning with paintings such as *The Persistence of Memory*, in which viscous clocks melt and flow in a dreamlike landscape

reminiscent of his native Catalonia, brought Dalí to the forefront of the Surrealist group, but they expelled him in 1934, largely because his politics didn't match their leftist views.

Visiting the US, he caused a stir with exhibitions of his paintings and with his outrageous public appearances, accompanied by Gala, his muse and future wife. Dalí's personal and artistic reputation soon spread to the international stage. Throughout his life, Dalí continued to break new ground in painting, photography, experimental filmmaking, performance art, sculpture and even furniture, with works such as his surrealist sofa in the form of Mae West's lips. With his technical brilliance and his audacious expression of the innermost workings of his mind in artistic form, Dalí set the standard for twentieth-century art, leaving a diverse legacy that adorns collections around the world.

◀ *Dali was involved with Surrealist artists in a variety of media. Here he is seen in the photograph "The Dali Atomicus," by Phillipe Halsam, in which objects were suspended off the floor using wires.*

◄◄ **REWRITING HISTORY**

Many musicians who played with Davis went on to create names for themselves and extend his influence indirectly. They include John Coltrane, Chick Corea, Red Garland, Kenny Garrett, Herbie Hancock, Keith Jarrett, John McLaughlin, John Scofield, Tony Williams, and Wayne Shorter and Joe Zawinul (who later formed fusion band Weather Report).

MILES DAVIS (1926–1991)

Jazz Composer and Musician

Developed a uniquely melodic and intimate style; contributed to all major movements in jazz throughout the second half of the twentieth century; his various bands nurtured up-and-coming talent, and many of his players went on to musical fame

In a career spanning five decades, trumpeter Miles Davis was a part, and usually in the vanguard, of every important development in jazz music. He had a playing talent that earned him recognition from the outset and a musical ear that enabled him continually to create new genres of jazz by bringing together unusual combinations of players.

Early Influences

Born in Alton, Illinois, in 1926, Miles Davis was brought up in East St Louis, Ill., across the Mississippi from St Louis, Missouri. His father was a well-to-do dentist, and the family also owned a ranch in Arkansas. At the age of 13 he was given a trumpet by his father, and had private lessons from his father's friend, school band teacher and St Louis jazz trumpeter Elwood Buchanan. Buchanan had a profound influence on Davis's playing, encouraging a relaxed, no-frills style to which Davis was to remain faithful.

On entering Lincoln High School, Davis joined the school band and was soon playing professionally outside school hours. In 1944, he had the thrill of playing with two of his heroes—Dizzy Gillespie and Charlie Parker—when the Billy Eckstine band (one of the first bebop bands) came to town and needed a third trumpet while Buddy Anderson was absent. Davis would have chosen to continue with the band had his parents not insisted that he continue his education, and on graduating he moved to New York and began studies at the Juilliard School of Music.

The New York Jazz Scene

Miles Davis quickly fulfilled his real purpose in moving to New York by meeting up with Dizzy Gillespie and Charlie Parker, learning from the masters and then spending three years as a full-time member of Parker's band. In 1948, working with arranger Gil Evans, he formed his first band—an innovative nine-piece group that included non-black players, including West Coast musicians, and unusual instruments such as French horn and tuba. Although the band appeared live on only a few occasions, the sound that it created was revolutionary. A radical departure from bebop, having a much smoother and more intricately arranged sound, the "cool jazz" recordings released as singles were not initially popular, but *Birth of the Cool*, on which these were compiled, became one of the most influential jazz albums.

Change Upon Change

In the early '50s Davis struggled with, and beat, heroin addiction, but was musically productive. It was at this time that he began using the Harmon mute and developed his signature sound, and his popularity soared after his 1955 Newport Jazz Festival performance. Miles Davis's "first quintet" (later a sextet) was formed at this time, producing several memorable studio albums, including *Milestones* and *Kind of Blue*, broadly considered his greatest work.

Through the '60s and '70s, Davis repeatedly reinvented his jazz style with the support of some of the greatest jazz musicians of the time, including Herbie Hancock, Wayne Shorter, and the young drummer Tony Williams in the "second quintet," which later included Dave Holland and Chick Corea, Joe Zawinul and John McLaughlin. Having introduced a more orchestral sound, and then flirted with flamenco, Davis moved increasingly toward the use of electric instruments, and by the early '70s was in the forefront of jazz-rock fusion with albums such as *Bitches Brew*, which rekindled popular interest in jazz, but a combination of ill-health and drug use led to his virtual retirement from the music scene in 1975.

He returned in the early '80s with a smaller band, and continued to adopt new musical technology and embrace new genres of music, including hip-hop, with albums such as *Tutu* and several movie soundtracks. Miles Davis died in 1991 of pneumonia and a stroke, but his musical influence continues to pervade the music scene well beyond the confines of jazz.

#11

Seen here performing at the legendary Ronnie Scott's jazz club in London's Soho in 1969 for a live broadcast of the BBC TV show, **Jazz Scene.** *Miles Davis performs with Chick Corea, Dave Holland, and Jacques de Johnette.*
▼

SIGMUND FREUD (1856–1939)

Austrian Neurologist and Psychologist

Founder of the "psychoanalytic" school of psychology; renowned for his theories about the role of the unconscious mind in mental and physical disorders; identified sexual desire as the driving force in human behavior; continues to influence psychiatry and the humanities

- Politics & Leadership
- **Science & Technology**
- Popular Culture & the Arts
- Business & Commerce
- Writers & Thinkers

REWRITING HISTORY

Breuer's patient and Freud's inspiration, Anna O. was later revealed to be a German-Jewish woman called Bertha Pappenheim, who became well known for her feminism and social work. Analysis of her symptoms has since suggested that, rather than hysteria, she was in fact suffering from temporal lobe epilepsy

Although he was not the first to posit the existence or importance of the conscious and the unconscious, Austrian neurologist Sigmund Freud popularized the concept and formulated a theory of mental development and processes, as well as clinical techniques for analyzing and resolving problems that he believed were rooted in the unconscious.

A Promising Child

Born of Jewish parents in the village of Freiberg in Moravia, Austria, Sigmund Freud was the first child of his father's second wife and was his mother's favorite. The family moved to Vienna when Sigmund was about five years old, and he was given privileges denied to his two older half-brothers and six younger siblings, including good schooling and his own room in which to study. He responded with hard work and an active mind, and he graduated with honors in 1873. After considering taking law, Freud enrolled in Vienna's prestigious medical school, where he was drawn to the experimental and investigative, rather than the clinical, side of medicine. He chose to extend the normal five years of study to seven, and worked in the zoological and anatomical laboratories of the famous physiology professor Ernst Wilhelm von Brücke, whose work had a strong influence on the young Freud. Together with Hermann von Helmholtz, best known for his work on thermodynamics, von Brücke proposed that the workings of living organisms could be explained in terms of physics and chemistry. Freud took von Brücke's concept of "psychodynamics"—which looked at the work of the conscious and unconscious mind in the forming on human behavior—and set out to apply this reductionist principle to the study of personality.

From Body to Mind

After receiving his doctor of medicine degree, the 24-year-old Freud chose to abandon his path as a researcher, primarily on financial grounds. He had met, and fallen deeply in love with, a young Viennese woman by the name of Martha Bernays, and von Brücke advised him to turn to clinical practice if he wanted the financial security needed to marry and start a family. He moved to Vienna's general hospital, and worked in several departments before spending a period in the psychiatry department working under the Austrian psychiatrist Theodor Meynert. Meynert's approach was neurological, studying the structure and pathology of the brain in order to ascertain the nature of the interaction between organic and psychological factors. In this approach to psychiatry, the patients' behavior was studied only as a symptom of an underlying pathological disorder rather than as something worth studying in itself.

The Talking Cure

In 1885 Freud went to study in Paris under the leading French neurologist Jean Martin Charcot, who was using hypnosis to treat "hysteria," a suite of physical and behavioral symptoms thought to have an underlying

psychological cause. In 1886 he returned to Vienna, finally marrying Martha Bernays after a four-year engagement and the exchange of some 900 love letters, and set up his own neuropsychiatry practice. He also collaborated with the Austrian physician Josef Breuer, and his work—especially his treatment of one particular patient—was to have a profound effect on the development of Freud's approach to psychology.

Several years earlier, a patient whom Breuer referred to as "Anna O." came to him suffering from apparent hysteria, the symptoms of which included headaches, hallucinations, visual disturbances, and partial paralysis. The onset of the symptoms coincided with the start of her father's serious illness, and when he died she became paralyzed and unable to eat. In the course of two years of treatment, it became clear to Breuer that when Anna O. talked about experiences that were troubling her, the symptoms diminished. She herself referred to the therapeutic sessions, during some of which she was in a state of self-induced hypnosis, as "chimney sweeping" and "the talking cure," while Breuer spoke of the sessions as catharsis.

Psychoanalysis

Breuer had found that Anna O. had difficulty talking about certain experiences, and Freud believed that this was due to a defense mechanism,

◀ *In 1909, Freud (bottom left) and Carl Jung (bottom right) were both invited to give a series of lectures on psychoanalysis at a conference held at Clark University in Worcester, Massachusetts. Freud's lectures brought him to the attention of a much wider audience.*

"What we call happiness in the strictest sense comes from the (preferably sudden) satisfaction of needs that have been dammed up to a high degree."
Sigmund Freud

actively repressing the acknowledgement or reenactment of unpleasant memories or experiences. In his account of the case, Breuer commented that sexuality appeared to play no part in the young woman's character or experiences, but Freud himself was convinced that, on the contrary, sexual development was at the heart of psychological tension and that in Anna O.'s case her hysteria was in response to childhood sexual abuse. Breuer and Freud co-wrote *Studies on Hysteria* (1895) based on Anna O., but their disagreement over the role of sexuality led to a rift between them.

Freud developed talk therapy as a treatment for mental illness, but preferred to work without the use of hypnosis, believing that the defense mechanisms were more easily overcome if the patient was awake. He encouraged patients to engage in a process that he called free association, and his psychoanalytic methods developed from this. He increasingly focused on sexual aspects of his patients' lives, but found that much of what was revealed was imaginary and appeared to be related to fantasies from childhood, and even infancy, leading him to believe in the primary role of the child's complex positive and negative relationships with its parents.

Freudian Theory

As well as continuing his work with his patients, Freud also undertook a detailed exploration of his own dreams and thoughts, and was able to document a process of personal emotional development. His work was published as *The Interpretation of Dreams*, in 1901, and in it he claimed that "The interpretation of dreams is the royal road to knowledge of the unconscious activities of the mind." Through his work, Freud came to formulate a theory of personality that has had a profound influence on the way we think about and treat psychological issues. Freud believed that the individual personality comprised three parts: the "id" (corresponding to our basic instincts, the source of our psychic energy); the "ego" (the rational aspect of our personality that develops in childhood and deals with the demands of reality); and the "superego" (the moral aspect of personality, the conscience, in some respects an internalization of social values).

The terms id, ego, and superego are now in common usage, with their specific psychoanalytic connotations, but they are actually latinized translations. Freud himself used the terms *das Es*, *das Ich*, and *das Über-Ich* (the It, the I, and the Over-I), which had self-evident meanings to his German audience. The superego and the ego are partly conscious, partly unconscious, but the id is wholly unconscious, and for Freud it is in the unconscious, which makes up the vast majority of the personality, that the most important psychological processes take place. The ego, trying to take reality into account, finds itself in conflicts between the amoral, instinctual demands of the id and the moral dictates of the superego. To resolve these conflicts, the ego uses defense mechanisms—distorting and interpreting reality in such a way as to evade the anxiety that the conflicts produce. Chief among these defense mechanisms, said Freud, is repression, pushing the id's unacceptable impulses into the unconscious mind and keeping them there, and chief among these impulses is sex.

Oedipus and Electra

Freud's formulation of the Oedipus complex provides a clear insight into his theoretical approach—as well as, it can be argued, his own emotional history. In Greek mythology, Oedipus fell in love with his mother and killed his father, and according to Freud, "It is the fate of all of us, perhaps, to direct our first sexual impulse towards our mother and our first hatred and our first murderous wish against our father. Our dreams convince us that this is so." Freud believed that in the course of their psychological development, between the ages of three and five, all boys go through an "Oedipal phase" in which the mother becomes the object of desire, leading the child to fear his father's anger and the possibility of castration. The resolution of the Oedipus complex is seen as important in the development of gender and of personal identity. Girls are thought to have the same (in this case homosexual) desire for their mothers, together with "penis envy" directed at the father, a situation that Carl Jung labeled the Electra complex. Freud's work in bringing sexuality to center stage earned him many opponents, but his perspective has had a profound effect on a wide range of academic studies and the fundamentals of his methods are still in use today.

◀ *Sigmund Freud was born in this house, close to the main square in the eastern Czech town of Pribor, in 1856. The town celebrated the 150th anniversary of his birth with a ceremony marking the official opening of the house as a museum.*

WILBUR WRIGHT (1867–1912) AND ORVILLE WRIGHT (1871–1948)

American Inventors of the Airplane

Made the first sustained, manned flight in a powered, heavier-than-air craft; approached flight scientifically; invented means of steering a craft in the air; built their own engine

- Politics & Leadership
- **Science & Technology**
- Popular Culture & the Arts
- Business & Commerce
- Writers & Thinkers

 REWRITING HISTORY

In the same month as the Wrights' first flight, Samuel P. Langley, funded by the Smithsonian Institution (of which he was secretary) tested his own craft, without success. Langley then secretly incorporated many of the Wrights' inventions, and the craft flew in September 1914. The Smithsonian then displayed it as the first heavier-than-air craft "capable" of manned powered flight, sparking a long feud with the Wright brothers.

Wilbur and Orville Wright, the inventors of the airplane, won the race to achieve powered flight because they brought together the right combination of qualities. As well as the pioneering spirit and a good deal of bravery, the brothers displayed original thinking, a mechanical aptitude, and the intelligence to apply rigorous scientific thinking to the problem—all with no formal education.

Practical Magic

Wilbur Wright, born near Millville, Indiana, and his brother Orville, born in Dayton, Ohio, were the sons of a clergyman (later Bishop) in the United Brethren church and a highly practical mother. The boys were encouraged to read the books, including scientific works, in their father's extensive library, and they both developed an early interest in things mechanical. The brothers later attributed their fascination with flying to a rubber-band-powered toy flying machine that their father gave to them in 1878. When the toy inevitably broke, Wilbur tried to build a larger version and soon found that the bigger it was, the harder it was to make it fly.

Even in their teens the boys displayed mechanical aptitude. Together they built a working lathe, and Orville started a printing business using a small press. Limited by its size, he and his brother then built their own much larger press, and in 1889 Orville began printing and publishing a local newspaper—the *West Side News*. The press's mechanism was so ingenious that it attracted the attention of a Denver printer. Neither of the brothers attended college, and when Orville left school, Wilbur joined him in the newspaper venture, but in 1892 the brothers returned to their interest in engineering and opened the Wright Cycle Shop in Dayton, later selling the newspaper.

Learning from the Master

The Wright brothers had been following the development of gliders since the early 1890s, and in 1896, spurred on by the untimely death of gliding pioneer Otto Lilienthal, they began their own practical investigation of flying. Given that neither of them had had any formal training in physics or engineering, their approach was remarkable, but it owed a good deal to the methods used by Lilienthal.

The German aviator was, like the Wrights, an engineer by inclination, and sales of a small engine that he had invented brought in sufficient income for him to spend his time developing gliders. Lilienthal can take the credit for showing that flight in heavier-than-air crafts was a practical possibility and not just a dream. He was effectively the inventor of the hang glider, and he made literally thousands of short successful flights in a total of 18 craft, each one incorporating the lessons of the last. Three of his gliders were biplanes,

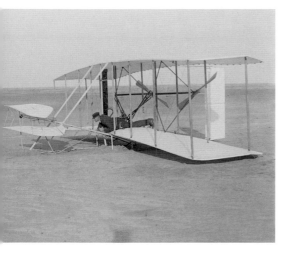

and he had invented a movable tail plane that could be raised to give upward thrust as the craft landed. He had also, after many uncomfortable landings (his gliders had a tendency to stall and then nose-dive), installed a "rebound bar" in front of the pilot to absorb the shock of a head first descent. Sadly, the device was not in place when the wing of his glider broke off and he plunged more than 50 feet (15.25 m) to the ground. The impact broke his spine and he died the following day.

When they began their own experiments in flying, the Wright brothers took on board Lilienthal's studious approach to the task. He had carried out careful experiments, recording the results, and even tabulating the amount of lift produced by different curvatures of wing, and the Wright brothers set out in a similarly thorough manner.

A Scientific Approach

Aviation research was taking place in many places, especially in Europe, and Wilbur and Orville collected as much information as they could while beginning their own work on a series of kites and gliders. By 1900 they had built several gliders up to 22 feet (6.7 m) in wingspan and had even solved the problem of controlling the tipping of the craft from side to side but, despite several decent flights at their chosen testing ground of Kitty Hawk in North Carolina, the results were disappointing. Using homemade measuring

◀ *Made of white spruce, ash, aluminum, platinum, tin, muslin, and steel, the 1903 Wright Flyer I had a wingspan of more than 40 feet (12 m) and weighed a little more than 700 pounds (317 kg). The pilot lay prone in the center of the lower wing.*

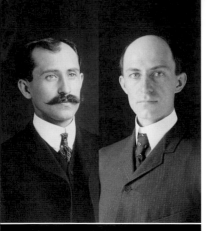

▶ *The Wright Brothers
initially applied for a
patent for their flying
machine in 1903, but
it was rejected. A new
application depicting their
1902 glider but featuring
their three-axis flight
control system was finally
successful in 1906, but
they soon found themselves
in legal wrangles with
manufacturers who wanted
to use elements of their
design without paying
them a fee.*

instruments, they found that the actual forces acting on the wings in flight didn't match the data from other would-be fliers, including Lilienthal's tables of forces. Their response to the problem took them from enthusiastic amateurs to truly scientific researchers: they developed a piece of apparatus that was to prove crucial to their endeavor—a wind tunnel. The wind tunnel itself and the mechanism they invented to measure the various forces were fairly crude, but the device provided them with important and accurate data and gave them a greater understanding of aerodynamics than anyone else in the field. By the Christmas of 1901 they had carefully tested more than 100 wing designs, and they then applied their results directly to their flying machines, enabling them to make consistent progress. In 1902 they flew their glider more than 600 feet (183 m) into a strong wind. The next challenge was powered flight.

The First Powered Flight

Unable to find a suitable lightweight engine for their aircraft, the Wright brothers took a typically independent step and built their own with the help of their bicycle store mechanic, Charlie Taylor. The four-cylinder gasoline engine, cast in aluminum and weighing just 170 lb (77 kg), produced 12 horsepower. They also had to design and build their own propellers, returning to the wind tunnel to create the most efficient shape.

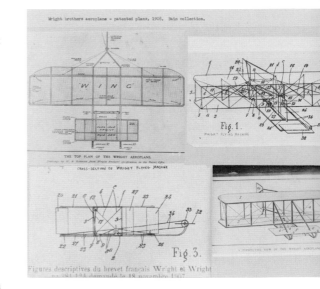

By the fall of 1903 the Wright Flyer I was ready for its first trial, and the brothers were confident. They knew that the craft was capable of flight, and from their "laboratory" studies they knew the power of the engine and the thrust that the two propellers (turning in opposite directions to avoid skewing the plane in flight) would produce. Now it was just a matter of getting it into the air. They prepared for the flight at Kitty Hawk and, after weeks of setbacks involving broken propeller shafts, on December 14th Wilbur won the toss of a coin and climbed into the craft. The engine stalled during takeoff and the airplane came down after just a few seconds, causing minor damage.

On December 17, 1903, with repairs completed, it was Orville's turn. The plane took off into a strong headwind and flew 120 feet (37 m) in 12 seconds at a height of about 10 feet (3m) with a ground speed of just under 7 miles per hour (11 km/h). Orville flew the craft again that morning, and Wilbur flew twice, each flight being longer than the one before and the longest being over 850 feet (260 m). The Wright brothers had succeeded—they had achieved the first sustained, controlled, manned, and powered flight in a heavier-than-air craft.

Onward and Upward

The response from the press and the public was remarkably cool. Many people tried to belittle or even deny the brothers' achievement, and over the next few years they encountered problems in registering patents for the various elements of their invention. Flyer I never took to the air again, but Flyers II and III were even more successful and the brothers gave many public demonstrations, including a flight around New York that solidly established their reputation. The Wright Company was incorporated in 1909 and, with Wilbur as president and Orville as vice president, the company set up a factory in Dayton and a flight school in Huffman Prairie. The company, under the name Curtiss-Wright Corporation still operates today, testing and manufacturing components for the aerospace industry. Interestingly, despite being officially recognized as the first people to achieve powered flight in a heavier-than-air craft, their designs proved less lucrative than would have perhaps been expected. The demand for aircraft at that time was virtually non-existent, and the brothers were forced to train a team of pilots to enter their machines in regional shows and competitions, in the expectation that they would collect the prize money on offer. It was a dangerous business. Of the nine people who were trained to operate the aircraft, two were killed at air shows, while a further four lost their lives in flying accidents after the enterprise had ended. Orville Wright was badly injured on September 17, 1908, after a propeller shaft snapped in mid-air, but he could consider himself lucky—his passenger, Army lieutenant Thomas Selfridge, was killed after he fractured his skull in the crash.

The Wright brothers sit alongside the truly great American inventors of the era, combining a sharp intellect and a stubborn determination that was shared by the likes of Edison and Ford. Without any formal education or great financial backing, the Wright brothers built their enterprise up from the ground. Their remarkably thorough scientific approach provided a platform for future advances and established practices that are still used today. Their legacy—that of human flight—continues to capture the popular imagination like no other.

"It is possible to fly without motors, but not without knowledge and skill. This I conceive to be fortunate, for man, by reason of his greater intellect, can more reasonably hope to equal birds in knowledge than to equal nature in the perfection of her machinery"
Wilbur Wright

MARTIN LUTHER KING (1929–1968)

Baptist Minister and Civil Rights Activist

High-profile leader of the African-American Civil Rights Movement; led the Montgomery Bus Boycott; helped found the Southern Christian Leadership Conference; Nobel Peace Prize winner

■ **Politics & Leadership**

■ Science & Technology

■ Popular Culture & the Arts

■ Business & Commerce

■ Writers & Thinkers

 REWRITING HISTORY

Martin Luther King was born the son of the Reverend Michael King, and he was originally named Michael King, Jr. In 1934, when the young boy was five years old, the King family traveled to Germany, and his father was inspired to change both their names to Martin Luther in honor of the German Protestant leader of the Reformation.

Civil rights activist Martin Luther King did more than anyone to advance the rights of African-Americans. His greatest gift lay in his power to electrify crowds with his impassioned speeches. Today's world leaders, including Barack Obama, the first black President in US history, continue to invoke his words.

Born into the Church

Martin Luther King was born in Atlanta, Georgia, the son (and grandson) of a pastor. Growing up in the heart of America's Deep South, King experienced racial discrimination at an early age. He attended segregated schools in Georgia before enrolling at Morehouse College to study sociology. King earned his BD at Crozer Theological Seminary in Pennsylvania in 1951, where he won a scholarship to study at Boston University. In 1953 King married Coretta Scott, with whom he had two sons and two daughters. He was awarded his doctorate in 1955. During his time in Boston, King was mentored by the civil rights leader Howard Thurman, a former classmate of King's father and the first black Dean of Marsh Chapel. Thurman had met with Mahatma Gandhi, who urged him to spread the use of nonviolent resistance as a form of protest. King himself later travelled to India to meet members of the Gandhi family, where he heard the message for himself. King joined the executive committee of the National Association for the Advancement of Colored People (NAACP) and began to work for black civil rights.

The Montgomery Bus Boycott

King took up the post of pastor at the Dexter Avenue Baptist Church in Montgomery, Alabama, while studying for his doctorate in 1954. Like many places in the Deep South, Montgomery had a policy of racial segregation on its public transit system. Blacks were required to sit in the back rows on buses, while whites took the front seats. If no white rows were available when a white boarded the bus, the blacks had to move back a row. In December, 1955, Rosa Parks was sitting in the front-most row for blacks, and when a white person demanded her row she refused to move. Her subsequent arrest triggered the boycott of the transit system, led by King. The Montgomery bus boycott lasted over a year, tensions in the community rose, and King's home was firebombed. Although he was arrested, King's commitment never wavered, and the boycott ended with a United States District Court ruling in December 1956 that declared segregation on buses as unconstitutional. From that day on, blacks and whites could ride on the buses as equals. King emerged from the boycott as America's preeminent black spokesman.

Peaceful Protests

In 1957, King helped form the Southern Christian Leadership Conference (SCLC). The SCLC took its modus operandi from Gandhi, hoping to harness the voice and power of black churches throughout the US in its peaceful crusade against racial discrimination. Despite threats against his life, phone tapping by the FBI—its director J. Edgar Hoover called him "the most dangerous man in America"—and attempted blackmail, King led the organization until his death. He applied Gandhi's nonviolent form of protest against segregation in the South, leading campaigns wherever he was needed.

King was an inspirational orator, gifted with the ability to move and uplift his audience, black and white alike. King drew upon his Christian faith when he spoke, frequently making Biblical references and delivering his speeches in the manner of a sermon. His speeches were free of hatred and revenge and instead focused on the way forward. Between 1957 and 1968, King wrote five books, spoke over 2,500 times, and traveled more than six million miles (9.5 million km) in his fight for justice. King's campaigns began to attract the attention of the world's media, who were shocked at the indignities endured by black Americans on a daily basis. In particular, the campaign against segregation in Birmingham, Alabama, in the spring of 1963, drew televisions crews from around the world, and the force of public opinion ensured that racial segregation became a national, not simply a local, issue.

▲
Martin Luther King became a pastor at the Dexter Avenue Baptist Church (now the Dexter Avenue King Memorial Baptist Church) in 1954. The church became a meeting place for Black American during the Montgomery bus boycott and is considered by many to be the birthplace of the civil rights movement in the US.

As King himself said of the Birmingham protests, "The purpose of … direct action is to create a situation so crisis-packed that it will inevitably open the door to negotiation." The events in Birmingham enhanced King's reputation considerably and he received the support of more than a quarter million people from different ethnic backgrounds during his March on Washington for Jobs and Freedom in the summer of 1963. His famous "I Have a Dream" speech delivered that day has gone down in history as one of the great speeches in the history of American oratory.

Time magazine named him their Man of the Year in 1963. The following year, 35-year-old King received the Nobel Prize for Peace, making him the then youngest recipient in Nobel history. King donated the $54,123 prize money to the civil rights movement. The passage of the Civil Rights Act of 1964 effectively ended racial prejudice in employment and public services in the US, and the Voting Rights Act of 1965 outlawed discriminatory voting practices. King later came under fire from the more radical sectors of the black community, who rejected his peaceful protest movement in favor of the more violent and radical leadership offered by the likes of Malcom X and Stokely Carmichael. He also faced mounting criticism for his opposition to the war in Vietnam. Undeterred, King continued his work, widening his focus to ending poverty among all sectors of society.

Assassination

Death threats continued to plague King, including a bomb threat against his plane as he prepared to fly to Memphis in April 1968 to support striking sanitation workers. When he finally reached Memphis, King addressed a rally at the Mason Temple, the World Headquarters of the Church of God in Christ, delivering his "I've Been to the Mountaintop" speech, which was to be his last. The speech refers to the death threat that he had received: "And then I got to Memphis. And some began to say the threats, or talk about the threats that were out. What would happen to me from some of our sick white brothers? Well, I don't know what will happen now. We've got some difficult days ahead. But it doesn't matter with me now. Because I've been to the mountaintop … I just want to do God's will. And He's allowed me to go up to the mountain. And I've looked over. And I've seen the promised land. I may not get there with you. But I want you to know tonight, that we, as a people, will get to the promised land." The following day, April 3, he was fatally shot while standing on the second floor balcony of the Lorraine Motel in Memphis, Tennessee. His assassination led to rioting in over 100 US cities. James Earl Ray later confessed to his murder and was sentenced to 99 years in prison, though Ray later recanted his confession and the conviction remains the subject of controversy and conspiracy theories. Indeed, the King family supported Ray's appeal for a retrial though it was never granted. Ray died in prison in 1998. After King's death, his widow Coretta Scott King opened the

Martin Luther King, Jr. Center for Nonviolent Social Change, an organization that works to preserve his legacy of nonviolent conflict resolution worldwide.

King's Legacy in America

Martin Luther King was posthumously awarded the Presidential Medal of Freedom in 1977 and the Congressional Gold Medal in 2004. Since 1986, his birthday is celebrated on the third Monday of January as a national holiday in the States. More than forty years after his death, King remains the symbolic head of America's fight for racial equality. Nearly every major city and neighborhood has a street, park, or building named after the civil rights leader. However, his legacy goes far deeper than that. Without King's leadership, the United States could still be in a state of apartheid, on par with pariah state South Africa prior to Nelson Mandela's release from jail. Before King, black Americans could not sit next to whites on a bus, nor go to the same school, nor eat at the same diner. King's Civil Rights Movement swept away the racial anachronisms that haunted America's Deep South and

◀ *King is seen here with fellow civil rights activist, Malcolm X, in Washington D.C. in 1964 shortly after attending a US Senate debate on the Civil Rights Bill. The two men had a different approach to winning support for African-Americans, with Malcolm X adopting more radical and violent methods.*

he advanced the rights of black Americans to the point where one of its own could win the ultimate prize—that of President of the United States.

JOHN F. KENNEDY (1917–1963)

President of the United States

35th US president; Pulitzer Prize-winning author; negotiated peaceful end to the Cuban Missile Crisis; escalated US involvement in Vietnam War; instigated new Civil Rights law; established the Peace Corps

- Politics & Leadership
- Science & Technology
- Popular Culture & the Arts
- Business & Commerce
- Writers & Thinkers

◀◀ REWRITING HISTORY

Elected at the age of 43, John F. Kennedy was the second youngest man to hold the post of President, after Theodore Roosevelt. However, he remains the youngest person ever elected president. Roosevelt was elected as vice president and only assumed the top post after the assassination of President McKinley in 1901.

With his elegant wife Jacqueline and two young children at his side, JFK brought a hitherto unseen freshness and glamor to the White House. JFK's assassination in 1963 shocked the world and brought an end to one of the most enduringly popular presidencies in US history. His untimely death ensured that the "Camelot" dynasty would remain fixed in the popular American imagination.

Formative Years

Of Irish descent, John Fitzgerald Kennedy was born in Brookline, Massachusetts, in 1917, the second son of Joseph Patrick Kennedy and Rose Fitzgerald. The family was already involved in politics and his father later served as ambassador to Great Britain. JFK graduated from Harvard University in 1940. His university thesis formed the basis of his best-selling book *Why England Slept*, an account of Britain's appeasement policy prior to World War II. JFK attended Stanford Graduate School of Business before joining the United States Navy in 1941. He was sent to the South Pacific in 1943, serving as commander of a patrol torpedo (PT) boat. When his PT boat was hit by a destroyer, JFK showed courage and leadership in saving the lives of his comrades, and was awarded a medal for bravery. He suffered severe spinal injuries in the process, further exacerbating already existing back problems that were to plague him for the remainder of his life.

Turning to Politics

JFK considered a career in journalism but the death of his elder brother Joe in the war left him as the family's political heir apparent. Encouraged by his father, JFK won election as a Democrat to the House of Representatives in 1946, where he remained for six years. In 1952, he was elected to the US Senate. The following year he married socialite Jacqueline Lee Bouvier. They had four children together but only two, John and Caroline, survived infancy. While recovering in 1956 from one of several spinal operations, JFK wrote the Pulitzer Prize-winning book *Profiles in Courage*. Kennedy narrowly lost the vice presidential nomination in the 1956 campaign but was reelected to the Senate for a second term in 1958. In 1960, JFK won the Democratic nomination for its presidential candidate and selected Lyndon B. Johnson as his running mate.

His Catholic faith presented JFK with a potential obstacle to winning the election—no Catholic had ever before, or since, been elected president—but Kennedy countered this by saying "I am not the Catholic candidate for President. I am the Democratic Party's candidate for President who also happens to be a Catholic." In September and October, JFK appeared with the Republican candidate, Vice President Richard Nixon, in the first televised presidential debates in history. Made up for television and at ease in the presence of the cameras, JFK gained instant advantage over a tense-looking Nixon, and the American audience warmed to the less experienced candidate. In one of the closest-fought contests in US history, JFK won by a margin of 34,226,925 votes to 34,108,662. In his inaugural speech in January 1961, JFK set the tone of his presidency with the words, "Ask not what your country can do for you—ask what you can do for your country."

Domestic Policy

In his election campaign, JFK promised African-Americans that he would implement a new Civil Rights Act. Consequently, over 70 percent of the black vote went to Kennedy. However, although he offered support to the rising Civil Rights Movement by sending federal marshals to protect the Freedom Riders in Alabama and the black students at Mississippi University, JFK's civil rights bill did not come before Congress until 1963. JFK had ambitious plans for a Medicare program to offer basic health coverage but was unable to persuade Congress to pass his bill. He had more success with the economy, presiding over a period of great economic growth and prosperity.

He also successfully established the Peace Corps, a volunteer program to send out the country's young people to serve for a two-year period in third world countries.

#7

John F. Kennedy meeting with West Berlin Mayor (later German Chancellor) Willy Brandt at the White House in 1961, the year that the Berlin Wall was erected. Two years later Kennedy visited West Berlin, where he delivered his famous "Ich Bin ein Berliner" speech.
▼

Kennedy was also eager to lead the way in the space race. In May 1961, Kennedy announced his commitment to the US landing a man on the Moon before the end of the decade. He approached Soviet premier Nikita Khrushchev twice about a joint venture in space exploration. Khrushchev refused the initial offer in 1961, largely due to the fact that the Soviets were well ahead in the race at the time. However, in late 1963 Khrushchev agreed to collaborate, but Kennedy was assassinated before an agreement could be formalized. Kennedy's dream came to fruition six years after his assassination, when the Apollo 11 astronauts landed on the moon on July 20, 1969.

Foreign Policy

JFK's foreign policy was largely preoccupied with containing the perceived threat presented by the spread of communism. Shortly after taking office, JFK authorized an invasion to overthrow Cuban leader Fidel Castro. Backed by the CIA, a force of Cuban exiles attempted to invade Cuba in an operation known as the Bay of Pigs in April 1961, but without direct support from the US military the invasion ended in abject failure with the killing or capture of all the exiles. After being held for 20 months, the captured soldiers were released in exchange for over US$50 million in food and medical supplies. The failed coup was a huge embarrassment for the Kennedy administration and only served to increase distrust between the two countries, with Cuba turning increasingly to Russia for help in improving its defenses.

In August 1961, construction of the Berlin Wall started. The wall divided West and East Berlin and symbolized the ideological divide between the capitalist West and Soviet East. In June 1963, Kennedy traveled to West Berlin to give a speech against the evils of communism, in which he spoke the now famous words "Ich Bin ein Berliner." A huge proportion of the West Berlin population went out onto the streets of the capital to hear the president speak, and the moment became an iconic symbol of the stark differences between East and West. Kennedy's casual demeanor and rhetorical eloquence provided a counterpoint to the repression of the communist regime, and the appeals of western "freedom" and "democracy" rarely looked so appealing as it did that day, against the backdrop of the monstrous wall.

In 1962, JFK confronted the prospect of nuclear war with the Soviets over the secret installation of Russian ballistic missiles in Cuba. As the world held its breath, JFK began negotiations with Soviet Premier Khrushchev that led to the removal of the missiles and the US promise to leave Cuba in peace. Following the Cuban Missile Crisis, JFK worked to slow down the arms race, resulting in the Partial Test Ban Treaty of 1963. In Vietnam, JFK continued the previous administration's policy when he provided limited military support as early as 1961 to the South Vietnamese government to fight the Communist forces led by Ho Chi Minh. From a policy of "containment" whereby the

US confronted communism indirectly via client states, the conflict escalated into one of direct US intervention and would become one of the defining issues of '60s America. Under Kennedy's presidency, the US military used napalm and the defoliant "Agent Orange" against the Vietnamese. It has been argued that Kennedy intended to pull US forces out of Vietnam before he was assassinated.

Assassination and Legacy

On November 22, 1963, at 12.30pm, JFK was traveling in an open-top motorcade through the streets of Dallas, Texas, when he was shot in the back, neck, and head. He was pronounced dead at 1pm by officials at the Parkland Memorial Hospital. Kennedy was given a state funeral and buried at Arlington National Cemetery, where his grave is lit by the "Eternal Flame." Lee Harvey Oswald was arrested for the assassination but he was murdered by Jack Ruby before he could be brought to trial. Conspiracy theories concerning the assassination abound—the conclusion of the 1964 Warren Commission that Lee Harvey Oswald had acted alone in killing JFK did little to dampen the speculation. Kennedy's assassination marked the beginning of a period of disillusionment with the political establishment in America, precipitated by the war in Vietnam. Kennedy was famous for his eloquent speeches, which

◀ *JFK was assassinated while on a trip to Dallas, Texas, on November 22, 1963. Kennedy was traveling in the presidential cavalcade with wife Jackie and Texas Governor John Connally and his wife when he received fatal shots to the back and head.*

played well with the media, and he features high on the list of America's most popular presidents. This remains the case despite holding office a relatively short time and failing to implement much in the way of major legislative change.

ADOLF HITLER (1889–1945)

Führer and Chancellor of Germany

Early member and subsequent leader of the National Socialist German Workers (Nazi) Party; attempted to take over the Bavarian government; appointed Chancellor of Germany; introduced anti-Semitic laws; initiated World War II by invading Poland; set in place "The Final Solution"

- Politics & Leadership
- Science & Technology
- Popular Culture & the Arts
- Business & Commerce
- Writers & Thinkers

◀◀ REWRITING HISTORY

Adolf Hitler initially wanted to become an artist, and he moved to Vienna to pursue his dream. Had he not been rejected twice by the Academy of Fine Arts in Vienna, Hitler may have remained in Austria and Europe would not have been plunged into World War II.

The Treaty of Versailles, which ended World War I, was a humiliation for Germany, and sowed the seeds of a growing resentment that later surfaced in bellicose nationalism. Hitler rose to power in the early-1930s on the back of resurgent national pride, and his incendiary speeches succeeded rapidly in endearing him to large numbers of the German people.

Formative Years

The son of a customs clerk and a housemaid, Adolf Hitler was born in 1889 in Braunau-am-Inn, Austria, close to the German border. He was an average student and left school before completing his education. He moved to Vienna, where he attempted unsuccessfully to make a living as an artist. Vienna had a large Jewish population at this time, including many Orthodox Jews, and Hitler began to formulate extreme anti-Semitic views. He is said to have been influenced by Vienna's fervently anti-Semitic mayor Karl Lueger. After being rejected for military service in Austria, Hitler became increasingly disenchanted with his homeland. In 1913, he moved to Munich in Germany, volunteering for military service at the outbreak of World War I. During the war he distinguished himself as a soldier in the 16th Bavarian Reserve Regiment, and was decorated for bravery.

Early Politics

Hitler remained in the army after the end of the war and worked as a police spy. Asked to infiltrate a local group of the German Workers' Party, Hitler was inspired by the anti-Semitic, nationalistic rhetoric of leader Anton Drexler and joined the party as its 55th member. Hitler's oratorical talents soon became apparent and he was made responsible for the party's publicity and propaganda. In February 1920, Hitler spoke to an audience of nearly 2,000 people in the Munich Hofbrauhaus and presented a 25-point program of ideas that formed the basis of the party's platform. The name of the party was changed to the National Socialist German Workers Party (NSDAP)—Nazi for short—on April 1, 1920. Hitler spoke before ever-increasing crowds, swelled by his tactic of sending out supporters to distribute leaflets before his meetings. In 1921, a disaffected element within the Nazi party—unhappy with Hitler's growing influence—made efforts to have him expelled, but this ultimately failed. Hitler's exceptional charisma as a speaker was central to the party's appeal and represented a key weapon in extending their influence. In the end, any vague feelings of unease with the man himself were outweighed by the collective desire to see National Socialism succeed. Adolf Hitler was appointed chairman of the NSDAP on July 29, 1921.

The Beer Hall Putsch

By 1923, Hitler's ambitions had grown and, influenced by Mussolini's March on Rome in 1922, he formulated plans to overthrow the Weimar Republic by force. On November 8, Hitler attempted to take over the Bavarian government. The plot, known as the Beer Hall Putsch, failed and Hitler was tried for high treason and imprisoned in Landsberg. During his time in jail, Hitler began work on his political tome, *Mein Kampf* (*My Struggle*), dictating its contents to his deputy Rudolf Hess. He was released less than a year later under a general amnesty. Although initially banned from public speaking after his release, Hitler worked hard to increase the appeal of the Nazi Party throughout Germany, particularly among the poor and the nationalistic. The Wall Street Crash of 1929 and subsequent world economic depression worked in Hitler's favor, and when elections were held in 1930, the Nazi party secured 6.4 million votes, making it the second largest party in Germany. In 1932, Hitler became a German citizen so that he could stand against Hindenburg in the 1932 presidential election. Although he failed to defeat Hindenburg in the election, Hitler became Chancellor the following year in a coalition government.

▲

Adolf Hitler performing the Nazi salute at a rally. The salute was adopted by the Nazi party as a symbol of loyalty and obedience to the Führer and was usually accompanied by the "Sieg Heil" greeting.

The Rise of Totalitarianism

The burning of the Reichstag (German Parliament) in February 1933 gave Hitler the excuse both to intern anyone he considered a threat to national security and to suppress free speech. The Enabling Act passed in March transferred all legislative powers from the Reichstag to Hitler's cabinet for a four-year period, effectively conferring dictatorial powers on the Führer, and in July the Nazi Party passed a law declaring itself the only legal party in Germany. In the Night of the Long Knives on June 30, 1934, Hitler ordered the arrest and execution of his opponents, including Ernst Röhm, the leader of the Sturmableilung (SA). After the death of President Hindenburg in August 1934, the role of President was abolished and the powers of head of

#6

- Politics & Leadership
- Science & Technology
- Popular Culture & the Arts
- Business & Commerce
- Writers & Thinkers

▶ *This Nazi propaganda poster calls on the women of Germany to do more in support of the war effort. Hitler reportedly said that the skilful use of propaganda could make people see "even heaven as hell."*

state were transferred to Hitler as Führer and Reich Chancellor. After gaining total power, Hitler quashed all public opposition through a policy known as *Gleichschaltung* ("bringing into line"), brutally enforced by the Gestapo. He set up concentration camps for dissidents and introduced the anti-Semitic Nuremburg Laws. Hitler then set about preparing Germany for military expansion.

Entry into War
Although Hitler preached peace, he was preparing for war. In contravention of the Versailles Treaty, Hitler began to build up the German army by conscripting five times its permitted manpower and also increasing armament production. This led to full employment, further reinforcing his popularity. He reoccupied the Rhineland in 1936 without meeting any opposition, forced the unification of Austria with Germany (the *Anschluss*), and "liberated" the Sudeten Germans in 1938. In signing the humiliating Munich Agreement of 1938, the British and French governments made it clear to Hitler that they did not have appetite for confrontation and that appeasement was the preferred policy. To avoid war on two fronts, Hitler negotiated a non-aggression pact with Stalin's Soviet Union. On September 1st, 1939, Germany invaded Poland, leading to the outbreak of World War II.

World War II
Hitler's military *Blitzkreig* tactics enjoyed great success during the first phase of the war and within a relatively short time Denmark, Norway, Luxembourg, Holland, Belgium, and France fell to the Germans. By June 1940, Hitler controlled most of Western Europe;

Britain alone remained unoccupied among the Allies. Hitler's plans to invade Britain faltered when the Luftwaffe failed to overcome the Royal Air Force during the Battle of Britain, and the ill-fated invasion of Soviet Russia in

1941 marked a decisive change in Hitler's fortunes. The entry of the US into the war in December 1941 further strengthened the Allied effort and from 1942 onward, the Allied forces began to inflict major defeats on the German Army. Early in 1942, Hitler implemented the "Final Solution of the Jewish Question" with the systematic deportation of Jews from all over Europe to extermination camps. Hitler's health deteriorated and his behavior became increasingly erratic; when it became clear that Germany could not win the war, Hitler retreated to his bunker in Berlin. On April 10th, 1945, Hitler committed suicide, together with his long-time mistress Eva Braun, whom he had married the previous day. His death marked the end of both Nazi rule in Germany and war in Europe.

Hitler's Legacy

Hitler is inevitably listed among the very worst dictators. His proposed "Thousand Year Reich" lasted a mere 12 years, yet in that short time he unleashed unprecedented horrors upon the world and arguably caused more suffering than any other individual in its history. The clinical extermination of Jews, Gypsies, homosexuals, and other minority groups carried out by his regime is without precedent in its shocking ambition and execution. The world continues to live with the legacy of the Holocaust. Hitler's dream of redeeming the Fatherland from the indignities of the Versailles Treaty and returning it to its rightful place as a world power turned into a nightmare that left Germany divided and subjugated.

Passionate debate continues to surround the extent to which the German people were complicit in the crimes of the Nazi party, yet the Nazi appeal was clear to see. For a long period in the 1930s, the regime oversaw rapid economic improvement, and imposed social order and a restored sense of national pride that many had felt to be missing from the Weimar era. At the pinnacle of this newly resurgent Germany stood Adolf Hitler. His vision of the new German empire combined a noxious blend of nationalism, militarism, and racist ideology that quickly won over the fanatical fringes of society. Effective use of state propaganda—as well as overt use of violence and coercion—helped retain the support of the majority of the German people, who placed their trust in the cult figure of the Führer. In the end, this trust led their country to destruction. In *Mein Kampf*, Hitler wrote that "Germany will either become a world power or will not continue to exist at all." Amidst the postwar ruins, with over 7 million Germans dead and the economy decimated, that fanatical vision was close to being realized.

▲
The Memorial to the Murdered Jews of Europe is situated in Berlin, one block south of the Brandenburg Gate. Designed by Peter Eisenman, the 4.7-acre (1.9-hectare) site contains 2,711 concrete slabs arranged in a grid pattern. There is also an underground "Place of Information," which contains the names of all known Jewish Holocaust victims.

ELVIS PRESLEY (1935–1977)

American Singer—The "King" of rock 'n' roll

A revolutionary figure in popular culture; defined a teen generation; the first American idol; one of the best-selling solo artists in the history of music, with sales of over one billion records; received 14 Grammy nominations and three awards

REWRITING HISTORY

Despite his rebellious image, when Elvis visited President Nixon at the White House in 1970 he expressed his contempt for hippie drug culture (an irony given the manner of his death) and accused The Beatles of stirring up anti-American sentiment.

Without any formal musical education, this Southern boy from a poor family brought together a range of black-American musical styles to create a new and revolutionary sound. The raw energy of his singing style and the unfettered sexuality of his presentation redefined what popular music could be.

The Edge of Poverty

Elvis Aaron Presley was born in a small "shotgun" house in East Tupelo, Mississippi. His twin brother was stillborn, and Elvis was raised an only child with strong ties to his mother. The Presley family lived barely above the poverty line, and when his father was sent to jail for several months they lost their home. Elvis was three years old when he and his mother went to live with her family. Elvis went to school in Tupela and regularly attended the local Pentecostal church with his mother, where he enjoyed the gospel singing, and when he was ten he was persuaded, despite being extremely shy, to enter a fairground singing competition in which he came fifth. For his eleventh birthday he was given a guitar, which he learned to play with the help of his father's brother and by playing along with music on the local radio station. When he was 12 he performed a song on the radio.

In 1948 the family moved to Memphis so that his father could find work, and possibly to evade the law, and there they lived in welfare-assisted housing, where Elvis—who played his guitar constantly—started a band with several of the young tenants. While he remained shy and somewhat tied to his mother's apron strings, he nonetheless began to cultivate a flamboyant look, with flashy clothes and long sideburns, which did nothing to enhance his popularity at high school although that didn't stop him from winning the school's singing competition in 1952.

The Big Break

After graduating from high school, Presley went to work as a truck driver, but he already had a musical career in mind and he spent a good deal of time listening to music in record stores and at the many gospel, blues, and hillbilly music venues. Memphis has a rich tradition of African-American music, Beale Street being a key location in the history of jazz, and in the early '50s the new genre of rhythm-and-blues was increasingly being featured on local radio stations.

In the summer of 1953 he made a sample recording at a studio owned by Sun Records, followed by another in early 1954. The sound of up-tempo blues numbers sung by a white guy caught the attention of the studio owner Sam Phillips, who had been looking for just such a combination to sell to the white market, and he invited the young truck driver in for an audition—which didn't go well. However, Elvis was asked back to sing with musicians Scotty Moore and Bill Black and, feeling more relaxed, he gave "That's All Right (Mama)" his own treatment and provided precisely what Phillips wanted. When the recording was played on the radio it provoked enormous interest, with many listeners assuming that the singer was black. It was released as a single in July 1954, and has since been hailed as the first true rock 'n' roll recording. Promoting the single, Elvis, together with Moore and Black, performed in various venues, including the outdoor Overton Park Shell in midtown Memphis, where the young singer's rhythmic leg movements elicited a hysterical response from the female members of the audience.

#5

Riding the Wave

Over the next 12 months further record releases and concerts followed, and his new style of music—and performance—grew in popularity. In August 1955 Tom Parker became Elvis's manager, and he soon signed a deal with

▶ *Elvis Presley performing in Honolulu, Hawaii, January 1973. His deteriorating physical condition led to increasingly critical reviews, fuelling speculation that his increasing weight had led to a loss of self-confidence.*

RCA Victor. His first recording on the RCA label, released in February 1956, was "Heartbreak Hotel," and within two months it had sold one million copies and hit the top of the US charts.

In the following months Elvis made television appearances on a succession of high-profile shows, from *Milton Berle* to *Ed Sullivan*, and released a string of singles, as well as an album that netted sales of one million dollars. Thus began the tumultuous love-hate relationship between the American public and what amounted to a revolution in popular music culture. Already the record company was smoothing off the rough edges of his earlier performances and aiming for the commercial market, but his live appearances had the crowds going wild. While the girls screamed and swooned, and the boys envied and emulated, conservative middle America regarded him as vulgar and obscene, an evil influence on the youth of the day inciting them to sexual deviance. The greased-back "duck's ass" hairstyle that he had picked up as a trucker, the raunchy, black-American-inspired singing style, his sultry good looks, and his overtly sexual rhythmic gyrations quickly came to symbolize rebellious and disaffected youth, an image that was fueled by parental disapproval across the US and even in the UK. In his television appearances, camera angles were carefully orchestrated to show only his top half, censoring the suggestive movements of "Elvis the Pelvis," and he was denounced by the popular press, by the Jesuits, and even by Frank Sinatra. The FBI regarded him as a threat to national security!

Into the Army

At the end of 1957 (the year in which he bought the Graceland estate outside Memphis), with his popularity at its height, he was drafted into the US Army, although his call-up was deferred for three months to allow him to finish the filming of *King Creole* for Paramount Pictures. After basic training in the US, he spent 18 months serving in Germany, during which time his mother died of heart failure, probably brought on by excessive drinking. Elvis made no new recordings while he was in the Army, but earlier recordings were steadily released to keep him in the public eye. The strategy certainly worked, as he returned in March 1960 to an ecstatic welcome from his fans. The recordings that followed included some of his most popular songs, but the thumping rock 'n' roll had been replaced by a more ballad-like style. Throughout the 1960s Elvis gave very few live performances, but he put his energies into the movie career that he had begun in the late '50s, with a series of movies that, although criticized for their banal plots and weak songs, were enormous box-office hits. In May 1967 he married Priscilla Beaulieu, the daughter of a US Air Force officer, after a long engagement. She and Elvis had met in Germany in 1959 when she was just 14. Their daughter Lisa Marie was born in 1968. (He and Priscilla separated in 1972 and were divorced the following year.)

Return and Decline

At the end of the '60s, when the emergence of new musical styles was dating his sound, his career was boosted by a television special, called simply *Elvis*, in which he returned to the rock 'n' roll style that had brought him such fame, and he soon resumed live performances. These continued throughout the 1970s, but Elvis himself was declining both physically and mentally, putting on weight at an alarming rate and becoming dependent on prescription drugs, on which he overdosed more than once. His performances suffered as a result, and he was increasingly unwilling or unable to make the recordings that RCA required of him. In 1976 he allowed his father to fire some of the closest members of his entourage, which isolated him still further and deprived him of friends that might have pulled him back from self-destruction. The following year he was unable to complete a concert tour, and on August 16, 1977, Elvis was found dead in his bathroom at Graceland, aged 42. The cause of death was given as a heart attack, but drug use was undoubtedly a factor.

In a career that lasted less than 25 years, Elvis had a greater cultural impact than almost any other singer, ushering in the rock 'n' roll era, changing the course of popular music, and helping a generation to differentiate and define itself.

#5

"When I first heard Elvis' voice, I just knew that I wasn't going to work for anybody, and nobody was going to be my boss. He is the deity supreme of rock and roll religion as it exists in today's form. Hearing him for the first time was like busting out of jail. I thank God for Elvis Presley."
Bob Dylan

WALT DISNEY (1901–1966)

Cofounder of Walt Disney Productions

Movie producer, director, screenwriter, voice actor, and animator; pioneer in the field of animation; produced the world's first full-length cartoon; multiple Academy Award winner; created Disneyland theme park

- Politics & Leadership
- Science & Technology
- **Popular Culture & the Arts**
- Business & Commerce
- Writers & Thinkers

REWRITING HISTORY

Too young to enlist in the military, the 16-year-old Walt Disney joined the war effort in 1918 as a Red Cross driver. He was sent overseas to France, where he decorated his ambulance from front to back with cartoons.

It is difficult to imagine a world without Walt Disney. His whimsical cartoon characters are recognizable the world over, featured on everything from pajamas to lunch boxes. An animator of supreme talent and imagination, Disney was also an astute businessman, creating a multibillion dollar empire in the interwar period.

Drawing on His Talents

Walter Elias Disney was born in 1901 in Chicago, Illinois. When he was four years old, the family moved to a farm in Marceline, Missouri. The seven-year-old Walt Disney showed enough talent as an artist to sell his drawings to friends and neighbors, and he frequently contributed cartoons to the school's newspaper during his high school years. A good mimic, he also entertained school friends with his impersonation of silent screen star Charlie Chaplin. After a brief spell working for the Red Cross during the latter part of World War I, Disney moved to Kansas City to pursue his dream of a career in commercial art. He began producing animated cartoons for local businesses and eventually set up his own Laugh-O-Grams company, supplying cartoons to theaters in the area. He began work on *The Alice Comedies*, which featured a real person in an animated world, but his company ran out of money.

Hollywood Calls

Undeterred, the young Walt set out for Hollywood to start anew. With the backing of his brother Roy, Walt set up another company and they secured a distribution deal for *The Alice Comedies* through New York distributor Margaret Winkler. Another series, *Oswald the Lucky Rabbit*, enjoyed great success but Disney lost rights to the character through a business disagreement with Universal Pictures. Universal also lured away the majority of Disney's talented animation team at the same time. Disney hit back with the creation of the character that perhaps more than any other defines the Walt Disney image—Mickey Mouse. Based on a pet mouse that Walt had once adopted in Kansas City, Mickey Mouse was drawn by Ubbe Iwerks and given voice and character by Walt himself. Mickey Mouse first appeared in a silent cartoon called *Plane Crazy* but the introduction of sound to the motion picture industry halted its release. Quickly catching up with the new technology, Disney introduced a talking Mickey Mouse to the world in *Steamboat Willie* on November 18, 1928, at the Colony Theater in New York. The mouse with the squeaky voice became an instant hit with the US public. Walt next released a series of musical shorts called *Silly Symphonies*, though these did not enjoy as much success as Mickey.

Full-Length Features

In 1932, Technicolor Corporation cofounder Herbert Kalmus persuaded Walt to redo his movie *Flowers and Trees*, originally shot in black-and-white, in three-strip Technicolor. Disney secured the sole rights to use Technicolor for a two-year period, allowing him to produce the only color cartoons. *Flowers and Trees* went on to win the first Academy Award for Best Short Subject: Cartoons in 1932. Disney was also awarded an Honorary Academy Award for the creation of Mickey Mouse that same year. Spin-off characters from the Mickey Mouse series, including Donald Duck, Goofy, and Pluto, went on to individual cartoon stardom in the 1930s. After Mickey Mouse, Donald Duck was the most successful of Disney's cartoon characters. The bad-tempered duck with the distinctive voice made his cinematic debut in a supporting role in "The Wise Little Hen" in 1934. He was later joined by love interest Daisy Duck and his three mischievous nephews, Huey, Dewey, and Louie. Determined to stay ahead of his rivals, Disney began plans for a full feature-length musical version of *Snow White* in 1934, despite the reservations of both his wife and his brother Roy. Dubbed "Disney's Folly" by the entertainment press, many predicted that it would cause the demise of the Disney studio. Ignoring his critics, Disney employed Chouinard Art Institute professor Don Graham to work with his animation team on new techniques. Using the *Silly Symphonies* series to experiment, they played around with special effects, worked on distinctive character animation, and introduced the multi-plane camera technique for the first time in *The Old Mill* (which won an Academy Award in 1937). Costing an unprecedented $1,499,000 to make, *Snow White* premiered at the Carthay Circle Theater in Los Angeles in December 1937. The audience gave it a standing ovation and the movie went on to earn over $8 million and win Disney an Academy Award.

#4

Walt Disney is pictured here with rocket technician Dr Wernher von Braun. Von Braun worked as a technical director at the Disney Studios in the 1950s, making TV programmes on space exploration. ▼

The success of *Snow White* enabled Disney to build a new studio at Burbank, which opened at the end of 1939. The feature-length animation staff worked on *Pinocchio*, *Fantasia*, *Bambi*, and *Dumbo*, all of which have become classics of their genre. The short-animation staff continued work on the Mickey Mouse, Donald Duck, Goofy, and Pluto cartoon series. Disney's staff at the Burbank studio swelled to more than a thousand but animation work was interrupted in 1941 by the entry of the US into World War II. During the war, much of Disney's talent was tied up in training and propaganda movies for the government, but he succeeded in producing a number of short comedy movies to keep the country's morale from flagging, including "Der Fuehrer's Face" (1943). The animation featured Donald Duck and won the 1943 Academy Award for Animated Short Film. In 1944, Disney re-released *Snow White*, so beginning the Disney tradition of seven-year reissues. In the 1950s, Disney collaborated with NASA rocket pioneer Wernher von Braun to produce *Man in Space* and *Man and the Moon* (both 1955), and *Mars and Beyond* (1957), which were designed to educate the public about the US space program.

The Postwar Period

In the early postwar period, the Disney Studios worked on relatively low-budget cartoon shorts. These were then combined in packages for movie theater release, the first of which was *Saludos Amigos* (1942). For its sequel *The Three Caballeros* (1945), Disney combined live action with animation for the first time, a process he repeated with *Song of the South* (1946) and later with the highly acclaimed *Mary Poppins* (1964). By the end of the 1940s, the studio had recovered enough financially to begin producing full-length features again. They produced *Cinderella* (1950) and completed *Alice in Wonderland* (1951) and *Peter Pan* (1953), both of which had been started before America entered the war. Disney also produced *Seal Island* in 1948, the first of his award-winning *True-Life Adventures*, a series of live-action nature movies.

Disneyland

In the late 1940s Disney turned his attention to the creation of an amusement park for the enjoyment of adults and children alike. He spent five years developing ideas for the park. His initial concept was for an eight-acre Mickey Mouse Park close to the Disney studios. However, his concept for the park grew grander and grander and he purchased a 160-acre plot of land in Anaheim, southeast of Los Angeles in Orange County. To raise money for the project, Disney created the show *Disneyland*, which he agreed to broadcast on ABC television in return for their investment in the park. Work on Disney's groundbreaking theme park began in July 1954 and it was completed exactly one year later at a cost of $17 million.

The Disney Brand

In the 1950s, Disney began expanding studio production to include full-length, live-action feature movies such as *Treasure Island* (1950), *Old Yeller* (1957), and *The Parent Trap* (1961). He also began to host the ABC weekly series *Disneyland*, and its later incarnation *The Wonderful World of Disney*. In 1955, he introduced the *Mickey Mouse Club*, which aired daily on American TV, and the following year he set up Disneyland Records. By the time of his death from cancer in 1966, Disney had established Walt Disney Productions as the world's leading family entertainment company. In total, Disney received a record 59 Academy Award nominations and won a record 26 Academy Awards, four of which were special awards. The Walt Disney Company continues to expand its operations into new entertainment technologies—in 2006, it acquired Pixar Animation Studios, a leading producer of CGI-animated features that has won numerous awards for hit movies such as *Toy Story* and *Finding Nemo*.

The acquisition of Pixar has cemented The Walt Disney Company's position as one of the most influential global entertainment corporations. Today, it is a multibillion dollar empire made up of motion picture studios, television networks, record labels, theme parks, hotels, and vacation resorts. It has produced unforgettable characters that are loved the world over, and helped shape the impact of American culture abroad. Not at all bad going for a smalltown farm boy from Missouri.

#4

◀ *Marketed as the "Happiest Place on Earth," the Disneyland theme park boasts a fairytale castle and plenty of fireworks. The amusement park was opened in 1955, and was the culmination of five years planning by Walt Disney.*

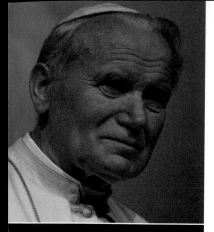

REWRITING HISTORY

In keeping with the importance that he gave to the "universal call to holiness," the Roman Catholic Church's teaching that all are called to live holy lives, Pope John Paul II canonized (declared to be a saint) 482 new saints and beatified (gave the title "Blessed") to 1,340 individuals, more than the total recognized in the previous five centuries.

POPE JOHN PAUL II (1920–2005)

Pope of the Catholic Church and Sovereign of Vatican City

Highly influential world leader; played a pivotal role in bringing an end to Communist rule in many European countries; improved relations between the Catholic Church and other world religions

Serving as head of the Roman Catholic Church for almost 27 years (only Pope Pius IX served longer), John Paul II was the first non-Italian Pope for almost 500 years, and he brought a new, more human and more inclusive face to one of the world's major religions.

Wartime Studies

Karol Józef Wojtyła was born in Wadowice, near Krakow, Poland, in 1920. After graduating from high school, he went to Jagiellonian University in Krakow in 1938, where he displayed a remarkable flair for learning languages, and also attended drama school. When the occupying Nazis closed the university the following year, to avoid being deported to Germany he went to work, including a stint of several years as a laborer in a quarry. During this time, attracted by the priesthood, he took courses given by Cardinal Adam Stefan Sapieha, Archbishop of Krakow, at a clandestine seminary and was a leading member of an underground theater group. He is also said to have helped Polish Jews find refuge from the Nazis.

Entering the Priesthood

His studies continued at the main seminary and at the faculty of theology of Jagiellonian University after World War II, and he was ordained into the priesthood by Cardinal Sapieha in 1946. Over the next 12 years he completed two doctorates in theology, worked as a priest among Polish immigrants in France, Holland, and Belgium, and taught moral theology and social ethics at the seminary of Krakow and in the Catholic University of Lublin.

In 1958, Pope Pius XII appointed him Bishop of Ombi and auxiliary of Krakow. In 1963, he was made Archbishop of Krakow by Pope Paul VI, and he became a Cardinal in 1967. In that year he was involved in the writing of Pope Paul VI's encyclical "Of Human Life," which re-stated the Church's traditional opposition to abortion and artificial birth control. Following the death of Pope Paul VI and the brief papacy of Pope John Paul I, the relatively young 58-year-old Polish Cardinal Wojtyła was chosen as the compromise candidate when neither of the two principal contenders could win the necessary majority, and he was elected as the 264th Pope on October 16, 1978. His inauguration took place six days later.

The People's Pope

From the start of his papacy, Pope John Paul II made it his mission to take the Christian message to the world, using jets, helicopters, and a range of "Pope-mobiles" to spread the Gospel and very traditional Catholic teachings in a style that had more than a touch of show business. He quickly became known for his openness and charity, and what has been described as simple friendliness, a quality that endeared him to a wide constituency in the course of more than 100 papal pilgrimages overseas and in meetings with hundreds of heads of state. A survivor of both Nazi occupation and Communist rule, he had a message for both the oppressed and the oppressors, and one of his first visits, made in 1979, was to his native Poland. There his presence and his message, in which he spoke of Poland's deep Christian roots and the transience of the Communist regime, are credited with giving rise to the Solidarity opposition movement that fought for human rights in Poland and ultimately led to the end of Soviet domination in Eastern Europe.

Pope John Paul II was the first Pope to go to the White House, meeting with President Carter in 1979—although he was always at pains to point out that while Communism leads to oppression, Capitalism too has its faults, and the rich have a responsibility to care for the poor. He was also the first Pope to visit Mexico and the United Kingdom. In the course of his 25-year world tour (he is probably the best-traveled leader of all time) Pope John Paul II brought together the largest ever gatherings of the faithful, most notably in 1995 when an estimated crowd of more than five million attended mass in Manila, Philippines.

Ecumenical Efforts

Throughout his papacy, Pope John Paul II made continual efforts to reach out to other religions, and in 1986 he organized the first World Day of Prayer for Peace in Assisi, Italy, which was attended by some 120 representatives from the various Christian denominations and almost all world religions. He extended a special hand of friendship toward Judaism. In Rome he became the first Pope to pray in a Jewish synagogue, and on his trip to Poland he went to the Nazi concentration camp of Auschwitz. In 1998 he publicly apologized for the failure of Catholics and the Catholic Church to take a stand on behalf of the Jewish people during the Nazi regime, and on a visit to Jerusalem in 2000 he visited

#3

In 1993, Madrid's Almudena Cathedral (which took more than 100 years to complete) was consecrated in person by Pope John Paul II. To commemorate the occasion, this statue of the Pope was erected in front of the cathedral.
▼

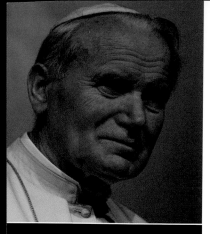

Yad Vashem, the Israeli Holocaust memorial. He also prayed at the Western (or Wailing) Wall, an important Jewish religious site, where he gave an address deploring anti-Semitism and the tragedy of the Holocaust. He later established diplomatic relations between the Holy See and Israel. In Syria he became the first Pope to pray in an Islamic mosque—the Grand Mosque of Damascus—where he actively called for cooperation between Jews, Muslims, and Christians, and in 2001, shortly after the 9-11 terrorist attacks, he flew to Kazakhstan and addressed a largely Muslim audience.

Pope John Paul II also worked to improve relationships with other Christian denominations. In 1982 he became the first pontiff to visit the United Kingdom, making a demanding six-day tour of England, Wales, and Scotland. On the second day of his visit he stood beside the Archbishop of Canterbury in Canterbury Cathedral and addressed the Church of England. In his speech he called for unity, and when the Church of England later elected to ordain women priests he expressed his disappointment over this divisive issue. The Pope also held talks with representatives of the Eastern Orthodox Church and met eight times—more than with any other leader—with the Dalai Lama, the spiritual leader of Tibetan Buddhism, who shared the Pope's experience of Communist occupation.

Gender and Sexuality

In 1995, the Pope apologized for injustices committed against women, the violation of women's rights, and the historical denigration of women, but his exhortation to women to take their rightful place in society clearly referred only to the secular sphere, and not to roles in the Church—or even within the family. He was roundly condemned by many for a firm and traditionalist stance on the ordination of women, and for maintaining the Church's opposition to artificial birth control, including condoms even as a means of protection against HIV/AIDS. Critics claimed the Pope's position led to the spread of the disease, and increased poverty by encouraging large families. He was also criticized by the gay rights movement for the Church's immovable attitude toward homosexual behavior, same-sex marriage, and for the exclusion of transgender individuals from ordination.

▶ In 2003, it was announced that Pope John Paul II was suffering from Parkinson's disease—a fact that had been kept secret for many years.

Assassination Attempts

On May 13, 1981, while being driven through the throng awaiting his address in St Peter's Square, Pope John Paul II was shot in the abdomen by a Turkish member of a militant group. The bullets tore through the Pope's intestines and caused massive bleeding, necessitating several hours of surgery. He put his eventual recovery down to the intervention of Our Lady of Fatima, an apparition of the Virgin Mary that was first witnessed in Fatima, Portugal, on May 13, 1917. The Pope visited the town of Fatima the following year, and on May 12 he was the target of an attack by a Spanish priest opposed to the changes that followed from the Second Vatican Council, in which Cardinal Wojtyła had been involved. A bodyguard prevented the attack. Pope John Paul II was also one of the targets of a thwarted Al-Qaeda-backed terrorist plot in 1995.

#3

Sanctification

Pope John Paul II died on April 2, 2005, having suffered from Parkinson's disease for several years. Within weeks, his successor Pope Benedict XVI announced that the process of beatification and canonization for Pope John Paul II would begin without the usual five-year waiting period. This process is still underway.

▲

In 1979, less than a year after his inauguration, Pope John Paul II paid a Papal visit to the US. He is seen here arriving at the Yankee Stadium in the Bronx to hold a mass for world justice and peace.

◄◄ REWRITING HISTORY

Henry Ford had an unlikely admirer in Adolf Hitler, who once told a Detroit news reporter that "I regard Henry Ford as my inspiration." Hitler kept a life-sized portrait of Ford next to his desk and in 1938 awarded him the Grand Cross of the German Eagle, the highest honor awarded by Nazi Germany to foreigners.

HENRY FORD (1863–1947)

Founder of the Ford Motor Company

Introduced the world's first mass-produced car; revolutionized the manufacturing process with the introduction of the moving assembly line; brought affordable cars to the masses; set up a dealer-franchise system to sell and service Ford motors

In 1900, the US was the only country in the world to be manufacturing cars, and it produced just 4,192 vehicles that year. By the turn of the twentieth century, there were over 600 million vehicles on the streets of the world. The car's evolution from an exclusive luxury to everyday necessity is largely the result of one man's dream—that of Henry Ford.

Turning his Back on the Rural Life

The eldest of six children, Henry Ford showed little interest in the family's prosperous farm, located in Dearborn, Michigan, preferring instead to spend his time tinkering with bits of old machinery. At the age of 16, Ford left home to work as an apprentice machinist in the nearby city of Detroit. After a three-year apprenticeship, Ford returned to Dearborn, where he divided his time between working on the family farm and operating and repairing Westinghouse steam engines. He also briefly ran a saw mill. Ford's heart, however, lay in industry, and in 1891 he joined the Edison Illuminating Company in Detroit as an engineer, leaving behind his rural roots for good. Two years later, his promotion to the post of Chief Engineer gave Ford the opportunity to experiment with one of his pet projects—the internal combustion engine. In 1896, he completed his own self-propelled vehicle, the Quadricycle. Encouraged by Thomas Edison, Ford continued his experiment to produce an efficient gas-powered car, building a second vehicle in 1898.

The Ford Motor Company

In 1899, Ford resigned from Edison to pursue the dream of establishing his own automobile company. His first two attempts failed, primarily due to disputes with his backers. However, in 1903 he founded the Ford Motor Company in partnership with Alexander Malcomson, James Couzens, the Dodge brothers, and others. They started with just $28,000 capital, and Ford acted as vice president and chief engineer of the new company. Four years later, Ford bought out his partners and the company became a family-run venture. Ford began work on designing a low-cost motor car, and in 1908 he introduced the Model T, the car that was to change the face of transportation.

Ford made sure that every newspaper in Detroit carried a story about his new car. Efficient and easy to drive, the Model T came with a price tag ($825 in 1908) that made it affordable to a wide range of consumers, and it was an instant hit with the US public. Ford also initiated a dealer-franchise system to market his automobile, and by 1912 there were some 7,000 Ford dealers throughout the US. Sales soared, and within a decade of its inception the Model T could boast 50 percent of the US automobile market. To keep up with consumer demand and further reduce costs, Ford looked for ways to improve production time, and in 1913, his workers came up with the idea of a moving assembly line. Previously a small group of workers had put together the entire vehicle, but with the introduction of the assembly line, workers stayed in one place adding components to the car as it passed them on the conveyor belt. By 1914, Ford's factory could put a car together every 93 minutes, and the price of the Model T dropped steadily; in 1916 the car cost only $360. To support the increase in automobile traffic, Ford also campaigned for improved automotive infrastructure—better roads and more gas stations. The Ford name became increasingly famous throughout the US, and in 1918 President Woodrow Wilson asked Ford to run for a Michigan seat in the US Senate, hoping that he would gain positive publicity for his League of Nations proposal. Although the country was at war, Ford ran on a peace ticket and he failed to gain election. In late 1918, Henry Ford turned over the everyday running of the company to his only child Edsel, though he continued to have the final word in decisions and frequently overruled his son. (Henry Ford resumed the presidency in 1943 after Edsel's premature death.) In the 1920s, Model T sales began to decline as other automobile manufacturers introduced new designs, as well as offering customer credit plans. Stubborn in nature, Ford initially refused to make any changes but ever-decreasing sales finally forced him to introduce a new design. In 1927, he presented the Ford Model A, which ran until 1931. Ford, though, remained vehemently opposed to any kind of payment plan until the 1930s, when he introduced the Universal Credit Corporation for Ford customers.

Fordism

In January 1914, Ford astonished the world with the introduction of a $5 per 8-hour-day minimum wage for his employees. The average wage for automobile workers had hitherto been $2.34 for a 9-hour day. Dubbed "Fordism" by the press, and greeted with scorn in *The Wall Street Journal* and

▲
The Ford Model T was produced by the Ford Motor Company between 1908 and 1927 and was the world's first low-cost car, enabling automobile use to spread to the general public. This 1921 model is parked outside the White House in Washington D.C.

▶ *Henry Ford with the Washington correspondent for the* **Detroit News**, *Jay G. Hayden.*

elsewhere, Ford's social philosophy maintained that his workers should be able to afford the cars that they produced. Never before had uneducated workers received such financial reward but Ford's vision paid off—skilled mechanics flocked to his factory and employee-turnover dropped, raising productivity and lowering costs still further. Simultaneously, Ford began to move his company toward economic independence by implementing a strategy known as vertical integration, whereby he controlled both upstream suppliers and downstream retailers. By the late 1920s, Ford had access to rubber plantations in Brazil, 16 coal mines, a fleet of ships, a railroad, iron-ore mines in Michigan and Minnesota as well as thousands of acres of timberland, and could boast complete self-sufficiency. Ford's massive Rouge Plant, located on the banks of the Rouge River in Dearborn, included its own steel mill and glass factory, as well as the automobile assembly line. This allowed all steps in the manufacturing process, from the refinement of raw materials right through to the assembly of the finished car, to take place at the plant.

The Age of the Consumer

Henry Ford did not invent the automobile. Nonetheless, he developed production techniques that allowed for its mass production at a cost that could be borne by the average wage earner. The primary innovation was the introduction of assembly lines, whereby labor was organized into specific tasks and completed by specially trained individuals. This resulted in shorter production times and lower unit costs, enabling a much more affordable price tag for the Model T. Perhaps Ford's greatest insight was to increase wages accordingly, so that his workforce would in theory be able to afford their own vehicle, making them direct beneficiaries of their labor—and also transforming them into new customers. The growing success of the enterprise necessitated a larger workforce, which in turn created yet more potential new customers. In this way, Henry Ford's revolutionary approach to car production introduced mass consumerism to the world and did more to create a new class of workers—the middle class— than anyone else in US history. The similarities between the story

of Ford and that of Ray Kroc (pp. 16–7) are evident. Taking products that already existed, they put in place a business model that helped turn their respective brands into huge global corporations, and symbolic powerhouses of the US economy.

The Man behind the Name

Ford was by no means perfect. Although a mechanical genius, he was very much set in his way. Critics point to his reluctance to make changes in his production system or to diversify—he didn't bring out another model until the Model A in 1927—and he is justly infamous for his "any color as long as it's black" quip. Eventually, the company's share in the automobile market plummeted and General Motors was able to take advantage of its fall.

He has also been lambasted for interfering too much with personal lives

◀ *Henry Ford began his career in engineering with the Edison Illuminating Company. Company boss Thomas Edison (left) encouraged the young Ford to pursue his experiments with automobile design. The two men are shown here, with US naturalist John Burroughs in the center, at Edison's home in Fort Myers, Florida.*

of his employees, fearful that they would spend their new-found wealth on booze and loose women, and for refusing to let his workers set up a labor organization for many years. He eventually agreed to allow the United Auto Workers to organize a plant in 1941 after being faced with the prospect of a strike. He has also been heavily criticized for making anti-Semitic comments. Ford was, however, a great philanthropist. In 1936, with help from his son Edsel, he established the Ford Foundation. Initially confined to the state of Michigan, the Foundation went national in 1950 and is now one of the world's richest philanthropic organizations.

ALBERT EINSTEIN (1879–1955)

Theoretical Physicist

Reformulated theoretical physics; discovered spacetime and the equivalence of energy and matter ($E=mc^2$); his discoveries made many technologies possible, including electronics, space travel, and nuclear energy and weapons.

- Politics & Leadership
- **Science & Technology**
- Popular Culture & the Arts
- Business & Commerce
- Writers & Thinkers

◀◀ REWRITING HISTORY

No Jewish person, not even a genius, was safe from the resurgence of anti-Semitism set in motion by the Nazis. When Hitler came to power in 1933, Einstein was lecturing in the US and he wisely chose to remain at Princeton, NJ, where he worked until his death in 1955.

The name Albert Einstein is synonymous with genius. His contributions to the field of physics were numerous and far-reaching, transforming our worldview and making many of the modern technologies we now take for granted possible. One much less desirable outcome of his research, however, was the development of the A-bomb.

Golden Compass

Albert Einstein was born into a Jewish family in Ulm, Germany, and was raised in Munich. The boy had a precocious intellectual talent, and the story goes that when the five-year-old Einstein saw a compass for the first time, he was struck by the idea that something invisible all around him was making the needle move to point north. Aged ten, he was already tackling Kant's *Critique of Pure Reason* and Euclid's *Elements*. While he performed indifferently at high school, by the age of 15 he had written his first scientific paper, "The Investigation of the State of Aether in Magnetic Fields" (1894). Disillusioned by the authoritarian education system, he left high school that year, but without a diploma he could not gain entrance to university, so he enrolled at school in Zurich. Impressed with the democratic values in Switzerland, he renounced his German citizenship and applied for Swiss nationality, which he received in 1901. Einstein graduated from college in 1900, and took a job at the Swiss Patent Office in Berne. Over the next few years, Einstein worked studiously on problems in physics, developing his revolutionary new ideas without any contact with the established academic community.

Annus Mirabilis

In 1905 Einstein published several scientific papers in the prestigious German *Annalen der Physik* (*Annals of Physics*). These pieces of work, which have become known as the "Annus Mirabilis [wonderful year] Papers," dealt with some of the most pressing issues in physics at the time, and they demonstrated the amazing originality of his thinking, as well as his willingness to accept results that contradicted contemporary theories and scientific consensus. In his paper on the subject of the production and transformation of light,

Einstein proposed that light was made up of packages, or "quanta," of energy and that the quantity of energy depended upon the frequency of the light. This contradicted the contemporary wave theory of light, and the idea that energy is infinitely divisible. It also suggested a return to the much earlier Newtonian theory of light as consisting of particles, and it was not immediately accepted. It turned out to be a crucial leap forward for the physical sciences, and Einstein received the Nobel Prize for this work in 1921.

He also published a paper on Brownian motion, the erratic motion of particles in suspension in a liquid. Starting from an entirely theoretical perspective, he made mathematical predictions about the motion that would be imparted by the kinetic energy of molecules and atoms in the liquid, and experimental observations that supported his predictions provided the first physical evidence for the existence of atoms.

Special Relativity

In his paper entitled "On the Electrodynamics of Moving Bodies" he put forward what was to become known as his special theory of relativity, stating that, contrary to the Newtonian view of the universe, time and space are relative to the observer, while the speed of light in vacuum is an absolute constant and is unchanging regardless of the speed of the observer or the emitting object.

In his final paper of that remarkable year he put forward the theory that mass and energy are interchangeable, an idea expressed in the famous equation $E = mc^2$ (energy = mass x the speed of light squared). This introduced a new kind of energy that was neither kinetic nor potential but was inherent in mass itself, and Einstein showed that, theoretically, the smallest particle could release huge quantities of energy. It was a discovery that would later come back to haunt him, as its destructive potential was put to use in the manufacture of the atomic bomb.

The publication of any one of these papers would have established Einstein as one of the leading theoretical physicists of the century. At the time, however, the establishment of the day did not realize their true significance. The ideas they contained were so far ahead of their time that the validity of some could

#1

◀ *Einstein renounced his German citizenship when he left the country for the US in 1933. He then applied to become a US citizen, and is seen here receiving his certificate of American citizenship from Judge Phillip Forman in 1940.*

"The most incomprehensible thing about the world is that it is comprehensible."
Albert Einstein

▶ *During the 1920s Einstein made frequent visits to Leiden, in the Netherlands, to speak at the University. Throughout his career he regularly gave lectures to academic groups.*

not be proven experimentally until many years after Einstein's death. In 1912 Einstein became professor of physics at the German University of Prague, where he continued his work, publishing papers on the effects of gravity on light. The paper challenged astronomers to find a way of detecting the deflection of light from the stars during a solar eclipse, and his prediction was indeed confirmed some years later.

Seeking Simplicity

In 1915, Einstein published his general theory of relativity, which brings together special relativity and the Newtonian model of gravity in a description of gravitation that is still used today, in which spacetime is distorted by massive objects such as stars and black holes. The theory now forms the foundation of our cosmological models of the universe.

During World War I and the interwar period, Einstein lived in Berlin, where he was director of the Kaiser Wilhelm Institute for Physics. Einstein's research after general relativity consisted primarily of a long series of attempts to generalize his theory of gravitation in order to unify and simplify the fundamental laws of physics. Einstein believed that the universe was orderly,

predictable, and fundamentally elegant, and he was therefore unwilling to accept the theories of "quantum mechanics" developed by scientists such as Niels Bohr. In response to their view that at the level of subatomic particles all is uncertainty and chance, Einstein famously said he could not believe that God plays dice with the universe.

The Looming War

When Adolf Hitler came to power and anti-Jewish sentiment began to make itself felt, Einstein resigned his position and took up residence in the US, where he remained for the rest of his career. In 1939, concerned at the advances in nuclear physics being made in Nazi Germany, and encouraged by the American scientific community, Einstein wrote a letter to President Roosevelt, urging that the US develop the nuclear bomb first. The Manhattan

Project, under Robert Oppenheimer, was established soon afterward in order to put the equation $E=mc^2$ to practical use, but Einstein refused to play an active role, fearing the consequences of nuclear energy for mankind. A pacifist and humanitarian, he was horrified by the dropping of nuclear weapons on Japan. After the war, his pacifist sentiments led to accusations that he harbored communist sympathies, and efforts were made to discredit both him and his work. FBI files reveal that the Immigration and Naturalization Service considered revoking his citizenship in 1951 when his secretary and housekeeper was suspected of being a Soviet agent.

The Einsteinian Revolution

Before Einstein, the planetary systems of the atom and of outer space ran on tidy, predictable lines; time was absolute and flowed in one direction and at the same rate for everyone. After him, the primary law of the physical universe was relativity. The discovery had as startling an effect on the human psyche and the subsequent development of human civilization as Copernicus's assertion that the Earth orbited the Sun. It is interesting to note that the greatest changes in the human worldview for the past four centuries have not been triggered by philosophers or social scientists, but by astronomers and physicists: Copernicus, Galileo, Newton, and Einstein.

Einstein's influence lives on into our own century, in our quest to unlock the most basic secrets of matter and the universe.

#1

◄ *Albert Einstein and the atomic physicist Niels Bohr (seen here in 1925) were close friends and intellectual colleagues. Einstein once wrote to him: "Not often in life has a man given me so much happiness by his mere presence as you have done. I have learned much from you, mainly from your sensitive approach to scientific problems."*

ENTRIES IN ALPHABETICAL ORDER

FURTHER READING

The Internet is an invaluable source of information if you want to read more about any of the topics covered in this book. Typing a keyword into any search engine will give you numerous links from which you can start your exploration. Alternatively, if you prefer to sit down with a book in your hands, we have suggested a number of titles that explore some of the key themes of the last century. This is by no means an exhaustive list, but you might want to use it as a helpful start point. The titles are arranged according to the categories set out in this book, starting with a selection that provide an historical overview of the twentieth century.

Hanhimäki, Jussi; Maiolo, Joseph A.; Schulze, Kirsten E.; Best, Antony. *International History of the Twentieth Century and Beyond*, Kentucky: Routledge 2008

Keyler, William R. *The Twentieth-Century World and Beyond: An International History since 1900*, New York: Oxford University Press USA 2005

Grenville, J. A. S. *A History of the World: From the 20th to the 21st Century*, Kentucky: Routledge 2005

Roberts, J. M. *The Penguin History of the Twentieth Century: The History of the World, 1901 to the Present*, New York: Penguin 2004

Howard, Michael. *The Oxford History of the Twentieth Century*, Oxford: Oxford University Press 2002

Hobsbawm, E. J. *Age of Extremes: The Short Twentieth Century 1914–1921*, London: Abacus 1995.

Politics & Leadership

Figes, Orlando. *A People's Tragedy: Russian Revolution, 1891–1924*, London: Pimlico 1997

Brown, Archie. *The Rise and Fall of Communism*, London: The Bodley Head 2009

LaFeber, Walter. *America, Russia and the Cold War 1945–2006*, Columbus: McGraw Hill Higher Education 2006

Blum, George P. *The Rise of Fascism in Europe (Greenwood Press Guides to Historic Events of the Twentieth Century)*, Santa Barbara: Greenwood Press 1998

Roberts, Andrew. *Masters and Commanders: The Military Geniuses Who Led the West to Victory in World War II*, New York: Penguin 2009

Fenby, Jonathan. *Alliance: The Inside Story of How Roosevelt, Stalin and Churchill Won One War and Began Another*, New York: Pocket Books 2008

Sweig, J. E. *Inside the Cuban Revolution: Fidel Castro and the Urban Underground*, Cambridge, Massachusetts: Harvard University Press 2004

Paterson, David; Willoughby, Doug; Willoughby, Susan. *Heinemann Advanced History: Civil Rights in the USA 1863–1980*, Portsmouth (USA): Heinneman 2001

Clark, Nancy L.; Worger, William H. South Africa: *The Rise and Fall of Apartheid (Seminar Studies In History)*, London: Longman 2004

Science & Technology

Preston, Diana. *Before the Fall-out: From Marie Curie to Hiroshima*, US: Corgi Books 2006

Feynman, Richard P. *Six Not-so-easy Pieces: Einstein's Relativity, Symmetry and Space-time* (Penguin Press Science), New York: Penguin 2007

Mackersey, Ian. *The Wright Brothers: The Aviation Pioneers Who Changed the World*, London: Little, Brown 2003

Farmelo, Graham. *It Must be Beautiful: Great Equations of Modern Science*, London: Granta Books 2003

Watson, James D. *DNA: The Secret of Life*, London: Arrow Books Ltd. 2004

French, Francis; Burgess, Colin. *Into That Silent Sea: Trailblazers of the Space Era, 1961-1965 (Outward Odyssey: A People's History of Spaceflight)*, Nebraska: University of Nebraska Press

Popular Culture & the Arts

Osborne, Harold. *The Oxford Companion to Twentieth Century Art*, Oxford: Oxford Paperbacks 1988

Stein, Gertrude. *Picasso*, USA: Dover Books 2000

Altschuler, Glenn C. *All Shook Up: How Rock 'n' Roll Changed America (Pivotal Moments in American History)*, New York: Oxford University Press USA 2004

Tirro, Frank. *The Birth of the Cool of Miles Davis and His Associates (CMS Sourcebooks in American Music)*, New York: Pendragon Press 2009

Maltby, Richard. *Hollywood Cinema*, New Jersey: Wiley Blackwell 2003

Belton, John. *American Cinema / American Culture*, Columbus: McGraw-Hill Higher Education 2009

Schaap, Jeremy. *Triumph: The Untold Story of Jesse Owens and Hitler's Olympics*, Boston: Mariner Books 2008

Hauser, Thomas. *Muhammad Ali: His Life and Times*, London: Robson Books 2004

Writers & Thinkers

Gupta, Suman; Johnson, David. *A Twentieth Century Literature Reader: Texts and Debates*, Kentucky: Routledge 2005

Boundas, Constantin V. *The Edinburgh Companion to Twentieth-century Philosophies*, Edinburgh: Edinburgh University Press 2007

Davidson, Paul. *John Maynard Keynes (Great Thinkers in Economics)*, Basingstoke: Palgrave Macmillan 2009

Friedman, Milton. *Milton Friedman on Economics: Selected Papers*, Chicago: Chicago University Press 2008

Frieden, J. A. *Global Capitalism: Its Fall and Rise in the Twentieth Century*, New York: W. W. Norton & Co. 2007

Aikman, David. *Billy Graham: His Life and Influence*, Nashville: Thomas Nelson Publishers 2007

Smailes, Gary. *Pope John Paul II*, Godalming: Waverley Books 2009

Levenson, Claude B. *The Dalai Lama: A Biography*, Delhi: Oxford University Press India 2002

Fishman, Charles. *The Wal-Mart Effect: How an Out-of-town Superstore Became a Superpower*, New York: Penguin 2007

Watson Jr., Thomas. *A Business and Its Beliefs*, Columbus: McGraw Hill 2003

Gates, Bill. *Business at the Speed of Thought: Succeeding in the Digital Economy (Penguin Business Library)*, New York: Penguin 2000

Business & Commerce

Brinkley, Douglas G. *Wheels for the World: Henry Ford, His Company, and a Century of Progress*, New York: Penguin Books 2004

Bartlett, Donald L. *Howard Hughes – His Life and Madness*, London: Andre Deutsch Ltd 2003

Love, John F. *McDonald's: Behind the Arches*, USA: Bantam 1995

INDEX

PICTURE CREDITS

(PD = public domain; LOC = US Library of Congress)

P9 © LOC
P16 © Getty Images
P17 © Shutterstock
P18 © Corbis
P19 © NASA
P20 © Sam Ogden/
Science Photo Library
P21 © Science Photo
Library
P22 © Science Photo
Library
P23 © NASA
P24 © PD
P25 © PD
P26 ©Time & Life | Getty
P27 ©Time & Life | Getty
P28 © Getty Images
P29 © Dreamstime
P30 © Dreamstime
P31 © Dreamstime
P32 © Getty Images
P33 © Dreamstime
P34 © Getty Images
P35 © LOC
P36 © Dreamstime
P37 © PD
P38 ©Time & Life | Getty
P39 © iStockphoto
P40 ©WireImage
P41 © LOC
P42 © PD
P43 © PD
P44 © NASA
P45 © NASA
P46 © Getty Images
P47 © iStockphoto
P48 © LOC
P49 © LOC
P50 © Getty Images

P51 © PD
P52 © PD
P53 © Getty Images
P54 © PD
P55 © Getty Images
P56 © Corbis
P57 © NASA
P58 © L. Giffard / Alamy
P59 © Dreamstime
P60 © AFP/Getty Images
P61 © Bill Anderson /
Science Photo Library
P62 © PD
P63 © Dreamstime
P64 © AFP/Getty Images
P65 © PD
P66 © Getty Images
P67 © Dreamstime
P68 © Nasa
P69 © Nasa
P70 © Nasa (Both)
P71 © Nasa
P72 © Getty Images
P73 © AFP/Getty Images
P74 © AFP/Getty Images
P75 © AFP/Getty Images
P76 © LOC
P77 © PD
P78 ©Time & Life | Getty
P79 © Dreamstime
P80 © PD
P81 © Getty Images
P82 © LOC
P83 © LOC
P84 © LOC
P85 © iStockphoto
P86 ©Time & Life | Getty
P87 © PD
P88 © AFP/Getty Images

P89 © Dreamstime
P90 © Dreamstime
P91 © PD Courtesy of
Reagan Library
P92 © Dreamstime
P93 © Dreamstime
P94 © LOC
P95 © LOC
P96 © PD
P97 © PD
P98 © Getty Images
P99 © LOC
P100 © Getty Images
P101 © Getty Images
P102 © LOC
P103 © NASA
P104 © LOC
P105 ©Time &
Life | Getty
P106 ©The Art Gallery
Collection / Alamy
P107 © LOC
P108 © Dreamstime
P109 © iStockphoto
P110 © LOC
P111 © LOC
P112 © Getty Images
P113 ©Time &
Life | Getty
P114 © Interphoto /
Alamy
P115 © iStockphoto
P116 © Getty Images
P117 © Getty Images
P118 © LOC
P119 © LOC
P120 ©Time &
Life | Getty
P121 © PD

P122 © LOC
P123 © LOC
P124 © LOC
P125 © LOC
P126 ©AFP/Getty
Images
P127 © PD
P128 © Pictorial Press
Ltd/Alamy
P129 © PD
P130 © AFP/Getty
Images
P131 © PD
P132 © LOC
P133 © LOC
P134 © Getty Images
P135 © PD
P136 © LOC
P137 © LOC
P138 © LOC
P139 © PD
P140 ©Time &
Life | Getty
P141 © Photos 12 /
Alamy
P142 © LOC
P143 © Pictorial Press
Ltd/ Alamy
P144 © Getty Images
P145 © Mary Evans/
SALAS COLLECTION
P146 ©Time &
Life | Getty
P147 © Getty Images
P148 © D. Levenson /
Alamy
P149 © M. Downey /
Alamy
P150 © Getty Images

255